John Wesley Hardin

Dark Angel of Texas

John Wesley Hardin

Dark Angel of Texas

LEON METZ

UNIVERSITY OF OKLAHOMA PRESS

Norman

Library of Congress Cataloging-in-Publication Data

Metz, Leon Claire.
    John Wesley Hardin : dark angel of Texas / Leon Metz. —
University of Oklahoma Press ed.
        p.   cm.
    Originally published: El Paso, Tex. : Mangan Books, 1996.
    Includes bibliographical references (p.   ) and index.
    ISBN 0-8061-2995-6
    1. Hardin, John Wesley, 1853–1895.   2. Outlaws—Texas—
Bibliography.   3. Texas—History—1846–1950.   I. Title.
F391.H27M49   1998
364.1′523′092—dc21
[B]   97-42244
                                                                            CIP

The paper in this book meets the guidelines for permanence and durability of the Committee on Production Guidelines for Book Longevity of the Council on Library Resources, Inc. ∞

Oklahoma Paperbacks edition published 1998 by University of Oklahoma Press, Norman, Publishing Division of the University, by arrangement with Mangan Books, 6245 Snowheights Court, El Paso, Texas 79912. Manufactured in the U.S.A. First printing of the University of Oklahoma Press edition, 1998.

3   4   5   6   7   8   9   10

To my brother, Ron
— a gunfighter when he had to be.
AND TO
Chuck Parsons, Margaret Waring,
Eddie Day Truitt, Joyce Hardin Cavett, Jo Foster,
Deen Underwood, and Oran Hardin.
They pointed the way.

BOOKS BY LEON C. METZ

John Selman: Gunfighter

Dallas Stoudenmire: El Paso Marshal

Pat Garrett: Story of a Western Lawman

The Shooters

City at the Pass

Fort Bliss: An Illustrated History

Turning Points in El Paso, Texas

Desert Army: Fort Bliss on the Texas Border

Border: The U.S.-Mexico Line

Southern New Mexico Empire

El Paso Chronicles

Roadside History of Texas

John Wesley Hardin: Dark Angel of Texas

Contents

Foreword

The devil himself
masquerades as an angel of light.

REVELATION 9:11

JOHN WESLEY HARDIN was a killer. The tools of his trade were six-shooters and shotguns. He was an expert, a professional with weapons. He spent his youth practicing with firearms. His career was, and would be, repeatedly interspersed with amazed comments by friends and strangers, outlaws and lawmen, regarding his astonishing dexterity with revolvers, how he spun them on his finger, performed various rolls, flips and other tricky, magical, near impossible exhibitions.

Killing people, putting all of that natural skill to use, was inherent in John Wesley Hardin. So he killed many men, perhaps as few as twenty or as many as fifty. Nobody knows the exact figure, but had he not killed, John Wesley Hardin would be just a name among a legion of names of Old West drifters and ne'er-do-wells. They briefly stormed across the pages of history and left no tracks.

But he killed—that is what he did, why he is remembered—and you have to wonder about a man who killed so massively, so methodically and so remorselessly.

You have to think of that grand Christian name of his, John Wesley, after the eighteenth century English divine who became the father of Methodism.

You have to think of the boy, John Wesley Hardin, being raised in a staunch religious tradition, steeped in Christian virtues, who became a sort of wrathful Old Testament figure, a dark angel slaying enemies, real and perceived.

You have to wonder about the wicked brew of ideas and ideals that bathed and shaped the mind of the boy, Hardin. He had a fierce fire and brimstone religiosity, a rigid code of family loyalty and that indelible sense of *honor* that was part and parcel of the lives of Southerners, rich and poor.

And you have to mix the brew with the awful period of Hardin's youth—those bloody times when the South lay beaten down, filled with hate and praying for vengeance. You realize that the Civil War song, "Oh, I'm a Good Old Rebel," reflected accurately the mind of a youngster like Wes Hardin.

> Oh, I'm a good ol' rebel, now that's just what I am,
> For this fair land of Freedom, I do not care a damn,
> I'm glad I fit against it, I only wish we'd won,
> And I don't want no pardon for anything I've done.
>
> I hates the constitution, this great Republic, too,
> I hates the Freedman's Bureau and uniforms of blue,
> I hates the nasty eagle with all its brags and fuss,
> The lyin' thievin' Yankees I hates them worse and worse.
>
> Three hundred thousand Yankees is still in Southern dust,
> We got three hundred thousand before they conquered us;
> They died of Southern fever and Southern steel and shot,
> I wish there was three million instead of what we got.

And the refrain, above all:

> I don't want no pardon for what I was and am,
> I won't be reconstructed and I don't care a damn.

I have lived most of my adult life in the town where Wes Hardin was killed. I have visited his grave at Concordia Cemetery, and have taken countless visitors there. As I stood gazing at earth so barren that only artificial flowers bloom, I have repeatedly asked myself, "What kind of man was he?" To family and friends, and much of today's world, he was a good man compelled to do bad deeds. To others, the easy smile and friendly handshake were simply masks obscuring evil so malevolent as to be unbelievable.

The man's appeal remains magical. After the turn of the century, the classic writer O'Henry used Hardin as the real-life model for his Cisco Kid in "The Caballero's Way." Cisco was the Hardin type of desperado, "killing for the love of it—because he was quick-tempered—to avoid arrest—for his own amusement—any reason that came to his mind would suffice."[1]

Phone calls and letters reach me from all over the world. The public requests photos and specific directions for finding the grave. Those who probe rarely know much about him except that he killed people. Yet, they perceive him as larger than life, a man more sinned against than a sinner himself.

Popular literature has treated Hardin not as a killer but as a gunfighter, and therein lies the difference. In our folklore, gunfighters wore white hats. They were practitioners of a code, the Code of the West, a code that never took unfair advantage. Gunfighters shot people only in self-defense.

While several gunmen left briefly written accounts of themselves, usually in letters, John Wesley Hardin recognized that his life warranted an autobiography. Since his death, *The Life of John Wesley Hardin* has remained almost continuously in print. The book established Hardin's reputation based on his own experiences, recollections and exaggerations.

That autobiography also is the greatest stumbling block to the writing of a book about John Wesley Hardin. Without it, there would be no way to piece his life together, for Hardin himself, one of the West's majestic manslayers, shot few people of any significance. The humanity that fell before his flaming revolvers were generally ciphers, non-entities, obscure, homeless ramblers and wanderers who would, in large part, never be remembered at all if Hardin had not killed them.

Hardin biographers use the autobiography as a primary source because without it, the writer is limited to obscure court records and skimpy newspaper files. Without his autobiography, 70 percent of Hardin's killings would go unrecorded. His comments, perhaps true, perhaps not, usually comprise the only record.

His autobiography has discouraged others from conducting serious research into his career. A century after his death, much of what is presently known about Hardin still springs from his self-composed life history. It remains the major research tool into his turbulent life because outside of his letters, his autobiography is the primary version of events. He is one of the few characters in Western history to explain himself, to discuss his motives, to define his core beliefs as a man, as a spiritual individual, and one of the coldest killers ever to walk the broken, sullied face of the earth.

Hardin's sense of character echoes loud and clear. He was intensely loyal to his friends. The man believed in spunk as well as the living God. He had a relentless desire to present himself in the best possible circumstances. In his own mind, he never shot a man who did not deserve it.

Hardin was a family man, and family meant parents, brothers and sisters, aunts, uncles, cousins, nephews, and their aunts, uncles, cousins, and nephews. The story of Hardin is a story of clannish individuals struggling for respect and power. After family and friends, everyone else was a stranger under suspicion.

Hardin's account of his career, his professed desire to seek God's righteousness, is filled with self-serving justification. Many of his versions are not as false as they are incomplete. In spite of his contradictions, John Wesley Hardin remains the best known, the most highly complex, homicidal desperado ever to prowl the back roads and cattle trails of Texas.

I have read what he wrote—his autobiography and his many letters—the newspaper articles and the court records—and thought deeply about who and what he was, and how and why he did the things he did. My first book chronicled the life and career of the gunman who killed him (*John Selman: Gunfighter*, University of Oklahoma Press). In those days, because of his autobiography and letters, I perceived that nothing of value remained to be written about Mr. Hardin.

I was wrong. It is insufficient to say that John Wesley Hardin was the most prolific, the most feared and fearless of all the Old West's killers.

There has to be more to the man, and that extra insight and knowledge is the rationale for this biography.

Leon C. Metz

El Paso, Texas
Aug. 19, 1996

Prologue

El Paso, Texas
August 1895

...the man who does not exercise the first law
of nature—that of self preservation—is not worthy
of living and breathing the breath of life.

JOHN WESLEY HARDIN

AUGUST HAD NOT BEEN AN EASY MONTH for John Wesley Hardin. He had reached El Paso more by accident than design. The middle-aged gunman had not planned to stay, but he had no where else to go either. El Paso was the far-western tip of Texas, but it might just as well have been the end of the earth.

Memories, fresh and ancient, sweet and painful, dark and thunderous, meandered through his mind. There was Jane, gone. Callie, gone. Beulah, gone. Parents, gone. Brother Joe, gone. Other brothers and sisters, dead, distant and scattered. Former companions, for the most part, dead and gone. Children, alive but alienated. The world he understood, gone, dead as surely as the fiercest of his enemies.

Had Hardin known then that many future biographers would regard El Paso as his last great effort to lead a quiet and orderly life, he would have laughed. He might even have roared. History plays its strange jokes.

El Paso was simply another destination along a tangled trail extending back forty-two stormy years. Along the way, Hardin had matured, but not reformed; he had changed but he was still the same. Still, once there had been exultation in his life. Heartache and some confusion had long-since replaced the joy.

Partial answers to his life lay in a pile of papers stacked on his desk alongside a couple of forgotten legal briefs. He referred to this manuscript as *The Autobiography of John Wesley Hardin.*

Somewhere inside the scribbled writing lay the heart and soul of John Wesley Hardin. To his credit, he had never thought of himself as a writer, which was just as well because he wasn't. Above and beyond a justification for his own violent career, a history of his life had its own significance. He had lived it; he had witnessed it; he had partaken of it. Never mind that his autobiography would be self-serving, incomplete, frequently inaccurate, often intentionally so. He recognized that he had survived tumultuous times in Texas, that his story was important, impossible to be written by anyone else. He would tell it his way, in his own words. And if in doing so, he omitted more than a few truths, and skipped over more than a few details, well, that is the way autobiographies have always been written. Authors are not ordinarily known as self-bashers.

Hardin had one other reason for his story. He had not corrected his lifestyle in El Paso, although at first he assumed or hoped he would. Time and circumstances had changed him, slowed him. It followed then that since he could not reform, and since he lacked the reflexes and nerves of youth, his compulsive path of errant behavior could only, inevitably, lead to the graveyard. He understood that as intuitively as he knew the sun would rise the next morning—that the birds would sing even if he would not.

He must have despaired at his unchanging destructive lifestyle, and concluded that writing a manuscript would force him to think about himself and what he had done. It might explain where and why he had veered off the trail. If he were lucky, his autobiography might offer insight for redemption. The real John Wesley Hardin—son, husband, father, friend, desperado, man-slayer, convict, attorney—might step from the shadows of his tormented soul. In sorting through the pages of his life, in seeking answers to the relentless question of who he was, he returned to the beginning. Through the filter of a whiskey-soaked mind, he mentally retraced his steps. In doing so, he once again ran the gauntlet of bodies and blood.

A Boy Named John

JOHN WESLEY HARDIN WAS BORN near the little North Texas town of Bonham on May 26, 1853, the second child of James and Elizabeth Hardin. His ancestors originated in Great Britain and reached Virginia during the 1600s. The family and their descendants migrated into North Carolina to Tennessee, to Mississippi, and finally to Texas.

James Gibson Hardin, the father of John, was born in Wayne County, Tennessee, on March 2, 1823. In September 1841, as a single man of eighteen, James applied to the Texas government and received 320 acres in northern Liberty County, Texas. However, farming and ranching never appealed. Although from a family predominantly Presbyterian, he converted at twenty-two years of age to Methodism, and became a preacher. Hardin moved to Richland, Navarro County, north of present-day Waco, for his initial stewardship.

As a likable, articulate, nice-looking man, James Gibson Hardin sported a thick but neat mustache and medium brown hair. He wore a tidy, conservative suit. Neighbors described him as average in height, and slender.

In the Richland Crossing area, Hardin met the frail Dr. William Dixon. (The name is often spelled Dixson.) With his wife, two sons, five daughters and four grandchildren, Dixon left Indiana after learning about free land in Texas. Two of these grandchildren were six-year-old William L. Barekman, and his four-year-old brother, Alexander Henry "Alec" Barekman. Both boys would eventually become cousins of John Wesley Hardin. The violent destinies of Alec Barekman and Wesley Hardin would intertwine.[1]

William Nicks Anderson, a physician, adventurer and sub-agent for the Mercer Colony in Texas, guided the Dixons to the Richland Crossing area. Doctor Dixon and his wife erected a tent on his land grant on Pisgah Ridge, which extended several miles through today's southwest Navarro County. But after their life was threatened, and their tent burned by neighbors resentful of newcomers, they moved into town. In January 1847, the Reverend James Gibson Hardin performed a marriage ceremony between the doctor's daughter, Susanna Louise Dixon, and William Anderson.[2] In the process, the Reverend Hardin also met Mary Elizabeth Dixon (usually called Elizabeth), the doctor's cultured daughter and eighth child. She was born on December 7, 1826 in Sullivan County, Indiana. Neighbors and relatives portrayed her as attractive, deeply religious and having long, honey-blond hair. Her bright blue eyes enhanced a beautiful smile.[3]

They married in Navarro County on May 19, 1847. She was twenty and James Hardin was twenty-four. Ten children resulted from the union, the firstborn dying on the day of birth.[4] The others were Joe Gibson (Jan. 5, 1850), John Wesley (May 26, 1853), Elizabeth "Lizzie" or "Sissie" (June 23, 1855), Martha Ann "Mattie" (April 17, 1857), Benjamin (1859), Jefferson Davis (Sept. 7, 1861), Nancy "Nannie" (March 31, 1856), and Barnett Gipson "Gip" Hardin (Aug. 15, 1874).[5]

When the Methodist Conference met in Paris, Texas in November 1849, James Hardin accepted a couple of assignments and then transferred to the First Methodist Church of Dallas as its fifth minister.[6]

James Hardin turned thirty-one-years-old in 1854, but the minutes of the Methodist Episcopal Church, South, no longer mentioned his name. Any position he might have held thereafter was not as an itinerant minister, but as a pastor assigned to a relatively permanent position called "locating." So although John Wesley Hardin described his father as a circuit rider, the evidence suggests the Reverend Hardin rode an established circuit

James Gibson Hardin, the Methodist preacher who fathered John Wesley Hardin. The father never approved of his son's killings, but he could never bring himself to condemn them either. (R. G. McCubbin Collection)

primarily during those initial stages of his religious calling.[7]

Because Hardin placed his name on the role for infirm or aged preachers, it has generally been assumed that his health deteriorated. The record does not support that. Judging by the manner in which the preacher moved about, opening and closing churches and schools, one would suspect that the good reverend was in sound if not robust health. His and his wife's letters never mention any substantial or recurring physical problems. The memoirs of his son, John Wesley Hardin, refer to no infirmities or weaknesses, no periods of hospitalization or inaction. However, Martha Ann "Mattie" a younger sister of John by four-years, said her father had survived a terrible attack of whooping cough in his youth. The recovery left his voice subject to severe coughing. Paroxysms so hampered his speech that he reduced his preaching load.[8]

Otherwise, the mind of James remained clear and sharp, his back generally strong and lithe. Though he died at fifty-three, considering the time and the hardships, that was not unusual.

JAMES GIBSON HARDIN NAMED his third child, and second son, John Wesley, after the founder of Methodism. Although John Wesley Hardin was born at Blair's Springs on Bois d'Arc Creek ten miles southwest of Bonham, Texas, he had little if any recollection of his youth there. Instead, his memoirs picked up in the East Texas piney woods of Polk County near the tiny community of Moscow when John was sixteen. James Hardin had a land grant on Long King Creek, three miles northwest of nearby Livingston. John Wesley Hardin and his brother Joe, with several slaves, split the rails, leveled the ground and constructed the buildings.[9]

John Wesley considered himself a child of nature. He took his gun and dogs into the fields, forests and swamps where he hunted raccoon, opossum, deer and wildcat.

He mentioned a family horse named Jack who strayed to the Robert Sikes place, three miles distant. At dusk, John went to fetch him and while returning in a drizzling rain, the dogs cornered four raccoons in a white oak tree. Since they would not come down, John went up. Hardin backed old Jack underneath the tree, and with a rope gradually squirmed his way to the top. At that point, John and the raccoons had climbed as far as either could go. Hardin tied himself to the trunk and broke off a limb for defense and offense. When the raccoons charged, John knocked one from the tree but lost his weapon. The battle then see-sawed as John fought blindly to dislodge the others. One by one the raccoons plummeted to the ground—a good fifty feet—where the dogs promptly did their job.

His clothing shredded and soaked with blood, Hardin slid down the trunk, tied the raccoons together, slung them across Jack's back, and patiently put up with Jack's bucking and kicking all the way home. When the boy stepped through the door, he looked worse than the dead raccoons. Many years later in El Paso, as Hardin mused on the experience, he depicted himself as surviving that encounter because of pluck, what Hardin defined as courage or spirit, resolution in the face of difficulties. "If there is any power to save a man, woman or child from harm, outside the power of the living God," he wrote, "it is this thing called 'pluck.'"[10]

But pluck could not save him from the ticks, and John described his father's farm as the "tickiest" locality in the state. Because of ticks and general disgust, the elder Hardin transferred his property rights, along with farm improvements, to his brother Barnett. James then moved his family to Sumpter in Trinity County in southeast Texas where he preached part-time and taught school.

Trinity County existed near today's Big Thicket in East Texas and included portions of the present Davy Crockett National Forest. With an economy based on timber, the area's forests contained stands of long and short leaf pine. Settlers arrived in the mid-1840s, and most residents initially lived as part-time lumbermen and part-time hunters. After clearing the land, they planted cotton fields. Freighters traded the cotton in Louisiana, the wagons reaching Shreveport by traversing trails winding through the tangle of vines, streams, swamps, bogs and thick underbrush.

The Big Thicket proved a wild—and sometimes scary—place for a young boy struggling to comprehend the meaning of pluck. Nevertheless, John Wesley developed an easy acquaintance with revolvers, shotguns, rifles and knives. Bravado and courage, plus an intense effort to constantly demonstrate them, would be Wes Hardin's trademark.

The village of Sumpter was organized in 1854, its residents living in log cabins. The schoolhouse lacked furniture, and the only text was a Bible. J. C. Landrum, a schoolmaster for whom the Hardin boys developed an affection, kept the school functioning. Their father, James Gibson Hardin, also taught on weekdays and preached on Sundays.

D. H. Hamilton, a Hardin neighbor, would later refer to John Wesley Hardin as "one of the most notorious outlaws Texas ever produced, an Absalom in the House of David." However, Hamilton described the Reverend Hardin as "a good and capable man" who came to Polk county in 1854. Hamilton considered the reverend a friend of "sterling character who did much for the religious welfare of the people. He stood for the best in society."[11]

In 1860, a fire in the Eureka Hotel prompted the Reverend Hardin to organize a fire brigade. He climbed to the roof and never backed away until extinguishing the blaze, thus saving not only the building but the town. When later praised for his heroism, Hardin modestly replied, "I preach a salvation through faith but I believe that faith must also be accompanied by works."[12] When the courthouse burned in 1872, however, Hardin was not present.

By the start of the Civil War, the Reverend Hardin had established an "Academy of Learning" in Livingston, one that soon moved to Sumpter. Fifteen male students attended, including John and Joe Hardin. Subjects included arithmetic and geography, plus heavy doses of classics and Bible studies. Headmasters Hardin and Landrum stressed the virtues of righteousness, bravery, of controlling one's passions, and of pluck and manhood. They spoke of a violent if forgiving God capable of calling a terrible retribution down upon his enemies.

Against this background, John likened himself as the chief scholar, a youngster at the head of his class. However, even scholars needed exercise, so he was first out of class to the playground. Since John's parents had taught him and Joe to be "honest, truthful and brave...to let no one call them liar", it naturally followed that John and Joe frequently defended their honor against boys reckless with truth and free with false charges. Had John Wesley Hardin lived in modern times, he would have been the classic football hero, a seducer of admiring young ladies, a Horatius at the Bridge in defense of justice and the American way.

Every boy also carried a pocket knife for whittling, mumbletypeg, cleaning fingernails, cutting pieces of leather, or for warding off marauding bears or lions that were not that common, but young men had to be prepared just in case. Attorney William B. Teagarden, less than a year younger than Hardin, grew up in Sumpter. He had attended the same school with John Wesley Hardin and wrote to Hardin's daughter Mollie in 1931. Teagarden described her father as "candid and honorable."

When an irate schoolteacher prepared to whip Teagarden with a hickory stick, Hardin stepped into the aisle, an open knife in his hand, and threatened to kill the tutor if the beating happened. "The teacher retreated...[because] everybody in the school knew that John meant what he said. There was not in his life or character a single sordid or dishonorable motive. All men who treated him fairly and decently were met more than half-way, but those who...treated him wrongfully or disrespectfully always had their challenges accepted. They usually got what was coming to them," Teagarden said.[13]

In another instance, Hardin mentioned a schoolmate who, "wanted to be boss among the boys. Of course I stood in his way." Charles Sloter, whom Hardin called a bully, accused John of writing rude verse on the blackboard about a female student named Sal. "I love Sal, and Sal loves mutton," the opening lines went, and they obviously did nothing to enhance Sal's charms. Hardin said Sloter wrote the lines himself, then accused John. When Hardin protested, Sloter struck him and pulled a knife. Hardin reacted by stabbing Sloter in the chest and back. The youth almost died, and the school board nearly expelled Hardin although it was his father's establishment. Hardin said later that Sloter lived long enough to be lynched by a mob in an adjoining county.[14]

The Hour
of the Gun

THE AUTOBIOGRAPHY of John Wesley Hardin reveals a man
untroubled by ambiguities. Indeed, on occasion he must have
seriously considered the ministry as a vocation since his contem-
plations were unwaveringly harsh, moralistic and reminiscent of
the Old Testament. His enemies were many, and his sword of
retribution, a six-shooter. Hardin's lifelong code, long on religion,
short on temper, demanded he do the right thing as he understood the right thing to be. Hardin was often wrong, but he was
never in doubt.

East Texas during the mid-to-late 1800s consisted primarily of
piney woods. In 1861, nearly two hundred thousand slaves lived
in that region. By the advent of the Civil War, every county in
East Texas contained 25 percent or more black people. Two thousand farms could be called plantations since they had at least
twenty slaves each.

The Hardins never possessed many slaves. Their families
owned modest land parcels and often engaged in professions such
as law or clergy. They treated the help paternalistically although
slaves worked from sunup to sundown, just as the masters did.
In the mysterious ways in which lives are often shaped, black
and white children—frequently suckled by the same mammies—

grew up together climbing trees, sliding off haystacks, teasing the animals and fishing in the creeks. They shared the same humor and dialect as well as similar attitudes and prejudices.

Their superstitions infiltrated East Texas with its dark, mysterious forests, its shadows and bogs. The Piney Woods created fears and beliefs fed easily during the long, hot summer evenings. Everybody gathered to swap tales about the things they had seen and understood and the things they had seen and could not explain. The light of a full moon was widely believed by whites as best for planting. Horseshoes belonged over doorways. Blacks carried charms for medicinal purposes. Voodoo had its adherents, and the sighting of apparitions was not an uncommon experience.[1]

"I never was afraid of anything except ghosts," John Wesley Hardin wrote, "and I have lived that down. Constant association with Negroes in my young days had made me superstitious in this respect, and I was well versed in old folklore about ghosts, spirits, dead men's shadows, graveyards, etc., and many a time then did I honestly believe I had seen them."[2]

As white and black children grew older, their status changed. The whites took command of the games played.

TEXAS JOINED THE UNION in 1845 and almost immediately had second thoughts. Sentiment for secession broke out during the Compromise of 1850 that established the present Texas boundaries. These rumblings increased during the congressional elections of 1854 and the governor's race of 1857. When Abraham Lincoln assumed the presidency in 1860, Texas considered his victory as practically a declaration of war against the South.

John Wesley Hardin said, "I grew up a rebel [seeing] Abraham Lincoln burned and shot to pieces in effigy so often that I looked upon him as a very devil incarnate...." When he was almost ten, John plotted to run off with an unidentified cousin to fight Yankees. His father terminated the scheme with a sound thrashing.[3]

Texas voted to break away on February 23, 1861, the ballots being nearly four to one for secession. When Governor Sam Houston opposed withdrawing from the Union, the Texas legislature removed him from office.

James Gibson Hardin, who passed his law studies and was

admitted to the Texas Bar in 1861, cast his ballot for the Union. Nevertheless, when the vote went against him, he put aside personal feelings. Like most professional men and planters, he anticipated marching with his neighbors into battle. Trinity County, with a population of three thousand, procured three companies of soldiers: Tulles Company, Kirksey Company and Company M. At Sumpter, the thirty-eight-year-old Hardin helped raise Company M in early 1862. The men elected him captain. However, John said community leaders convinced the elder Hardin that he could be "of more use at home than off fighting Yankees." Reverend Hardin thus stepped aside and Captain Howard Ballinger, an attorney, took command.[4]

Of these three Texas units, only Company M and its one hundred and twenty soldiers left a written history. The troopers' ages varied between sixteen and sixty, about half being seventeen to twenty-one. They trained by marching on the courthouse lawn. On the evening of May 4, 1862, Sumpter residents organized a grand ball. Company M danced all night and vowed it would never dance again until the establishment of the Southern Confederacy. At 2:30 the next afternoon, with excited hurrahs and fiddlers striking up brisk martial tunes, the boys tramped off to war. Had they known the horror that awaited, neither they nor the kinfolks they gaily left behind, could have borne it.

Company M joined Hood's Texas Brigade and served in Robert E. Lee's Army of Northern Virginia, as well as in James Longstreet's Second Corps. It fought at Gettysburg, at Gaines' Mill, Eltham's Landing, Second Manassas, Antietam, Chickamauga, in twenty-four of the war's bloodiest battles. When at last the cannons grew silent, of the original one hundred and twenty men, dozens had been maimed and dismissed. A few had been captured and spent time in federal prisons. Most died in battle. Only six were still on their feet and present during the surrender at Appomattox. Captain Ballinger, disabled by disease and discharged, returned to Sumpter and died in Waco.[5]

THE WAR DESTROYED the plantation economy. Wealthy planters no longer existed in Texas. They had borne the war's expense, and much of the suffering and dying. With their economy devastated, they blamed their miseries on the blacks as well as

President Lincoln. Land before the war had been worth two dollars an acre. A young, healthy black male sold for five hundred dollars. Thus, residents were never wealthy in land, only in slaves. Now the slaves were free, and the land was still worth two dollars an acre. At a crossroads of culture, the economic and social world of Texas had gone topsy-turvy.

Texans had always viewed themselves as a special people. They had thumped the Mexicans, pushed back the Indians, and fought blizzard and drought to a standstill. They were accustomed to being conquerors, and now they were subjugated. Texas offered no resistance to the end of slavery, recognizing that human bondage had disappeared as surely as secession. Still, they watched in humiliation and confused hatred as lines of Union bluecoats marched in and occupied their hard-won soil. Texans found defeat especially galling because theirs was the only portion of the Confederacy never successfully invaded. Texas had not formally surrendered. Even the last battle of the Civil War had been fought in southeast Texas at Palmito Hill, and the Texans won.

DURING THE WAR YEARS in Sumpter, young Hardin witnessed his first killing, the slaying of Turner Evans, a prominent landowner who had lent money to John Ruff. When Ruff could not repay the debt, Evans downed several drinks and thrashed Ruff with his cane. Ruff then pulled a Bowie knife and, shrugging off bystanders, severed Evans's jugular. Hardin seemed neither shocked, sickened, nor outraged. Years later he used the event for moralizing. "Readers," he wrote in recounting the murder, "if you wish to be successful in life, be temperate and control your passions; if you don't, ruin and death is the inevitable result."[6]

John did not realize it then, but his own life would become a textbook example of a failure to control passions.

HARDIN'S UNCLE BARNETT lived four miles north of Livingston. Although Polk County was Big Thicket country, Barnett Hardin made his living with cotton (see Appendix B). He had sufficient land to consider himself a planter, and his home a modest plantation. He formerly owned perhaps a half-dozen slaves, small by regional standards.

When the fifteen-year-old John Wesley Hardin visited his

Uncle Barnett in November 1868, the boy carried what would become a favorite firearm, a Colt .44 cap-and-ball six-shooter. This 1860 Army model gained wide acceptance during the War Between the States. At two pounds and eleven ounces with an eight-inch barrel, the .44 balanced superbly.[7]

Thus far in his life, other than the knife incident in school, no known propensity for violence had surfaced. Exuberance and boastful moralizing seemed Hardin's strength as well as his weakness.

During those relatively quiet, transitional days, families often gathered outside in the evening to discuss the day's events or to release pent-up energy through horseplay and games. During this November visit by John Wesley, a cousin of Hardin's named Barnett Jones, matched himself and John against Major "Mage" Holshousen. Mage was a freedman who lived near Moscow and had once belonged to Judge Claiborne Holshousen, a brother of Uncle Barnett Hardin's wife. (Slaves frequently took the last name of their former owners.)

On the surface this competition appears patently unfair, two against one. But the match wasn't meant to be taken seriously. No championship belts were at stake here. Mage was probably a large, mature man with a reputation as the best wrestler in the neighborhood. The boys were young, likely skinny, inexperienced, and individually no match against Mage. Two against one therefore made it more equal, and certainly more entertaining for the crowd. A problem with such scraps however, was that the participants too often placed pride on the line.

Chances are that the black man successfully pinned both boys. Hardin in particular ached to get even.

He claimed that the two of them twice threw Holshousen, the second time bringing blood to his face. An angry Mage threatened a brawl, warning Hardin that "he would kill me or die himself; that no white boy could draw his blood and live; that a bird never flew too high not to come to the ground."[8] Uncle Barnett ordered Mage off the plantation.

Early the next morning Hardin left his Uncle Barnett's place and headed home, riding out of his way to convey a message from his father to a local farmer, Captain Sam Rowes. Following a meandering creek road that curved sharply for a hundred yards, he spotted Mage stepping briskly along a pathway and carrying a big stick.

Mage heard hoofbeats, turned and recognized Hardin. The two shouted obscenities. Hardin whipped Old Paint into a trot, but the black man raced to the other side of the road, grabbed the bridle and brought the horse to a halt. Hardin dismounted and shot Mage with the big .44. Mage reeled, then lurched forward again. Hardin fired until "I shot him loose" from the bridle and he went down.

Hardin left to fetch his uncle, Claiborne Holshousen. Claiborne, with a neighbor and John Wesley, hurried to the scene and found a badly-wounded but still feisty Mage calling John a liar. Had it not been for his uncle, Hardin would have shot Mage again. Holshousen handed his nephew a $20 gold piece and directed him to go home and explain the incident to his father. Twenty dollars for killing a man was a lot of money.

Hardin suggests coincidence in his encounter with Mage, but instead of happenstance, it seems more likely that Hardin stalked the black man. But whatever the circumstances of their confrontation, Mage died in November 1868 after a brief period of suffering. Hardin had slain his first person. At fifteen, he was a fugitive.[9]

JOHN'S BOYHOOD FRIEND AND CLASSMATE, attorney William B. Teagarden, who would outlive Hardin by forty years, wrote Hardin's daughter Mollie a letter in 1931. He offered insight into the early times of her father's career, explaining that, in those days "it was not, under any circumstances, permissible for a Negro to assault a white man, and death was always the penalty. That was the result in this Negro's case."[10]

STILL, THE SLAYING OF MAGE did not go unnoticed by the authorities. The Bureau of Refugees, Freedmen and Abandoned Lands—commonly known as the Freedmen's Bureau—attempted to establish civil rights for former slaves: education, voting, jury duty and the holding of political office. The Bureau sought to initiate labor, wage and employment practices equitable to all concerned.

Charles Schmidt of the Freedmen's Bureau kept a Complaint

Register as well as a record of violent crimes occurring between January 1867 and December 1868. Schmidt identified Mage as Major Holshousen. He said the killing took place ten miles from Moscow in Polk County: "Hardin, a mere lad, shot f.m. [freed man] without cause as the latter did not like the abuse of Hardin. He shot f.m. five times, every wound dangerous."[11]

Various lawmen also took note of the slaying, although none of them knew Hardin's correct age. Sheriff Thomas H. Kenley of Trinity County shortly thereafter described Hardin as a "very quarrelsome...boy about 19 years old and heavy-set." He had "killed a Freed boy of color in Polk County. We presume he is indicted in Polk. His father is a Methodist preacher."[12]

On July 16, 1870, Sheriff G. W. Barfield of Polk County sent a notice to James Davidson, chief of the Texas State Police. Barfield mentioned a John Hardin, wanted for murder in 1869. The letter described Hardin as about twenty-two-years-old, dark hair and eyes, standing 5 feet 8, and weighing 140 pounds. Barfield said "pursuit was made immediately after the murder but he escaped."[13]

Hardin actually was seventeen (in 1870), skinny, about 5 feet 8, dark-complexioned and weighing 130 pounds. He was a strangely alluring combination of the attractive and the deadly. Although few realized it, pound-for-pound and inch-for-inch, John Wesley Hardin was becoming the most dangerous man in Texas.

A Reputation Builds

T O JOHN WESLEY HARDIN, "the killing of a Negro meant certain death at the hands of a court backed by Northern bayonets; hence my father told me to keep in hiding until the Yankee bayonet should cease to govern. Thus, unwillingly, I became a fugitive, not from justice be it known, but from the injustice and misrule of the people who had subjugated the South." His father believed that once the democrats were back in political control, John would be assured of a fair trial.[1]

Reality was different, of course. Southern whites comprised the juries, and a jury rarely convicted a Texan for killing a black man. Had he gone to trial, John Wesley Hardin probably would have gone free. However, he preferred the life of a fugitive to that of a farmer, and killing a black man provided an excuse for breaking free from family restraints.

Still, he took his father's advice and fled to Logallis Prairie, twenty-five miles north of Sumpter, Texas, in Trinity County. His eighteen-year-old brother, Joseph Gibson Hardin, taught school there.

Suspecting Joe's home might be watched by the military, John Hardin stayed nearby at "old man Morgan's" place and spent his time hunting wild cattle and game. One afternoon, in December 1868, six weeks following the shooting of Mage, Joe warned him that three soldiers of Company B, Sixth Cavalry stationed in Livingston, were asking questions about Hardin's whereabouts.

Taking a double-barreled shotgun and his Colt .44 cap-and-ball revolver, Hardin waited for them alongside the brushy, deep bed of Hickory Creek Crossing. (A cap-and-ball six-gun had a paper cartridge whereby powder was poured in one end, and the bullet was glued on.)[2]

"I waylaid them where I knew they would cross the creek," Hardin later wrote. He killed two white soldiers with one blast each from the shotgun. A black soldier fled, but Hardin "ran up to him and demanded his surrender in the name of the Southern Confederacy." The soldier fired wildly, wounding Hardin in the arm. Hardin shot him down. "I had no mercy on men whom I knew only wanted to get my body to torture and kill," he said.[3]

Farmers sympathetic to John buried the soldiers in the creek bed one hundred yards downstream. Thus, in the winter of 1868, the fifteen-year-old Hardin had slain four men, and had been wounded once.[4]

In serious trouble, Hardin fled to Pisgah Ridge where Susanna Dixon Anderson, his widowed aunt—a sister of Hardin's mother, lived. Years earlier, on February 8, 1855, an Anderson neighbor, Captain William Love, killed Susanna's husband, Dr. William Anderson, over a land dispute. The two men passed in a road junction, and a bullet struck Anderson in the back. Although he made it home, he died painfully thirty-six hours later.

At the funeral, Susanna Anderson, his thirty-two-year-old widow with a fifth child in her womb, cried aloud for justice. "Someday, this baby in my body will avenge the murder of its father," she wailed. A jury acquitted Love, an ex-ranger, Indian fighter and spokesman for Texans who resented newcomers.[5]

SUSANNA LIVED in this blackland, agricultural community in Navarro County south of Corsicana. Pisgah extended as a ridge of high ground, and took its name for the biblical Mount Pisgah, a range in Jordan northeast of the Dead Sea where Moses saw the Promised Land from Mount Nebo, the highest point. Pisgah in East Texas consisted of broken country, and a few general stores catering to drifters flowing between Dallas and San Antonio.

In January, 1869, Susanna Anderson opened Nash School, a small, log building substituting as a church, in Navarro County. She needed a teacher, and John Wesley Hardin needed a hideout. He took charge of twenty-five scholars, boys and girls between the ages of six and sixteen. One female student said "John Wesley Hardin prayed before class every morning."[6]

HARDIN'S FATHER WROTE his sister-in-law Susanna Anderson on March 20, 1869. He mentioned his sons, Benjamin who had died of natural causes a year earlier at the age of nine, and John, both of whom had left the family, the first by death, the other by the consequences of his own violent actions. Of them, the saddened James Gibson wrote, "Benny is in heaven no doubt happy with the good [Lord]." Of his wayward son, he said to Susanna, "John is with you. We expect to [carry] on till we embrace them both."

The father hoped that Alec Dixon, Susanna's brother, "or some honorable persons" would get John out of Texas. The elder Hardin suspected the Army had contacts all over the state regarding fugitives from justice. The military "will send orders for the arrest of all persons who had anything to do with [the slaying of Mage] the Negro."[7]

After three months, John quit teaching and went to live with the Barekman brothers and his (and their) Uncle Alec Dixon, an older brother of Hardin's mother. Sixteen-year-old John in particular looked up to twenty-six-year-old Alec Barekman, a Civil War veteran. Barekman and Hardin became enamored with the open and independent life of the man on horseback and their Uncle Alec Dixon of Navarro County hired them as cowboys. Becoming a cowboy represented liberation from responsibility, not that either cousin had ever practiced it. They would become cowboys because cowboys roamed free and gambled.

The Barekman brothers moved livestock across the state, and Hardin, without being specific, said he learned "to drive cattle to shipping points." Under the tutelage of the Barekmans and cowboys not much older than himself, Hardin played poker, seven-up and euchre. He wagered on horse races, dog and cockfights. He bet on who could spit tobacco juice closest to a specific mark.[8]

The gambling may have disturbed his Methodist parents more than his killings. The latter he might outgrow; gambling could become a serious lifelong habit.

IN 1869, HARDIN MET the notorious desperado Frank Polk who also worked as a cowhand for Uncle Alec Dixon. While Hardin obviously admired Polk, and to a certain extent patterned his life after him, Polk died too quickly to build a lasting legend. He and Hardin allegedly killed a man named Tom Brady.

A group of Yankee soldiers rode down from Corsicana to arrest both men. The soldiers did not get Hardin but they captured Polk and briefly jailed him. Upon being freed, Frank went to Wortham and died there in Freestone County while attempting to murder Mayor W. M. Zely. Polk and City Marshal Charles Powers shot each other to death.[9]

FURTHER NORTH, NEAR THE RED RIVER, the Peacock-Lee Feud (see Appendix C) was winding down, primarily because most of the participants were dead. Hardin referred to the solitary survivor, Simp Dixon, as a cousin, although no tie-in with Hardin's mother, Mary Elizabeth Dixon Hardin, or her family, has ever been made. Hardin said Simp was a member of the "Ku Kluck Klan" and had "sworn to kill Yankee soldiers for as long as he lived."[10]

Within a brief time, Simp had his opportunity. A squad of soldiers attacked him and Hardin in the Richland Creek bottom. The resultant "free and fast fight" ended with two soldiers dead and the others fleeing. Hardin claimed to have killed one; Simp killed the other.[11]

No identifiable military records mention any such scrap, although this is not to say that it never happened. It does seem unlikely, however, that such a squad, even if unseasoned, armed with rifles and having a superiority in numbers, should be the ones fleeing. It is far more probable that Hardin and Dixon fired a few rounds and departed. That two military deaths occurred is perhaps boastful wishing rather than factual accounting, and Hardin's brief, almost lackadaisical mention of the action is in itself suspect.

In February 1870 a squad of United States soldiers, led by a Sergeant Dasch, caught up with Simp in Limestone County. The sergeant shot Simp with a carbine, and Union soldiers buried him at the Fort Parker Memorial Cemetery near Mexia, placing him oblique to the others because he was "crossways with the world." Hardin called Simp "one of the most dangerous men in Texas," and described him as "about 19 years old at the time of his death."[12]

BY THE FALL OF 1869, Hardin's killing count had reached five, and perhaps twice that if some of his implications are given credence. He and brother Joe left Navarro County and resided briefly at Hillsboro with their Aunt Ann Hardin. The Hardin boys then moseyed down the Brazos to visit people John described as "some relatives of ours named Page." Old Jim Page, the only reference Hardin made of him, lived near Towash, twenty miles west of Hillsboro, on the left bank of the Brazos River in Hill County.[13]

Hardin spent his idle time playing poker and seven-up, and betting on the pony races at the Old Boles Racetrack near Towash. His father visited the Page settlement on December 24, 1869, and urged John to rejoin the family in Navarro County. John agreed to go—after one more fling. On January 4, 1870, he borrowed his father's horse, and with James Collins, a twenty-year-old farmer who had married a Hardin cousin, he headed for the race track and won $75 on the horses. Feeling lucky and carrying $325, he caroused and gambled with Benjamin B. Bradley and Hamp Davis when a Judge Moore suggested a private game of poker.[14]

Hardin, cousin Collins, Bradley, Davis and Moore retired to a tiny, doorless, one-room hovel with a non-functioning fireplace providing the only entrance and exit. Everybody was armed except Collins who had earlier lost his weapon, and money, to Bradley. For comfort, Hardin removed his boots and tossed them and his six-shooter into a corner. After a few hours of gambling, Hardin and Bradley argued. Bradley drew a knife. As John Wesley began drunkenly slipping, sliding and lurching backwards, Jim Collins saved Hardin's life by stepping between him and Bradley. Bradley then drew a six-shooter, but could not use it because Collins grappled with him, all the while screaming for Hardin to get out through the fireplace.

On a frigid night with a bright full moon, Hardin hit the frosty ground running in his stocking feet. He ducked behind a tree. An out-of-breath Collins pounded right behind him. "Let's go home," Collins panted. "We are in a hell of a scrape."

"I am not going home to face my father in this condition," Hardin replied. "I want my boots, my money and my pistol." Collins reluctantly returned to the room, but through reason and cajoling, recovered only Hardin's footwear. Judge Moore had charge of the money as well as Hardin's weapon. He declined to return either. As Hardin slipped on his boots, Bradley and Davis derisively screamed profanities, yelling that Hardin was a coward and a cheat. Calling Hardin a coward and a cheat was like saying "sic-em" to a pit bull.

Meanwhile, a crowd gathered as Hardin stumbled from person to person, trying to borrow a gun. Everybody refused because of Hardin's intoxication. This left only the reliable Cousin James Collins who obtained a six-shooter from a friend, swapped it with Bradley for his own gun, and gave the weapon to Hardin in exchange for John's promise to leave for home.

As Hardin and Collins headed for their horses, Bradley, Hamp Davis and several bystanders intercepted them. Bradley and Hardin commenced firing. Bradley staggered, crying, "Oh, Lordy, don't shoot me any more." But Hardin repeatedly pulled the trigger because he did not want to "take chances on a reaction." The crowd scattered as Hardin stood in the frozen mud and taunted them as cowards.

Another version involves an 1895 *El Paso Daily Herald* story published with a Hill County dateline. According to a witness, Hardin and Benjamin Bradley quarreled over a card game, but the two men separated as friends. Later, Hardin accused Bradley of stealing money. Hardin and Collins left the house to visit a saloon. On the way they met Bradley walking with his horse. "Is that you, Ben?" Hardin reportedly asked. Bradley answered "yes," and Hardin shot him.[15]

In October 1872, a grand jury indicted Hardin for the murder of Benjamin Bradley although why the State waited nearly three years is unknown. The charges were later dismissed.

The killing also earned Hardin a spot on the 1878 *List of Texas Fugitives From Justice*, sometimes known as *The Rangers Bible*. The terse statement merely said, "Hardin, John. Murder. He is the notorious desperado, John Wesley Hardin."

Judge Moore disappeared after the Bradley slaying. Historian Chuck Parsons suspects Hardin killed him also. To execute someone like Bradley was perhaps commendable, but to kill a respected jurist was something else. Historian Parsons believes Hardin ignored Moore's death because he could not justify it.

The August 30, 1877 edition of the *Daily Democratic Statesman* of Austin mentioned an 1872 affidavit by Texas Ranger commander George W. Baylor. Baylor said Hardin had confessed to killing two men in Peoria, Hill County, Texas around 1869 or '70. One of those likely was Bradley. Moore was probably the other.

Nevertheless, without evidence, or a Hardin written confession, Moore's death is questionable. In shooting Bradley, however, the sixteen-year-old Hardin had now notched his sixth victim.[16]

At two o'clock that night, Hardin slipped back to Page's house and rationalized the shootout to his father. Both Hardins decided this would be a good time to seek other relatives. John, not wishing to unduly expose his father to danger, suggested they flee along opposite banks of the Brazos. An hour or so later, John bedded down in a cotton gin. Across the river, posses kept the father under such surveillance that James Gibson Hardin sent a Masonic friend to advise his son of the law's presence. However, the posse trailed the courier, and surrounded Hardin's hideout.

There are certain periods in the Hardin memoirs during which his sincerity and passion seem genuine, but his explanations are ludicrous. Hardin said the posse dispatched two armed men inside the cotton gin to discuss surrender terms. Hardin and a shotgun relieved them of two six-shooters, a rifle and two derringers, plus a double-barreled weapon similar to his own. Then, he ordered the prisoners to shout to their friends that Hardin would meet them at old man Page's. The posse accepted this and left. Hardin told his two prisoners to head for Page's too, that he (Hardin) would be along shortly. He chuckled twenty years later, writing "I reckon they are waiting for me there yet."[17]

John Wesley Hardin rode to Pisgah in Navarro County where his parents, brothers and sisters greeted him warmly. His father cautioned that armed men were searching for him, so Hardin and several friends caught up with the lawmen six miles from Pisgah

Nancy Brinson (Dixon) Hardin and her husband Robert E. Hardin. Robert epitomized the average Hardin: farmer, hard-working, religious, honest, fair, diligent, and kind. When called upon, he could even be a civic or political leader. (Joyce Hardin Cavett Collection)

on the west bank of Pin Oak Creek. The posse denied seeking Hardin, and at his suggestion, returned to Hillsboro. These must have been the most timid lawmen in the West.

ON JANUARY 20, 1870, John Wesley, accompanied by cousin Alec Barekman, fled toward Uncle Bob Hardin's place at Brenham. After twenty miles, the two riders reached Horn Hill, shaped like a ram's horn, in central Limestone County. With no room at the inn, Hardin sought the comfort of a circus campfire. In the process he bumped the arm of a roustabout lighting his pipe. Hardin apologized as the man threatened to smash his nose. "I told him to smash and be damned, that I was a...smasher myself." The circus employee struck Hardin, and Hardin sent a .45 ball crashing through the man's head. Barekman covered the crowd while he and Hardin backed away. Number seven had now fallen before Hardin's gun.[18]

The cousins then separated. Alec Barekman returned to Pisgah, and Hardin rode toward Brenham by way of Kosse, Calvert and Bryan. Kosse, in southwestern Limestone County, existed as the terminus of the Houston and Texas Central Railroad.

At Kosse by chance, Hardin rendezvoused at the room of a local girl, and had just gotten comfortable when her sweetheart or husband or friend stormed into the house and demanded a hundred dollars to appease his loss of personal honor. Obviously he and the girl had joined in a conspiracy to set up Hardin who probably had been gambling and bragging about his winnings.

Pretending to be shaking with terror, and protesting that he did not have that much money on his person, John rummaged through his pockets and deliberately dropped a gold coin on the floor. As the "boyfriend" snatched the money off the floor, the last thing he saw was Hardin's mirthless smile and the dark hole of a six-shooter. "The ball struck him between the eyes and he fell over, a dead robber," Hardin wrote. Number eight went down.[19]

THE SIXTEEN-YEAR-OLD Hardin arrived at Brenham during the last of January 1870, and lived with his Uncle Robert Echison Hardin (see Appendix D), who persuaded John Wesley to help with the crops. "I thus became a farmer and made a good plough boy and hoer," John wrote.[20]

But Hardin was to farming what blueberries were to apple jelly. He relinquished his money to his Aunt Nancy, and she doled it out. Even so, he manipulated her. Gradually, the economic barriers crumbled. Hardin "borrowed" money for clothing, and spent it on the sporting life.

Once while drinking and gambling, he and his cousin Will, the son of Nancy and Robert Hardin, tied their horses to the Brenham courthouse fence. Someone stole them. Hardin said he rode over a hundred miles in search of those mounts, all without success.[21]

IN BRENHAM, Hardin met Phil Coe, a tall, dexterous gambler. Phil Coe came out of Gonzales County, Texas, where he was born in 1839. He stood at least six feet four inches, had cold gray eyes, a bushy goatee and a bullet-shaped head topped by coal black hair. His haircut was a bad example of barbering even by Texas

Philip H. Coe.
Coe was a gambler,
occasionally a
shooter, and always
a scoundrel. (Chuck
Parsons Collection)

standards. Coe weighed over two hundred pounds. He had served in the Confederate Army, but spent much of his service absent without leave or in the General Hospital in Houston with gonorrhea. Somewhere along the way he also became a gambler well-known in Texas. He carried a revolver—a weapon almost as necessary as cards in his profession—but he was never a gunman in the sense that Hardin was, in the traditional gunfighter/ desperado mode.[22]

Historian Chuck Parsons believes Coe tagged Hardin as "Young Seven-up," a nickname the boy cherished. Seven-up referred to a popular card game between two or more players. Any one person, or set of partners, needed seven points to win. The game has also been called "All Fours" and "Pitch."[23]

FROM BRENHAM, Hardin frequently rode to Evergreen, forty miles west. There he met the fifty-one-year-old Tennessean, Ben Hinds. In the early summer of 1870, Hinds claimed to be a peaceful farmer although a grand jury had indicted him for aggravated assault and battery upon an eight-year-old boy. He had also slashed the throat of a Fayette County deputy. Somehow, he escaped these charges although he eventually served five years in the Texas penitentiary for horse theft. A newspaper described him as "of medium height, square made, iron-gray hair, cold, stern blue eyes, and a reckless resolute expression." Hinds emerged in 1881 as "an old man, bluff but candid in manner, and quite communicative."

In the spring of 1870, somewhere around Hardin's seventeenth birthday, he and Hinds squatted around an Evergreen dry goods box and played seven-up until Hardin won $20 and quit. Ben objected to the abrupt withdrawal. They exchanged words, and Hinds snarled that if Hardin were not a mere boy he would beat him to death. Hardin responded that Hinds "should not spoil good intentions on account of my youth." Hinds reached for Hardin and found himself staring into a revolver barrel. The young gunman snapped that he liked fighting too, but "I use lead."

Since the bystanders supported Hinds, Hardin drew another pistol, the first known instance of his becoming a two-gun man. "The first person that makes a move or draws a gun, I'll kill him," he snapped. The crowd backed away. Hinds reportedly apologized.[24]

LATER THAT AFTERNOON, as the swollen afternoon sun dropped behind Evergreen's tall pines, Hardin claimed he encountered the six-foot, slender and dark, William Preston Longley. (Later newspaper correspondence indicates that the two never met.) Bill Longley, born in Austin County and a year older than Hardin, claimed the title of "the most successful outlaw who ever lived in Texas."

Bill Longley edged up to Hardin, introduced himself and said, "If you don't watch out, you will be shot all to pieces before you know it." Hardin responded that as long as enemies such as the aforementioned Hinds, stayed in front, he would be all right. "All I ask is a fair fight," he growled, and "I want you to understand that you can't bulldoze or scare me either."[25] The wary relationship of Hardin and Longley continued into a poker game. With over $200 on the blanket, Longley said, "I call you for $220. I have an ace full," meaning three aces and two of something else.

"Hold on. I have two pair," Hardin responded.

"They are not worth a damn."

"I reckon two pair of jacks [four jacks] are good," Hardin retorted. He raked in the pot.[26]

The two desperadoes never met again. However, as their reputations and notoriety increased—and the newspapers drew comparisons—they grew to jealously detest one another.

Death Ride

THE JAMES GIBSON HARDIN FAMILY never really had a home. They spent their lives as Texas wayfarers, drifting from one relative to another, staying with whoever took them in. And so it was in August 1870, that the Hardin family, James, his wife Elizabeth, his younger children and their older brother, Joe, were rolling northwest out of Pisgah with no particular destination in mind. A wagon wheel collapsed three miles from Mount Calm, a tiny hamlet in today's southern Hill County.

Joe thought the broken wagon might be God's way of advising the Hardins to spend time in Mount Calm. As providence would have it, the good people of Mount Calm had just built a schoolhouse, one awaiting a yet-to-be-named teacher. Louisa Rush—better known as Sister Rush—a widow with four children, provided shelter for the Hardin family. They spent the next two months in her home. She pleaded with the Hardins to put down roots in Mount Calm.

James Gibson did some fast estimating and concluded he could recruit seventy-five scholars locally to fill seats in the schoolhouse. The students would be worth $140 a month to Master Hardin since he anticipated two dollars each for youngsters in the lower grades and three dollars for older students. Based on these figures, Hardin signed a contract to teach ten months of school beginning the first Monday in October. In addition, he agreed to preach on Sunday and whenever else necessary. Hardin purchased six acres alongside what he called "The Mount Calm Institute."

A week later, Elizabeth Hardin wrote her brother Alec Dixon, saying her husband had hired several hands to cut timber in the nearby bottom lands. It rained the first day, and James briefly came down with chills and vomiting.

Meanwhile, the family remained with Sister Rush although Joe attended another school in Round Rock. Schoolmaster J. C. Landrum told Joe that John Wesley planned to meet his parents at Richland Crossing. Joe passed the word along, and his mother therefore included references to John in her letter to Alec: "If my sweet Johnny is there, tell him to come to us immediately [at Mount Calm]," she wrote.[1] "His Pa says so. We want to see him so bad. Tell him to come quickly. John, if you are at Pisgah, come home to Ma! I could tell you a great many things though I hope to see you face to face ere long. The children want to see you bad. Come home, sweet John. Come Johnny."

Johnny did visit Mount Calm. He peddled cattle hides, then rode over to Round Rock, attended class for one day with Joe and passed the final examination. Joe returned to Mount Calm where he became a lawyer, probably by studying with his father, and assisted as a school teacher.

JOHN DRIFTED to Longview, Texas where on January 9, 1871, Lieutenant E. T. Stakes of the State Police charged him with stealing a horse from S. C. Clinton, plus four counts of unspecified murder.[2] The State Police planned to convey him to Marshall, but inexplicably released him. He had barely reached the streets, however, when the authorities remanded him back to jail. They planned to transfer him to Waco in McLennan County, where he would stand trial for horse theft, as well as murdering a man named Hoffman in a barber shop. Hardin denied the accusations.[3]

Longview authorities imprisoned Hardin with three others charged with unrelated crimes, in a log building with iron cells. John bought whiskey and tobacco for himself and his cell mates. One sold him a smuggled .45 Colt with four loaded chambers. Hardin gave him $10 and a $25 overcoat. He then tried to talk his

Mary Elizabeth (Dixon) Hardin, mother of John
Wesley Hardin. She was religious, attractive,
resilient, and possessed a tough, unyielding core that
united the family. She never lost faith that her son
Johnny was a good boy. (R. G. McCubbin Collection)

new friends into a jail-break. Hardin proposed killing the jailer,
then rushing the front of the building and overwhelming anyone
else. The three prisoners declined, believing they would soon be
released anyway. So Hardin concealed the weapon and awaited
his transfer to Waco.

Within a few days, the black female cook opened the cell door
and slid three supper plates inside. When the prisoners yelled

for the other one, she explained, "One of you is leaving tonight." Hardin realized this had to be him, so he took a clothing inventory. He had a heavy fur coat, a medium sack coat, two undershirts and two white shirts. John stripped, tied the pistol under his left arm, put a shirt over that and went to bed. A few hours later, when lawmen banged on the door, Hardin expressed irritation and alarm at being awakened out of a sound sleep and forced to leave so unexpectedly. Guards ordered what appeared to be a frightened Hardin into his clothes for the trip to Waco. He asked Lieutenant E. T. Stakes and Private Jim Smalley about the possibility of mob action from friends of the man whom Hardin had supposedly killed.[4]

Stakes and Smalley reassured him, so he dressed and dropped a jar of pickles into his overcoat pocket. A 175-mile trip to Waco, with snow on the ground, lay ahead, and the two officers briefly frisked Hardin, finding no weapons. Next they led him to a small black pony covered only with a worn blanket. Hardin tried to purchase a saddle from the jailer, but was rebuffed. However, he did get an additional blanket before officers lashed his legs under the pony. With Smalley holding the reins of Hardin's mount, the Waco trek commenced.

Hardin described the procession thus: "When daylight came, they untied my legs and allowed me to guide the little black pony. If you had met our party that day, you would have seen a small white man about forty-five-years-old, who was a captain of police named Stokes [Stakes], a middle-weight, dark-looking man, one-fourth Negro, one-fourth Mexican, and one-half white,… leading a small black pony with a boy seventeen-year-old tied thereon and shivering with cold."[5] An L. B. Anderson accompanied the procession. He rode the recovered horse back toward Waco where it would be introduced in evidence at the trial.

Stakes threatened to shoot John if he tried to run. Jim Smalley said he would kill him if Stakes gave the word. Hardin responded by being polite and suitably frightened. He rambled constantly about morality and religion, saying he was "strictly down on lawlessness."

Upon approaching flood waters in the Sabine River, the lawmen again lashed Hardin securely to the pony, and placed him in the middle of the procession. Stakes led. Hardin wrote later that

East Texas. John Wesley Hardin country during his early years before driving cattle to Abilene, Kansas. Considering his fast gun and multiple killings, he had to move around a lot.

the black pony swam like a duck. Except for everybody being frozen and wet, the crossing was uneventful.

The group halted after two more miles. Smalley searched for wood and fodder. Stakes borrowed an ax from a nearby rancher and ordered Hardin to chop kindling. The chore made Hardin uneasy because he feared the revolver might drop out of his shirt every time he raised his arm. After the deputy returned, the entire party clustered around the crackling fire and slept until morning.

On the following day, a boat ferried them across the muddy, swirling Trinity River. The party slogged on horseback through swampy bogs. Again the officers tied Hardin securely to the pony until reaching dry land.

On the evening of January 22, 1871, as the group approached within a few miles of Waco, Stakes and Anderson left to requisition corn and fodder from a farmhouse. Smalley tethered the animals and squatted on a stump while cursing Hardin. Hardin walked over to the opposite side of his pony, laid his head against the animal and pretended to be crying while loosening the Colt .45 from beneath his left arm. When the gun pulled free, Hardin stepped toward Smalley as the private reached for his revolver. Hardin shot him dead, saying later that Smalley died "because he did not have sense enough to throw up his hands at the point of a pistol."[6] Victim number nine had fallen.

John Wesley Hardin leaped on Smalley's sorrel mare, rode hard and never stopped until he reached Mount Calm and explained the events to his father. Oddly, the cavalcade had been traveling in the general direction of Mount Calm anyway, since the tiny community was only twenty miles northeast of Waco. The sorrowful preacher gave his son another horse, and sent the sorrel back to the dead man's family.

THE *FLAKES DAILY BULLETIN*, published in Galveston on February 4, 1871, described Hardin's escape somewhat differently than he later recalled it. When two miles out of Fairfield, Texas, while Stakes and Anderson gathered firewood, Smalley, who led the prisoner's pony, dismounted at the camp site and sat down. At that instant, Hardin "drew a repeater" and shot him in the back. Smalley rose, turned, and attempted to draw his own revolver as Hardin shot him in the stomach. As Smalley fell, Hardin climbed on the deputy's horse and fled. An aged black woman witnessed the killing.

Stakes and Anderson arrived in camp just as Hardin departed. Stakes's horse was too jaded to pursue. Anderson, still on the animal Hardin had supposedly stolen, followed the trail until his mount came up lame. According to the newspapers, Hill County authorities offered $1100 for Hardin's apprehension.

Hardin's father advised him to take refuge in Mexico, but John had barely left his parents residence before another group of officers arrested him between Belton and Waco. The young gunman referred to these policemen as Smith, Jones and Davis. While these names might have been actual, the possibility of three lawmen answering to such common monikers is as unlikely as square dancing buffalo. Hardin probably coined these names later because he could not remember the real ones. Anyway, the lawmen planned to incarcerate him in Austin, but the night closed down ten miles from Belton and they camped. Smith would take the first guard, Jones the second, and Davis the last. The guards had been drinking heavily, and Hardin carefully noted where they laid their weapons.

Davis and Jones dropped off to sleep. Smith (the guard) nodded before bracing his elbows on his knees and starting to snore. Carefully, Hardin picked up Davis' double-barreled shotgun and Jones's six-shooter. He fired one shotgun round at Smith's head and emptied the other barrel into Jones. Davis rose and groggily screamed, "What's the matter?" Hardin thumbed the six-shooter, and although Davis "begged and hollered, I kept on shooting until I was satisfied he was dead." A seventeen-year-old boy now had twelve dead men on his back trail.[7]

JOHN WESLEY HARDIN AGAIN RETURNED HOME to explain that the latest killings were not his fault, that the three men had arrested him while he was asleep. "Son," his father responded, "never tell this to mortal man. I don't believe you, but go to Mexico and go at once."[8]

John Wesley slept that night in the cellar of his folks' home and spent the next day in an abandoned outhouse. He and his father left Mount Calm on the following evening and traveled through Waco. His father rode part way to Mexico with John since he wanted to be certain his rebellious son had truly fled the country. At Belton they parted. The father returned to Mount Calm. The son promptly forgot his promise, and turned his horse toward relatives in Gonzales County. He knew he would be welcome.

A Dead Man
Every Mile

AFTER RECONSTRUCTION started, Texas was a law and order wasteland where desperadoes trusted no one but family. This explains why, when in trouble, John Wesley Hardin always turned toward relatives. It also explains why, although some relatives may have been appalled by Hardin's bloody activities, they never turned him in. He was family, and despite what he had done, in their eyes he had not sunk as low as the government.

Back when the Hardins were first entering Texas, Martha Balch Hardin, a sister of James Gibson Hardin, married Emanual Clements, Sr. and lived in Limestone County (now Freestone). Emanual became county clerk, and also the first sheriff of Limestone County. Their eleven children would become cousins and contemporaries of John Wesley Hardin.[1]

Hardin's memoirs mentioned four of his Clements first cousins: James, Emanuel, Jr. (called "Manning" by Hardin but "Mannen" by everyone else)[2], Joseph, and John, the latter usually called "Gip." The cousins asked Hardin to participate in a Kansas trail drive. The Clements' were gathering livestock for Jake Johnson, Columbus Carroll and Crawford "Doc" Burnett.

James Clements. The Clements and the Hardin clans meshed together like sweet corn and butter. (Chuck Parsons Collection)

History calls the Jake Johnsons, the Columbus Carrolls and the Doc Burnetts "cattlemen," but a more accurate term would have been "trail driving contractors." Few ranchers could afford to send employees toward Kansas with a trail herd. Contractors hired out-of-work cowboys, or men on the run looking for employment and a new identity. Trailing cattle north to Kansas was a business.[3]

Cowboys and cattle drives started their rise to national and world-wide fame with the ruinous, bitter end of the Civil War. The cotton economy lay in shambles, due in part to over-worked land and the boll weevil, but primarily from a lack of laborers to pick the crop. With no one to tend livestock during the early and mid 1860s, the animals ranged wild in the dense thickets of south-central Texas. Young Texas men, penniless and jobless, returned from the War and saw opportunity in those untamed cows.

But who needed the beef? The South did, but it was financially prostrate. California was too distant, and lacked a sufficient market. That left the North, economically thriving and desperately craving foodstuffs, especially beef. The shortest distance between Texas and the Chicago stockyards was north to Kansas where the railhead had recently penetrated. Between the two (Texas and the railhead) lay only open range, rich with grama grass. Cattle furnished their own transportation.

Cattlemen contractors, particularly in South Texas, frequently employed Mexican vaqueros. Since Hardin had only begun to consider himself a cowboy, and had worked only on his uncle's ranch, he had little Hispanic contact. One February day in 1871, Hardin and his Clements cousins visited a Mexican camp where someone suggested a diversion called Spanish Monte. A blanket immediately hit the ground. Although Hardin did not completely understand the game, and understood Spanish even less, he put up his money. During one round he nodded to the Mexican dealer, tapped his card and said "Pay the queen." When the dealer tried to explain that in Spanish Monte, the Queen lost, the young cowboy banged him over the head with a six-shooter. Two nearby players drew knives, and Hardin shot one in the arm and the other through the lungs. The gunman and his cousins later chuckled about the bloody events, Hardin noting that "the best people in the vicinity said I did a good thing."[4]

Assuming the story happened the way Hardin claimed it did, and the seriously wounded vaquero died, Hardin had now killed thirteen men.

MEANWHILE, CARROLL AND JAKE JOHNSON took sixteen hundred head up the Chisholm Trail toward Abilene, Kansas. Since Columbus Carroll liked Hardin's no-nonsense grit, he placed the boy in charge of a second trail herd being readied for the Kansas market. It pulled out a week or so after Carroll's exit.

As Hardin gathered the livestock, a black man, Bob King, tried to remove beeves he claimed Hardin and his cowboys had "inadvertently" accumulated. So "I rode up to him," Hardin said, "and struck him over the head with my pistol and told him to get out of my herd." King left.[5]

During early March 1871, with Hardin and Jim Clements earning $150 a month (ordinary cowboys received $20), the herd started north for Abilene, Kansas. Gip and Joe Clements followed with cattle belonging to Doc Burnett.

The original herd, divided between Hardin and Columbus Carroll, totaled nearly three thousand head. Each party used a dozen hands and twice as many horses. A herd averaged between eight and fifteen miles during daylight. It usually grazed in the morning until eight o'clock, then traveled until about eleven, after which it stopped and grazed until two. The line of march continued until five o'clock when the herd again grazed. As darkness fell, the cattle were bunched together and bedded down. One-third of the cowboys pulled guard duty, awakening the next shift five hours later. If the cattle stampeded, everyone did some furious, risky riding. An ordinary Texas to Abilene journey took between sixty and ninety days.

In Williamson County, all trail hands caught the measles except Hardin and Jim Clements. The drovers camped two miles south of Corn Hill in the north-central part of the county. Hardin and Clements cooked and nursed the cowboys.

With the herd resting, the outfit absorbed a few strays from outfits passing by. Trail bosses seldom worried about it since settlements occurred when the drives ended. However, a rambunctious white steer disrupted Hardin's cattle, and he fired his .45 at the animal's nose, intending to stun and scare him off. Instead, the bullet struck the steer in the eye and instantly killed him. Hardin wrote later that while the animal caused no further difficulties, "his owner gave me no end of trouble in the courts. I think that ox cost me about $200."

What a curious statement, since courts were as scarce as big cities. Given Hardin's temperament, it is difficult to see how such a dispute could have ended any other way than with funeral services. Anyway, Hardin's probable record now stood at thirteen dead men and one steer.

The trail hands recovered from the measles in ten days, and the herd crossed into Oklahoma at Red River Station, sometimes called Red River Bluff. Here the Chisholm Trail exited Texas.

THE CHISHOLM CONTINUED through Indian Territory better known to cowboys as the Nations, a series of Oklahoma areas containing reservation tribes. The route into Fort Sill went through the Kiowa, Comanche, and Apache nations. After that came the Wichita and Caddo, the Shawnee, Seminole, Creek, Cherokee and Osage.

Hardin described the trail as just one long line of livestock. Fifteen herds crossed the Red River on the same day. The Chisholm had become one great turbulent interstate dedicated to cattle.[6]

Wildlife thrived everywhere. Hardin shot antelope for a change of diet, and once wounded a wolf in the hips. He roped and pulled it into camp where everybody took a shot, one bullet severing the line. The wolf escaped. The entire outfit now had wolf fever as everybody tried to snag one. Nothing came of it except tired men and crippled horses.[7]

ONE AFTERNOON on the South Canadian River, about half-way through Oklahoma, Hardin's horse shied away from a clump of bushes. Hardin glanced up just as an Indian unleashed an arrow. Hardin jerked his revolver and fired. The arrow went wild, but the bullet hit the Indian squarely in the forehead. Back at camp, the cowboys expressed an interest in the dead man, so Hardin led them to the corpse. Some of the boys wanted his bow and arrows, but John demurred. With a spade and axe, they dug a shallow grave and buried the Indian with his weapons.

Whether the incident happened as Hardin described it is a matter of conjecture. Hardin probably killed an Indian, and returned with his companions to view the body. The question is, was the encounter really one of self-defense? Hardin said earlier that upon crossing the Red River, the story circulated that Indians had recently slain two white men. "Of course, all the talk was Indians, and everybody dreaded them. I was just about as much afraid of an Indian as I was of a raccoon. In fact, I was anxious to meet some on the warpath," he added.

With Hardin thinking like that, any Indian who wasn't firing arrows at him, perhaps intended to. So killing one, regardless of provocation, was self-defense. Fourteen men had now perished in front of the steady, relentless gun-hand of the barely eighteen-year-old John Wesley Hardin.[8]

Up ahead, the Osage Nation was the last Indian reservation in Oklahoma before entering Kansas. Each Nation attempted to extract a tax of ten cents a head for passage through. Some cattle-men paid, and some did not. Hardin did not. With most of the hands and Hardin absent from camp one morning, the Osages took a fancy silver bridle belonging to Hardin.

Later that afternoon, the Osage began cutting out cattle. One man had a silver bridle. Hardin offered him $5 for it. The Indian grunted, and handed over the item. Hardin then claimed some-one had stolen it from his cow camp. The Indian frowned and reached for the bridle. Hardin jabbed him with a pistol, then clubbed him over the head with the weapon. Another Indian selected an exceptionally large steer, and attempted to drive it off. When Hardin warned him away, the Osage said if he could not have the steer he would kill it. Hardin drew his six-shooter and warned the man that if he killed the animal, Hardin would kill him.

"Well," wrote Hardin, "he killed the beef and I killed him. The other Indians promptly vanished." Hardin mounted the dead warrior on the steer's back. The body count now numbered fifteen.[9]

As Hardin crossed into Kansas and approached Cowskin Creek (which he called Cow House) twenty miles south of Wichita, a delegation of businessmen encouraged the cowboys to visit a new community. Hardin reached Park City on May 28, 1871, by fol-lowing a plow furrow and veering west of the Chisholm Trail. The new avenue became the Park City Trail. Hardin's crew took advantage of sin and whiskey before returning to the Chisholm and pointing again toward Abilene.[10]

The Killing Trail

AFTER FORDING THE LITTLE ARKANSAS RIVER where the trail narrowed, Hardin's herd approached Newton Prairie near today's Valley Center, Kansas. Here, the trail widened from one to three miles on the flatland, thus permitting ample grazing and "passing zones."

A Mexican drive approaching from behind penetrated into Hardin's livestock and both herds partially merged. The boss vaquero, known as José, which Hardin spelled "Hosea" (and is pronounced ho-SAY), accused Hardin of delaying the Mexican progress. Hardin yelled for José to go around.

This angered the Hispanic trail boss, and he retreated to the rear of his herd. With no one guiding the oncoming Mexican livestock, the cattle again approached the Texans. Hardin's cowboys turned them to the left. José cursed Hardin in Spanish and went to the wagon for his rifle.

When a hundred yards short of Hardin, José fired. The bullet flicked off John Wesley's hat. The vaquero aimed again, but this time the rifle misfired. José shifted the weapon to his left hand, pulled a revolver with his right and advanced, shooting every few steps while he screamed for his companions. Hardin yelled for Jim Clements.

An artist's rendition of the fight with the Mexican cowboys.
(*The Life of John Wesley Hardin*)

Hardin's pistol—an ancient cap-and-ball—wobbled due to excessive shooting. The cylinder had to be steadied with one hand while pulling the trigger. Nevertheless, Hardin fired several times from horseback, and missed. When he dismounted to shoot, he still missed. From the sidelines, Jim Clements yelled, "turn the horse loose and hold the cylinder."

Hardin did so, fired and grazed the vaquero in the thigh, aimed and pulled the trigger again. The gun misfired when the firing pin struck between chambered rounds. Both men now grappled. Other vaqueros clustered around. Jim Clements, screaming for the Mexicans not to shoot, jumped between the combatants and separated them, explaining "they were both drunk and did not know what they were doing."

In spite of Hardin's never-ending ache for confrontation, he wasn't a fool even when his blood was running hot. He thus agreed to a truce because his cap-and-ball pistol refused to function, and Jim Clements had not even loaded his weapon. The antagonists momentarily withdrew.

Back in camp, Hardin and Clements glowered when the vaqueros moved up again. The two men armed themselves with better revolvers.

Seven vaqueros, including José, circled around toward the Texans. Hardin changed horses and blocked their path. As the adversaries closed, José fired and missed. Hardin dropped his reins, spurred his horse and charged, all the while firing. The first

A cattle drive that must have looked like hundreds of others
on their way to Abilene. (R. G. McCubbin Collection)

bullet struck José in the heart. Blood gushed from his mouth as
he slumped over the saddle horn.

While Clements stripped two pistols from José, Hardin grabbed
the horse.

Both groups converged. Hardin shot a steer through the nose
and stampeded the herd. In the melee the vaqueros scattered.
Only one stood his ground, and Hardin shot him in the head.

The remaining vaqueros sought refuge with nearby outfits.
Clements and Hardin captured two men each. The last two denied any involvement, and claimed their companions must have
been drunk. Hardin accepted the story and released them. The
others, however, pulled pistols and fired point-blank at John
Wesley. They missed. Hardin retaliated, writing "The first I shot
through the heart, and he dropped dead. The second I shot
through the lungs and Jim shot him too. He fell off his horse, and
I was going to shoot him again when he begged and held up both
hands. I could not shoot a man...begging and down. Besides, I
knew he would die anyway."

"In comparing notes after the fight, we [Hardin and Jim Clements] agreed that I had killed five of the six dead Mexicans." John Wesley Hardin had now accounted for twenty dead men, the last five within a day or two of his eighteenth birthday.[1]

Of course, Hardin's account had its discrepancies. The *Wichita Tribune* of June 1, 1871, carried a garbled version of a gunfight on the Little Arkansas. It blamed intoxication, and told a morality tale suggesting possible consequences when herds by-pass Wichita for the Park City Trail.[2]

> A herd arrived at Park City last Sunday [May 28], and as near as we can learn, both joy and bad whiskey was unconfined. The cattle left unguarded roamed at will, and their will led them onto a cornfield. A boy was sent to drive them off, and while in the act of driving them away, one of the herders came up and threatened to kill the boy. His threat was heard by another herder who had just come up, and by a single shot brought him to the ground. This act was witnessed by a third party, who soon dispatched him to the spirit world. Another man coming up in time to witness the effects of the last shot, done likewise and another saddle was emptied. The whole matter ended up with two men being killed and one mortally wounded. This was more shooting than human flesh could endure.

Waldo E. Koop, a Kansas historian, suspects that "a [newspaper] story reporting six victims might have seemed so exaggerated that it would have been discounted entirely." So the article mentioned only two deaths. Koop also cited "orally repeated legends still recalled by descendants of pioneers of the area where the fight occurred." Those supported the Hardin version of events. One person pointed out a flood control project to Koop. In his youth, before water covered the area, he had been shown the grave site of six Mexican cowboys.[3]

Frederick "Fred" Christoph Duderstadt, two years older than Hardin, a Prussian and a stockman of DeWitt County, Texas, drove cattle only a short distance behind Hardin. Duderstadt mentioned how these killings led to the rise of Hardin's stature among his cowboy peers.

The stockman described Hardin as becoming the talk of the trail, as cowboys "stopped by the Hardin night camps just to get a glimpse of the famed kid gunman, or maybe to talk with him." Duderstadt said cowmen with "the status of cattle kings also made it a point to meet Wes."[4]

John Wesley Hardin forever after would be known, especially in Kansas, as "Little Arkansas," a reference not to Hardin's height, but to the Little Arkansas River where the killings took place. The name made him feared, prominent, and respected. And Hardin loved it.

Within a few days Hardin's cattle reached the bed grounds of the Chisholm Trail thirty miles south of Abilene, Kansas, on the North Fork of the Cottonwood River. Here the herd rested alongside one hundred thousand other Texas cattle awaiting sale and shipment east.

Columbus Carroll had brought the first Texas herd of the season to Abilene, arriving on May 10, 1871.[5] He sent word for Hardin and his wranglers to join him in town, receive their pay, and be discharged.

John rode into Abilene on or about June 1, 1871, and described the village as filled with sporting men and women, gamblers, cowboys, and desperados. "I have seen many fast towns," he said, "but I think Abilene beat them all."[6]

The Junction City *Union* agreed with him:

> For two or three things Abilene is noted. It is the principal rendezvous for the Texas cattle trade drovers, buyers, sellers and shippers. It handles more money than any town its size in the West, and has a class of transient men decidedly rough and reckless. Cut loose from all of the refining influences and enjoyment of life, these herdsmen toil for tedious months behind their slow herds, seeing scarcely a house, garden, woman or child for nearly 1,000 miles, like a cargo of sea-worn sailors coming into port, they must have—when released—some kind of entertainment. In the absence of something better, they at once fall into the liquor and gambling saloons at hand.[7]

Hardin posed for an itinerant photographer. He looked his eighteen years, a boy-going-on-a-man, lean and angular, 140 pounds and about 5-foot-9-inches in height, average for the time. A metal neck fastener protruded on his left side. It held him perfectly still and probably accounted for his sober expression. The boots, riding heels at least two inches high and "set under well," as the catalogs used to say, made him appear leaner and taller. A touch of jauntiness enriched the casual pose. A white hat with a high Texas peak perched on dark hair. His ears snuggled close to the head while the muscular hands and rugged face suggested outdoor activity. The fuzzy cheeks revealed a cleft chin, straight nose and steady eyes. Hardin removed the suffocating collar attachment. The "long roll cutaway" suit, inexpensive and store-bought, of lightweight wool, was of a generic dark color, common attire on Abilene streets. With no fancy trim in evidence (hatband, spurs, weapons or other decorative gear), Hardin split the difference between resembling a working cowboy and a successful businessman of standing.[8]

Abilene, Kansas

THE VILLAGE OF ABILENE, built upon productive, loamy soil and high, luxuriant grasses, arose in 1857 on the north bank of Mud Creek. Surveyors finished laying out lots in 1861, and a year later, Abilene became a county seat with a dozen log huts. In 1867, eastern Kansas refused to accept Texas cattle because of the Texas Tick, a bug that did not affect the Longhorns but destroyed domesticated cattle. So the Texans drove their stock further west and shipped them through the Union Pacific Railroad at Abilene.

Abilene's status as a wide-open cattle town was assured by 1868. Texas Street ran east and west, parallel to the railroad. South of that—and sometimes north—wild elements defined as Texan did their best to shake off the loneliness and dust of the trail.[1]

The Junction City, Kansas, *Union* described Abilene as a town cut in half by the railroad. The churches, real estate offices, banks, and courthouse, existed on one side, while a museum of wonders laid claim to the other. The *Union* called the cowboys "citizens who live temporarily in Texas, or on the trails between Kansas and that State, but spend most of their time in this lively miniature city."[2]

Wild Bill Hickok. Wild Bill was never as homicidal as Wes Hardin, but he was every bit as dangerous. (R. G. McCubbin Collection)

Ben Thompson. Ben is better known as a Wild West gunman than his list of shootouts tends to justify. (R. G. McCubbin Collection)

IN ONE WEEK ALONE, the Great Western Stock Yards shipped fifty-eight carloads of livestock to market. One-year-old steers brought between $5 to $8 each. Two-year-olds were worth $9 to $12, and three-year-olds from $16 to $20. Cows went for $14 to $18 each.[3]

Forty-three responsible citizens in 1869 pushed through a petition incorporating Abilene. The town elected a mayor, and in the spring of 1870 created a marshal's office. Tom Smith was an outstanding peace officer until a homesteader nearly severed his head with an axe on November 2, 1870. After an interim, the city fathers appointed James Butler "Wild Bill" Hickok as marshal on April 15, 1871. He chose his own deputies, drew a monthly stipend of $150, plus 25 percent of all fines collected and fifty cents for each dog shot. He had been on the job six weeks when John Wesley Hardin hit town.

Hickok was a month short of his thirty-fourth birthday, and was at least six feet tall, every inch composed of complexities.

His lean and muscular frame suggested athletic prowess. A dandy in dress, and fastidious in habits, he had chestnut hair parted in the middle. A droopy mustache dangled beneath a thin nose and blue-gray eyes. Two guns jutted openly from leather holsters, or sometimes from a sash. The marshal favored .36-caliber Colt Navy 1851 revolvers. Like Hardin, he had a pronounced expertise with hand guns, and gambling was his passion.[4]

HARDIN GRAVITATED TO a large warehouse-appearing structure with a single word ALAMO splashed on the front. The *Union* newspaper out of Junction City, Kansas, referred glowingly to the Alamo's namesake in San Antonio, Texas, and noted in this slightly edited statement that this Alamo drew attention in Kansas:

> At night it is brilliantly illuminated. Crowds swarm within and about its doors. There are tables covered with the green cloth. On them are piled the checks of ivory, gold and silver. About the bar are costly mirrors, pyramids of sparkling glasses, and vases of the choicest flowers give the place an air of elegance. The harmonious strains of piano and violin temper the intense excitement of the games with a sort of weird enchantment.[5]

Ordinarily when a herd hit town, the cattlemen paid off the hired help, retaining only sufficient manpower to guard the beeves until they were sold. The trail hands returned home, sometimes immediately and sometimes after losing their money in the Abilene saloons, brothels and gambling halls.

Columbus Carroll and Jake Johnson offered Hardin $150 a month, and Jim Clements $140 a month to continue looking after the cattle until buyers had shipped them out. Clements turned down the offer, and left for Texas.[6]

Carroll "squared" Hardin with the officials. A system existed in Abilene, as in most cattle towns, by which a man could be "posted" "fixed" or "squared" (all meant essentially the same thing) with the city marshal. A herd owner slipped the marshal a few dollars and purchased the officer's indulgence for a cowboy's indiscretions. Posting could last for a night, a weekend or the few days that a trail hand would be in town. A drunken, unruly cowboy who was "squared" would be guided to a flophouse instead of clubbed over the head and dragged off to jail. The marshal also looked the other way when the fees for "squaring" equaled any rewards offered. Of course, everyone understood that the man being "posted" would not commit a serious crime, and all damages would be guaranteed by the poster. While Hardin had lines he could not cross, his misdemeanor problems such as drunkenness and brawling would be treated leniently, even ignored if serious injuries did not occur.

Columbus Carroll should have spent some of that "squaring" money for his own benefit, although he likely considered himself automatically posted since he paid the bribe. As Hardin and Carroll caroused in "a notorious resort," deputy Tom Carson, a nephew of Kit Carson, pulled a gun on Carroll. Hardin pulled one on Carson. Hardin forced the lawman from the premises, and told him to fetch Wild Bill. Carson left. Neither he nor Hickok returned, nor did anyone comment when both parties passed each other on the street the next morning.[7]

BY NOW, HARDIN HAD reacquainted himself with Phil Coe and Ben Thompson, two notorious gambler/gunmen he had previously met in Texas.

Ben Thompson, the son of a sailor, was born on November 2, 1843, in Knottingley, County York, England. Thompson grew up as a short, feisty individual in Austin, Texas. Although he learned the printing trade as a young man, his profession rarely varied from that of a gambler and manslayer. He spent a lifetime as one of the most dangerous men in Texas although most of his victims walked away only with wounds. While Thompson was neither a Hardin nor a Hickok when it came to gunplay, he was not far behind.

Both Phil Coe and Ben Thompson arrived at Abilene, Kansas in the spring of 1871, about the time Hickok accepted employment as city marshal. They surfaced as gamblers intent on acquiring money not through saddlesweat but by relieving Texas cowboys of their earnings. After pooling their assets, they opened the Bull's Head Saloon on First Street. A sign featuring a virile bull swung from the front. The placard was offensive to respectable people, so Marshal Hickok sent painters to dab over the obvious masculine aspects.[8]

From then on Hickok and the two gamblers and saloon

owners were at odds. Hickok fueled the quarrel by claiming the two men cheated Texas drovers, whereas Coe and Thompson rebutted that Hickok disliked Texans.[9]

Meanwhile, with Wes Hardin being the talk of the saloons regarding the number of men he had killed, and Ben Thompson having cowboy connections, it was not long before Hardin and Thompson had a serious discussion. Ben Thompson railed about Reconstruction, about the hated Union and how Marshal Hickok epitomized the Northern suppression of the South. Hardin said Thompson "tried to prejudice me every way he could against Bill, and told me how Bill, being a Yankee, always picked out Southern men to kill, especially Texans. I told him, 'I am not doing anybody's fighting now except my own, but I know how to stick to a friend. If Bill needs killing, why don't you kill him yourself?'"

Thompson replied, "I would rather get someone else to do it. I told him then that he had struck the wrong man."[10]

Although Hardin was a killer, he liked to think that he killed only in self-defense, or for manliness, or because it was the right thing to do.

Some historians discount Hardin's story, arguing persuasively that Thompson was a brave man with proven credentials. He would not farm out his killings. Perhaps. But brave men are not necessarily foolhardy. Courageous men, especially if they are gamblers, instinctively understand the odds in any given situation. They knew anyone challenging Hickok, no matter how lucky he felt, would likely wind up in the cemetery.

In Hardin, Thompson recognized a dangerous, ruthless, cocky youth who just might take the marshal. If he did, good. If he did not, too bad.

While Hardin would relish a Hickok confrontation, it would be on his (Hardin's) terms, and not some third party's. "I had not yet met Bill Heycox [sic]," Hardin wrote, and "really wished for a chance to have a set-to with him."[11]

Fred Duderstadt arrived in Kansas only a week or so behind Hardin. He confirmed that Texas men not only on the trail but in Abilene were constantly making bets over who would win a showdown between Hickok and Hardin. "Wes was a hero" to the other cowboys, Duderstadt wrote. "He had been publicly

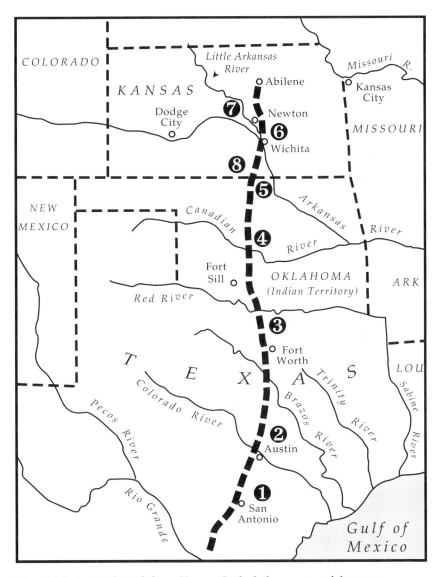

The Chisholm Trail to Abilene, Kansas. Included are some of the more
obscure places that Hardin made famous by shooting people.
(1.) Hardin trail herd starts from here. (2.) Hardin's drovers catch measles.
(3.) Red River Station. (4.) Hardin kills one Indian. (5.) Hardin kills Osage
Indian. (6.) Park City. (7.) Little Arkansas River. Five Mexican cowboys
killed. (8.) Hardin kills Bideno.

applauded for thinning out occupation troops and the State Police. He had a reputation as the world's fastest man with six-guns, and he also had a reputation for shooting in the head, where it counted. There was [intense] speculation [as to] what might happen if Wes and Wild Bill came together."[12]

Hardin and Hickok met in a wine room where they discussed the illegality of carrying firearms in Abilene. Hickok offered to be Hardin's friend. Hardin replied that he was charmed by the marshal's liberal views. They parted without resolving the issue of weapons, since Hardin still openly displayed his. Obviously, Hickok was permitting Hardin a flexibility that other cowboys did not enjoy.

IN ABILENE, KANSAS, carrying a revolver drew a penalty of not more than seventy-five dollars. The *discharge* of any weapon cost "not less than ten nor more than three hundred dollars."[13]

Hardin's *two* revolvers automatically made him a lightning rod of attention, especially since Hickok posted printed notices forbidding firearms inside the city. While Hardin was not the only armed cowboy, he rubbed it in by flaunting two six-shooters while he rolled tenpins and gambled at poker, faro and seven-up.

On one occasion, Wild Bill told Hardin to remove his pistols. Hickok then strolled outside, and Hardin followed, the high-heeled boots of both men making audible clumps on the boardwalk. An aggravated Hickok turned and snapped, "What are you doing with those pistols on?"

"I'm just taking in the town."

An exasperated Hickok jerked a weapon and said, "Take those pistols off. I arrest you."

Hardin pulled them from scabbards and held the guns out to Hickok, butts forward. Then Hardin simply rolled the guns over in his hands and stuck them, fully cocked, in Hickok's face. Since Hardin wrote the only account, his statement is worth evaluating:

> While he [Hickok] was reaching for them Hardin said, "I reversed and whirled them over on him with the muzzles in his face, springing back at the same time. I told him to put his pistols up, which he did. I cursed him for a long-haired scoundrel that would shoot a boy with his back to him (as I had been told he

intended to do with me). He said, "Little Arkansaw, you have been wrongly informed."

I shouted [to the bystanders], "This is my fight and I'll kill the first man that fires a gun."

Bill said, "You are the gamest and quickest boy I ever saw. Let us compromise this matter and I will be your friend. Let us go in here and take a drink, as I want to talk to you and give you some advice."

The two men entered the Apple Jack Saloon for a long discussion in a private room. Again, they parted buddies.[14]

SO THE QUESTION ARISES: did Hardin perform the Border Roll on Wild Bill Hickok? Most historians, using substantial, reasoned logic, do not think so. And yet the reality has to be a resounding "Yes!"

There is no evidence that Hardin lied. There is only speculation and conjecture, most of it taking place a century or so after the fact and offered by people who were not present.

Alfred Iverson "Babe" Moye, who went up the trail with Hardin, did not mention any face-off between Hardin and Hickok. In his memoirs, Babe described an incident where Hardin was standing at a bar drinking and toying with his gun. Hickok passed by and remarked, "Arkansas, you should put that pistol up before you let it go off and hurt somebody. Hardin complied without a word and didn't seem to get mad about it."[15]

Gip Clements, who arrived in Abilene shortly after the Border Roll incident, claimed "he never heard Hardin say anything about the trick." Clements did say, however, that "Wes had faced Bill down," and "Bill would have given both his eyes to take Wes, and he didn't do it."[16]

As for Hickok, if he ever commented on Hardin's Border Roll, no one recorded it. The local newspapers did not mention it. Contemporaries of both antagonists made no known published references to it. All of which proves only that if the event happened, it did not generate publicity.

Hardin's autobiography is contradictory. Sometimes he and Hickok are friends; sometimes they are enemies. However, since Hardin believed Hickok often wanted him dead, one can wonder why Hardin did not fire when his revolvers came right side up. It is also significant that Hickok, knowing he was facing a

Cowboys Gibson Clements, Eph Baker and Fred Duderstadt (left), ca. 1871.
At right, Alfred Iverson "Babe" Moye. Abilene, Kansas, 1871.
(Chuck Parsons Collection)

dangerous, perhaps unstable youth, did not pull his own triggers and dispatch Hardin to that Promised Land so often preached about by John's father.

Therefore, rolling the weapons over in his hands could have been Hardin's way of showing an old dog a new trick, and an old dog's way of saying that he was not impressed. Such tactics were dangerous but not improbable.[17]

In the end, the strongest confirmation that this Border Roll took place is Hardin himself. The Roll wasn't something Hardin tried on a whim. He rehearsed that technique in Texas, and mastered it during the long trail drive. While Hardin did not design it specifically with anyone in mind, he always knew that somewhere, someone would come along. When he did, Hardin would be prepared. This attitude explains why Hardin wore his guns to Abilene. Hickok was the opponent of a lifetime. At eighteen, Hardin realized that both men were at their peak. A showdown with Hickok represented the best meeting the best.

Furthermore, this Roll, this dexterity with weapons, was never meant to kill Hickok, or even to intimidate him. It was meant to impress him.

Hardin's whole life was an affirmation of who he was, and what he aspired to be. Backing down Wild Bill Hickok was the consummate juncture thus far in his spiraling, man-killing career. Hardin had arrived. Until now, he had faced dregs and toughs, people for the most part hopelessly outmatched. Killing had been easy. Hardin had fired and walked away.

A dead Hickok would have proven nothing, except perhaps that Hardin was lucky. A live Hickok would know for the rest of his life who was the better man. Hardin realized even before he entered Abilene that he would never depart without a Hickok showdown, that he would never vacate the town without knowing in his own mind who was the better man. How and when it would take place, he never realized until the second it happened. When he looked across those twin barrels into the unflinching gray eyes of Hickok, Wes Hardin knew he had won, and furthermore he knew that Hickok also knew he had won. It was over. Nothing remained to be proved.

As for Hickok, he had nothing to prove anyway. The long-haired marshal probably shook his head, shrugged his shoulders, and never gave the incident a second thought.

THE BORDER ROLL OCCURRED before noon. Hardin himself admitted he drank a lot that day, so all things considered he had much to be hyper about that same evening when he and a one-armed Texas friend named Pain seated themselves in a restaurant. A group of rowdy customers entered. They cursed Texans. Leaving Pain at the table, Hardin slipped around the room to a better advantage, and softly said to one of them, "I'm a Texan."

Both men jerked their revolvers and fired. The opponent missed. Hardin's bullet missed, too. It plowed into Pain's good arm. The opponent then scurried outside, but Hardin shot him as he cleared the doorway, the bullet striking behind the left ear and exiting through the mouth. Teeth scattered all over the street. Hardin sprang through the doorway, jumped over the dead man and encountered a deputy. "Hands up," Hardin screamed as he stuck his pistol into the officer's face. The policeman promptly complied. Hardin then vaulted onto his horse and raced south to his outfit on the bedding grounds of the Cottonwood River.

Hardin had now roughly accounted for twenty-one men. Throughout this early part of his life, the young gunman seemed to possess a limitless supply of bullets and luck.

Prairie Justice

*A*T COTTONWOOD RIVER Hardin mingled with other cowboys, all of whom gambled, argued and drank away their boredom. One of them was a Hispanic vaquero named Bideno who killed William "Billy" Cohron, a twenty-two-year-old cowboy. Cohron had come up the trail as boss herder for Colonel O. W. Wheeler, a California entrepreneur who purchased Texas cattle and drove them to wherever a market existed.

John Hardin described the slaying as "foul and treacherous." The *Abilene Chronicle* filled in a few details, saying Cohron had given an order that angered the Mexican. They quarreled and the vaquero "slipped up behind Cohron and shot him in the back, inflicting a wound from which he died shortly afterwards."[1]

Services took place in the Abilene Drover's Cottage. A new hearse led a procession followed by twenty-four carriages and thirty-eight horsemen. It was one of the largest funerals ever seen in Abilene.

Bideno dashed south, eluding cowboys who attempted to arrest or kill him.

Recognizing Hardin's talent for blood-letting, several prominent cattlemen urged him to apprehend the slayer. In response, Hardin requested letters of introduction to outfits coming up the

John Wesley Hardin in an Abilene, Kansas store-bought suit, June 1871. Here he appears more like a modest businessman who left his guns at home, than a drover at the end of the trail. (R. G. McCubbin Collection)

trail so that he might draw on them for information and support, as well as additional horseflesh.

Hardin left the North Cottonwood with Jim Rogers, another cowboy, at sunrise on or about July 6, 1871. They hoped to catch Bideno prior to the Nations (Oklahoma), and certainly before Texas. Late that afternoon, near the village of Newton, they encountered John Cohron, a brother of Billy, riding up the Chisholm Trail with another herd. John Cohron and Hugh Anderson, a cowboy from Salado, Bell County, Texas, joined the avengers. With fresh horses, the four men reached Wichita—eighty-five miles south of Abilene—at eleven o'clock that night.

Early the next morning, the posse passed alongside Wichita, making inquiries and riding hard. They changed horses every few miles. Bideno, wearing a broad-brimmed hat and riding two hundred yards off the trail, galloped toward Texas at a steady lope.

Near modern-day Wellington in Sumner County, Kansas, twenty miles north of the Oklahoma line, Hardin and his companions approached Sumner City. The town owed its existence to cattle drives fording the nearby Slate Creek.[2] (After the drives ended, so did the town.) Here, Hardin and friends caught up with Bideno.

The road forked, one route bypassing Sumner City with its ramshackle buildings, the other curving through it. Anderson and Hardin planned to check out the community while Cohron and Rogers circled around. Thus, they would simultaneously cover both routes. If neither found anything, they would rendezvous in the Indian Nations across the Oklahoma line. Hardin and Anderson had barely entered town, however, when they confirmed Bideno's presence. They signaled with six-shooters, and Cohron and Rogers joined them.

The posse rode into Sumner City like cowboys out for a good time, hitched their horses and divided into two parties. Anderson and Hardin entered a saloon where Hardin asked if a Mexican herder happened to be in the restaurant portion. Someone said "yes." Both men unsheathed their revolvers and opened the restaurant door. Hardin recognized his man. "I am after you to surrender," Hardin recalled saying to Bideno. "I do not wish to hurt you, and you will not be hurt while you are in my hands."

Bideno grabbed for his gun, and Hardin fired across the table, the bullet smacking Bideno in the forehead.

Across the street, Cohron and Rogers heard the firing, and rushed over. Cohron wanted to shoot Bideno again, but Hardin prevented it. Cohron seized Bideno's hat as a trophy.

As the avengers reentered the saloon, the frightened bartender croaked, "take what you want." They grabbed some good whiskey at no charge.

Outside, Hardin explained what happened to a gathering crowd. "They all commended our actions," Hardin claimed, "and I gave those people $20 to bury him."[3]

Other than Hardin's story, one additional reference mentioned Bideno's death. Sumner City had no newspaper but nearby Oxford did. The *Oxford Times* of July 13, published the following:

> A man was shot dead while sitting at the table in the dining room of the Southwestern Hotel, at Sumner City, at noon last Friday, by a man who called himself Conway, [Cohron] from Cottonwood River. Conway claimed that the man whom he shot without warning killed his brother a short time before. He (Conway) had followed him until he overtook him at Sumner, where he had stopped to take dinner. The murdered man was supposed to be a Mexican. His name was not ascertained...nor [do we have many] particulars of the incentives Conway had in thus taking the law in his own hands—if, indeed, he had any other motive than obtaining a fine horse ridden by the murdered man, which he asserted belonged to his brother. The Mexican being instantly killed, of course could not give his side of the story.
>
> The shot took effect in the forehead, passing through the head and the partition, barely missing a lady in the next room. It flattened against the stove. The so-called Mexican was totally unconscious of danger. Though facing the door fairly in which the assassin stood, [he] was struck down while drinking coffee, with the cup to his lips.
>
> Conway apologized for the confusion the shooting occasioned. He handed the proprietors of the hotel five dollars, remarking that would pay for cleaning up, and left, taking with him the horse before mentioned.[4]

Conway was undoubtedly John Cohron whom the newspaper incorrectly assumed killed the man. The *Oxford Times* did not mention Hardin, Anderson, and Rogers. The horse Bideno rode from the bedding grounds was not the same one confiscated by the posse. However, with its owner dead, since the animal had to go somewhere, where else but with the men who had tracked down its rider.

It makes sense that John Cohron would avenge his brother's murder. Yet, around Abilene, Hardin's execution of Bideno was such common knowledge that it seems unlikely for anyone else to have pulled the trigger. Bideno almost certainly was victim twenty-two for the eighteen-year-old John Wesley Hardin.

ON THEIR WAY BACK TO ABILENE, the posse stopped in Newton, Kansas, and drunkenly bullied the town. Two newspaper accounts reported that a group of Texans shot up a combination saloon-dancehall-brothel owned by Perry Tuttle and his common-law wife, Lyda Howell. They riddled the brothel with bullets, forced the girls "to stretch themselves at full length upon the prairie," and chased the brothel manager momentarily out of the city.[5]

HARDIN CLAIMED PEOPLE IN ABILENE clamored to meet the man who killed the murderer of Billy Cohron. Several residents handed him $20, $50 and $100 bills. "I did not want to take the money at first," he said, "but I finally concluded there was nothing wrong with it, so I took it as proof of their friendship and gratitude for what I had done." Hardin received roughly a thousand dollars for one execution.[6]

Hardin's surprised but easy acceptance of money being "pushed" on him, was his way of playing coy with the reader. At the beginning of this episode, he claimed that "many prominent cowmen came to me and urged me to follow the murderer." This was undoubtedly true, but it left unexplored the subject of funds. Hardin wrote only that he "expected to have my expenses paid." When he returned to Abilene, "some wealthy cowmen made up a purse and gave me $600." Hardin had indelibly learned that given the proper circumstances, the right people would not only pat you on the back, they would also compensate you for killing undesirable citizens.

Since leaving Texas a couple of months earlier, John Wesley Hardin had now killed nine "known" individuals in four separate incidents: five Mexican herders, two Indians, a rowdy in an

Abilene restaurant, and now Bideno. Any one of these episodes could have been avoided if Hardin had utilized a different choice of words, or walked away. Yet, Hardin preferred to meet the confrontations head on, in the process giving his opponents no option except to die. An ordinary man might have suffered remorse, some occasional pangs of guilt. He might have had trouble sleeping. In the quiet of the darkness, he might have second guessed his own actions and motives, wondering why he had not chosen alternatives.

This Kansas blood money signified, if nothing else, the total loss of innocence for John Wesley Hardin. Back in Texas, he had murdered men for a variety of reasons, some of them legitimate. In November 1868, when Hardin killed his first person, the black man Mage, Uncle Claiborne Holshousen handed his nephew $20 and told him to go home and explain the incident to his father. Mage may have been Hardin's first killing for hire, the wrestling match just a clever ruse building the case for justification. Now Hardin was killing nasties-of-the-earth for additional compensation, and his conscience never shuddered. In his mind, every one of those dead men had it coming. They lay in silent graves not because of what he did, but of what they did. They had opposed him. They had challenged him. They died because they deserved to die. He felt no contrition. A death payment of money was no different than a cattle payment, or a win at the gambling tables. Any of the three could make you feel good, put an extra spring in the step.

UPON APPROACHING ABILENE, Hardin swore that if Wild Bill tried to arrest him, he would kill the marshal. Cohron, Anderson and Rogers all pledged to stick by their companion.

The confrontation happened quickly. "Wild Bill came in [a saloon] and asked me if I remembered our talk in the Apple Jack," Hardin said. "Well," said he, "you cannot hurrah me, and I am not going to have it." Hurrah meant to intimidate with wild, threatening talk, and/or the flourishing of weapons.

"I told him, I don't wish to hurrah you; but I have come to stay, regardless of you."

Hickok probably weighed the odds against disarming Hardin, and decided it wasn't worth it. One or both men could get killed, and that would resolve nothing. On top of that, Hardin was a popular street figure. Nobody seemed to resent his being armed, and as a cowboy he would be moving on soon anyway.

"Well," Hickok said, "you can stay and wear your guns, but those other fellows must pull them off. You are in no danger here. I congratulate you on getting your Mexican. Come in and invite your friends. We will open a bottle of wine."

Hardin and his companions, all heavily armed, entered the saloon with Hickok and had a drink. The marshal left. Hardin then told his associates "that Bill was my friend and had asked me to see that they took their pistols off. They asked me why I did not pull mine off. I told them that the marshal had not demanded that of me, but I knew he was our friend and would protect us all, and if he did not, I would. Well, they said that if Wild Bill was all right with me, they would [leave], which they did."[8]

Hugh Anderson should have stuck with Hardin. As the son of a wealthy Texas cattleman, he had allegedly slain two black men and one white man in Texas. After riding out of Abilene, he returned to Newton, Kansas and the same whorehouse he, Hardin and the boys had shot up weeks earlier. Anderson and hooligan Mike McCluskie engaged in a wild gunfight that left McCluskie dead, Anderson seriously wounded, and four or five others dying. Kansas newspapers referred to it as "The General Massacre."[9]

In June of 1873, a fully recovered Anderson, now known as a Texas desperado, horse thief and murderer, was in Medicine Lodge, Kansas. While Anderson was dealing cards, Arthur McCluskie, the brother of Mike, sent word that he expected satisfaction for Mike's death. The two men met that night in an empty lot and while the whole mesmerized town watched, they fought a bloody gun duel. Each down and dying, their revolvers empty, they painfully crawled across the grass and stabbed each other to death.[10]

A FEW DAYS AFTER John Wesley Hardin parted with his comrades, his cousins Emanuel "Manning" and Gip Clements arrived in Abilene specifically to see Hardin. The three men entered a private room where Manning blurted out, "Wes, I killed Joe and Dolph Shadden last night, but I was justified."

Manning Clements,
a cousin to John Wesley
Hardin and one of
Hardin's closest friends.
(R. G. McCubbin Collection)

The Shadden boys had come up the trail from Gonzales, Texas with a herd Manning managed for Doc Burnett. The Shaddens did a fair job until they crossed the Red River. Then they became arrogant, declined to do night duty and demanded their pay, which the Clements refused to give. All through the Nations, the Shaddens threatened their boss.

One evening during the night shift on or about July 10, 1871, Manning realized the Shaddens planned to murder him after he turned in. He rode back to camp wearing his slicker, a pistol underneath. Joe Shadden heard him coming and jumped up. Manning shot him in the head. Dolph Shadden fired at Manning, the ball passing through the slicker and vest. Dolph and Clements then rushed together. During a hand-to-hand struggle, Manning shot Dolph Shadden through the heart.

The Clements turned the herd over to one of the hands, and rode immediately to Abilene. They asked cousin John Wesley Hardin for help.

The episode is one of the longer stories in the Hardin narrative. It is also one of the most puzzling, filled with inconsistencies. It does not make sense that Hardin would spin a tale as complex as this if it were not substantially true, although he would naturally give his cousins any benefit of doubt.

Kansas newspapers reported that at Slate Creek, on July 9, "a herdsman named Lee was killed by another herdsman named Clements." Another newspaper said "One J. H. Lee was killed at Burnes's Ranch on Slate Creek, in the southwestern part of that State, on the 9th instant. It grew out of a drunk among cattle drovers."[11]

HARDIN TOLD THE CLEMENTS, "I have had a heap of trouble, but I stand square in Abilene. Wild Bill is my particular friend, and he is the one to help you here if papers come from Texas. Now, Manning, pull off your pistols until I see Bill and fix him." Hardin made Gip do the same.[12]

Hardin asked Texas cattlemen Columbus Carroll and Jake Johnson to post the Clements boys with the marshal. Carroll promised he would.

Later, while Hardin and his cousins gambled, Hickok walked into the saloon and said, "Hello, Little Arkansaw." Then Hickok began wagering with the House's money and ignored the cowboys, who strolled over to the American House for supper. Within the hour, Wild Bill and deputy J. H. McDonald entered. Hardin immediately knew why.

The marshal asked Clements if he had finished eating. Manning—a man with dark hair, mustache and goatee—nodded. Hickok then said, "I have a telegram here to arrest Manning Clements, so consider yourself under arrest." Hardin asked McDonald to guard the prisoner while he pulled Hickok aside. He asked if Columbus Carroll had posted Manning.

"No," said Hickok, "he [Carroll] is drunk. Why did you not post me yourself?"

At this point, Hardin's convoluted narrative has both himself and Hickok acknowledging that Manning should be freed, but it should be done carefully to protect Hickok's "reputation as an officer." Therefore, they agreed that the marshal would place Manning in the lockup but release him precisely at midnight.

Hardin and Hickok spent the next few hours gambling. During this period, chief deputy Tom Carson arrested and jailed two of their favorite prostitutes. Hickok growled that the girls should be freed, and Carson should be thrashed.

The two men estimated they won $1,000 apiece that night with casino money. When they reached the jail at the end of their spree, deputy Carson handed the key to Hickok. The marshal released all of the prisoners, including the ladies and Manning Clements. Manning left. An incredulous Carson asked Hickok why he did that, and Hickok knocked Carson to the floor and gave him the worst beating Hardin had ever witnessed. An hour or so later, Clements returned to the jail. He, Hardin and Hickok drank a bottle of wine.[13]

Hardin and Clements rode out of town soon afterwards, pausing at the Smokey Hill River where John Wesley handed Manning a wad of traveling expenses. They promised to rendezvous at Barnett Hardin's farm in Hill County, Texas. Manning's younger brother Gip remained with Hardin, and they returned to Abilene at three in the morning. Why Hardin and Gip did not go to Texas with the others, no one said.[14]

9

Death by Snoring

BACK IN ABILENE ON AUGUST 6, John Wesley Hardin and Gip Clements, both drunk, entered the American Hotel and stumbled up the rickety stairs to their room on the second floor. Pulling off clothes, they collapsed into bed. Hardin later said he had almost dropped off to sleep when he heard the bedroom door unlatch. A figure Hardin described as armed with a dagger, snatched his trousers.

The intruder had barely eased back through the open door when Hardin's six-shooter thundered four times. The man stumbled a few steps down the corridor and fell dead.

Hardin hastily arose in his night clothes and motioned for Gip to follow. They opened a window and scrambled out onto the portico (roof) overlooking the main street. Below, Hickok and four policemen, summoned by gunfire, arrived in a hack and hastened inside the hotel. As they disappeared into the lobby, the two cowboys leaped to the ground.

Gip sought out a friend, while Hardin raced down the street to a cornfield and clawed his way inside a haystack. When daylight arrived, Hardin challenged a passing cowboy for his horse, and took it at pistol point. He galloped south to his cow camp on the North Fork of the Cottonwood. Somehow or the other, deputies Tom Carson and another lawman picked up the trail, although

Artist's sketch of John Wesley Hardin leaving his Abilene hotel in his nightclothes. (*The Life of John Wesley Hardin*)

neither realized their quarry rode but a few miles ahead. Hardin arrived at the camp in ample time to arm himself and bolt down food. When he heard his pursuers approaching, he dropped down alongside the riverbank and watched as the hungry deputies reined up and requested food. As they commenced eating, Hardin surprised them with a Winchester rifle. After forcing them to disrobe, he sent them back to town. The young gunman dressed himself with the lawmen's clothes.

Twenty-five-years later, when Hardin wrote his autobiography, he rationalized the events that had just transpired, as well as his reasons for not promptly surrendering. "All the bridges were guarded," he stated, "and the country was out after me, believing I had killed a man in cold blood, instead of a dirty, low-down, would-be assassin."[1]

Hardin did not explain why authorities would regard the easily understood killing of a burglar as murder. After all, a dead thief with a knife in one hand and trousers not his own in the other, were sufficient evidence of theft. A sneak thief, as Hardin called him, would have been fair game for any armed, outraged citizen in America. No grand jury would have indicted, because no court in the land would have convicted. Hickok would have yawned.

Furthermore Hardin and Hickok were the best of friends according to Hardin, having just the evening before drunk Abilene dry and released Manning Clements from jail. Yet, having said that, Hardin felt compelled to assert that if Wild Bill found him now in such a defenseless condition, he would "kill me to add to his reputation."[2]

As is often the fact, Hardin's autobiographical explanations frequently strain and blur reality. They rarely tell the whole gospel, but they invariably include intriguing details otherwise unavailable. Someone certainly died that night in the American Hotel. Since several newspapers, such as the *Abilene Chronicle*, printed nothing about a dead sneak thief littering the hallway of a downtown hostel, it is relevant to read about a body that the newspapers did discuss. The *Chronicle* identified the slayer as "Wesley Clements alias Arkansas." Everybody in town knew John Wesley Hardin by both names:

> The most fiendish murder was perpetrated at the American House, in this place, on the night of the 6th inst. The murdered man's name was Charles Couger, and that of the murderer Wesley Clements, alias "Arkansas." Couger was a boss cattle herder, and said to be a gentleman; Clements is from Mississippi. Couger was in his room sitting upon the bed reading the newspaper. Four shots were fired at him through a board partition, one of which struck him in the fleshy part of the left arm, passing through

the third rib and entering the heart, cutting a piece of it entirely off, and killing Couger almost immediately. The murderer escaped, and has thus far eluded his pursuers. If caught, he will probably be killed on sight. Coroner J. M. Shepard held an inquest on the body of the deceased, and the jury rendered a verdict to the effect that Charles Couger came to his death from a bullet fired from a pistol by Wesley Clements. No cause for the murder is yet known....[3]

A week later the *Chronicle* referred to the earlier slaying of William Cohron. On this occasion the newspaper spoke only of a tombstone arriving for the grave of Billy Cohron:

> To make this [tombstone] item more interesting, the man who killed Charles Couger on the 6th inst., in this place, also shot and instantly killed the Mexican who killed young Cohron.[4]

Other newspapers alluded to the possibility of additional slayers:

> A man was shot in Abilene last Saturday night. Two men in disguise entered his room, at the American House, and fired two shots into his breast. The assassins escaped and had not been re- ported captured at last accounts. They are supposed to have been former partners of the murdered man and took this method of ridding themselves of pecuniary obligations.[5]

A FINAL REASON FOR COUGER'S DEATH is the most colorful and intriguing of all, one accepted by most historians.[6] For over a century, a legend has lingered that Hardin killed a man in Abilene for snoring.[7]

A "death by snoring" version persisted through word-of-mouth and newspapers almost from the time Hardin returned to Texas. Jack Duncan, a Texas detective involved in Hardin's capture some years in the future, believed it. Duncan accused Hardin of "kill- ing several men in Kansas, one because he snored."[8]

The *Denison Daily Herald* also believed the story, writing that "J. Wesley Hardin, the desperado, is a very finely organized per- son. One of his victims he killed for snoring. He did not like to be disturbed in his sleep, and so he arose in the silent night and slew the snorer."[9]

It could very well be that Hardin, Clements and Couger had spent the evening drinking and gambling. They returned very drunk to their side-by-side rooms at the American House in Abilene. Couger arrived a few minutes earlier. Clements and Hardin disrobed and crashed headlong onto the lumpy mattress as Couger's raucous snoring ripped through the paper-thin walls. At first, Hardin and Clements drunkenly shouted for the man to roll over. Couger may have sat up in bed and tried to read a newspaper. Then he dozed off again. The snoring restarted, this time louder and more aggravating. To get Couger's serious attention, Hardin and Clements fired a few rounds through the wall. The bullets were likely intended to demonstrate the limits of their exasperation, rather than kill Couger. However, when the snoring abruptly stopped, and a cold silence echoed from the adjoining room, the two cowboys realized they had fired a little low. Knowing Hickok would not understand, Hardin and Gip Clements decided this might be a good time to depart for Texas.

THERE IS ONE ADDITIONAL PIECE OF EVIDENCE for "death by snoring." In 1963, Joe Clements, a nephew of Gip Clements, and his wife Helen, passed through El Paso, Texas. Local historians C. L. Sonnichsen and Robert N. "Bob" Mullin interviewed them at the Paso del Norte Hotel. Joe described his Uncle Gip as a small, wiry, dried-up man who had religion. Gip frequently stayed at Joe's house and told stories by the hour. This one has been edited for clarity:

> He [Gip] said they [Hardin and Gip] had a little trouble [in Abilene] and came back to the old board hotel. They went to bed. In the middle of the night, they heard somebody trying the door. Then there was a knock and they were told to open up [by] officers. The [young men] did not want to be arrested, so they went out the window without stopping to dress. They slid out onto a porch roof, [jumped to the ground] and entered a cab. At the outskirts of town [they] hid in a corn field. Finally…Wes went down the road where he waylaid a soldier, who was in the search party. Wes shot him off his horse. Wes got on the horse, rode it out of town to the cow camp. Then…he went back and got Gip.

Gip's stories, combined with Abilene newspaper comments, add more credibility than Hardin's awkward efforts to explain away a brutal murder. Couger had become number twenty-three on John Wesley Hardin's death list. Maybe the soldier should be twenty-four.

A Three-Gun Man

*A*S HARDIN AND GIP TURNED their (probably stolen) horses toward home, they rode through Emporium and Parsons, Kansas, passing through the Thayer-Cherryvale area where the notorious Bender family operated a store and inn. They consisted of John Bender, his wife, and two grown children, all of whom made a meager living through the buying and selling of trade goods, plus fortune-telling. Their chief source of income, however, consisted of murdering and robbing travelers. Graves scattered around the yard attested to their success.

Gip Clements and Wes Hardin spent one night with the Benders. During supper, the Benders seated the two men with their backs to a curtain. Hardin grew uneasy. He picked up his plate and moved to the other side of the table. Early the next morning, the two gunmen continued south.[1] At the time, they never realized how close they were to death. Of course, maybe the Benders didn't realize how close to death they were also.

By now, Hardin had reached another milestone. His family called him "John" or "Johnny," and judging by William Teagarden's letters, most childhood friends referred to him as "John." Now eighteen years old and shaving, John was maturing.

Somewhere during the early 1870s, people other than family just naturally started calling him "Wes." The name "Wes Hardin" resonated with a certain authoritative cadence like Billy the Kid, John Ringo, and Wild Bill Hickok.

When Wes Hardin returned to Texas in August 1871, he had not yet achieved broad celebrity status. Texas had essentially ignored his string of killings for several reasons: the state had not yet recovered from war, or completely shrugged off Reconstruction. Legal documents offered vague descriptions, uncertainties and ambiguities not only about him, but about the men he killed. Furthermore, while many figures in the state considered John Wesley Hardin a dangerous, homicidal threat to public safety, the authorities also recognized that many potential jurors believed Hardin's slaughter of blacks, Northern sympathizers and Union soldiers fell under the category of public services rather than crimes.

Even with an "estimated" twenty-three dead men lying behind him, Hardin had a final opportunity in Texas—with luck and an honest resolve—to seek peace and happiness in comparative security. But Hardin disdained that route.

Partly through circumstances, but primarily through deliberate intentions, John Wesley Hardin chose a bloody continuation of the same dark trail he had always followed. Until returning to Texas, John Wesley Hardin had been more or less a wild cowboy with an addiction to murder. Now, he would rapidly rise to become the most celebrated desperado in the state.

WES HARDIN AND GIP CLEMENTS SPENT maybe a week in August of 1871 with their cousin Barnett Hardin in Hill County. From there they rode over to Gonzales County where the Clements family resided. The *Galveston Daily News* described the Clements home as"a small fortress or block house, pierced by numerous port-holes on each side," a haven for fugitives from justice.[2]

One afternoon on October 6, a black state policemen caught up with John Wesley Hardin in Nopal. Hardin was munching cheese and crackers inside a small grocery owned by Neill Bowen, Hardin's future father-in-law.

The confrontation started when officer Green Paramore,

growled, "Throw up your hands or die." Hardin turned and stared into the barrel of a cocked revolver with a black, tight, nervous finger on the trigger.

"Look out, you will let that pistol go off, and I don't want to be killed accidentally."

"Give me those pistols," snapped the policeman.

"All right," Hardin responded, and he handed both Colt .45s toward the policeman, butts forward.

Suddenly one of those six-shooters did a somersault, spun firmly in Hardin's right hand and instantly spat lead. Down went the officer, quivering in his own blood, a bullet buried six inches in his head.[3]

Glancing through the window, Hardin saw John Lackey, another black policeman, sitting astride a mule. Both commenced firing, and the black man tumbled off his mount as Hardin raced through the rear door toward his own horse. In the confusion, the black officer struggled back onto his mule and escaped. Records identified him as a thirty-five-year-old mulatto blacksmith from Tennessee.[4]

Although the indictment for murder against Hardin referred to Paramore only as a "freed man of color,"[5] Paramore and Lackey comprised two of thirty "special policemen," auxiliaries to the State Police and stationed in Gonzales. They lived off fees for serving papers, rewards (bounties), and civilian occupations such as farming.

The black community in Gonzales County raged over Paramore's death and threatened "with torch and knife [to] depopulate the entire country." Cooler heads prevailed.[6]

The *San Antonio Daily Herald* said:

> Gonzales County has narrowly escaped martial law. Green Paramore was recently murdered in that county and John Lackey, both freedmen, severely wounded by an armed body of men. The freedmen assembled in numbers, armed and wanted to go after the bodies of their comrades. The Sheriff of the county and the mayor of Gonzales interfered and prevented the proceedings. Every effort is being made by the good people of the county to bring the murderers to justice. The two freedmen were members of the State Police.[7]

Over in Austin, the murder of Paramore outraged Governor

These confident black Texans were probably state policemen.
(R. G. McCubbin Collection)

Edmund Davis. On November 5, 1871, Davis proclaimed that "the said Wesley Clements, alias Wesley Harden, is now at large and a fugitive from justice." The governor offered a $400 reward "for the arrest and delivery to the Sheriff of Gonzales county, of one Wesley Clements alias Wesley Harden, charged with murdering one Green Paramore on the 8th of October."[8]

Authorities still had not gotten it straight regarding Hardin's proper name. But they were learning.

For the second time, Hardin claimed to have performed the so-called Border Roll, often known as the Road Agent Spin, and although this was a stunt where Hardin practically had a patent, the name was deceiving. A Road Agent was someone who robbed travelers, especially in stagecoaches. That wasn't Hardin. Nor did he use, or invent, the terms, "Border Roll" or "Road Agent Spin." Popular writers coined the phrases for him. Wild Bill Hickok earlier had survived because—Hardin's statements to the contrary—Hickok probably had his weapons sheathed when the engagement happened. Paramore had his six-shooter out and pointed, and died for it.

Anyway, Hardin never explained "exactly" how he did it. With reference to Hickok, he said, upon being ordered to turn over his weapons, "I said all right and pulled them out of the scabbard, but while he was reaching for them, I reversed them and whirled them over on him with the muzzles in his face...." With regards to Paramore, Hardin wrote that when the officer asked for the revolvers, "I said all right and handed him the pistols, handle foremost. One of the pistols turned a somersault in my hand and went off."

The killing of Green Paramore started an unprecedented fad. In an extraordinarily brief time, the Border Roll became a Texas craze. With his singular slaying of Green Paramore, the eighteen-year-old John Wesley Hardin evolved into a luminary among youthful male groupies perceiving him as a role model. The practice of flipping a six-shooter around in one's hand became a popular pastime for gangly boys struggling with rites of passage out behind the barn.

The *San Antonio Express* with tongue-in-cheek twisted some of its facts in an 1892 editorial. Even so, its moral concerns were on target. In speaking of John Wesley Hardin and his agility with weapons, especially the Border Roll, the newspaper reported:

> It is probable that no desperado who ever drew the breath of life has killed so many men. Some fifteen or twenty have fallen before the smoking muzzle of his revolver, but these are not a drop in the bucket to the number who have vicariously died by his hand. Some years ago, when a sheriff [state policeman] had him covered and requested him to dismount and come to jail, a happy thought flashed through the brain of Mr. Hardin. He extended his pistol butt foremost to the officer. As the latter reached to take it, Mr. Hardin, by a quick turn of his wrist, whirled the weapon around and shot the [policeman] dead. Then...he gallantly rode away. In endeavoring to imitate this masterly maneuver of the Hon. Hardin, one hundred thousand [sic] noble Texans have bitten the dust. They invariably shoot themselves just above the navel. They invariably look around with a pained and puzzled expression of countenance, then they draw their coat-tails over their faces and die. They are still at it. Every now and then the

fool-killer lays down his club and invites some tangle-footed youth to show him the 'John Wesley Hardin trick.' He does so, to the complete satisfaction of every one save himself.[9]

MEANWHILE, "A POSSE OF NEGROES" rode down from Austin, and Hardin killed three. The remainder went home. Evidence—other than Hardin's word regarding this fight— is non-existent. Hardin implied they were State Police but did not specifically say so.[10]

The time was September 1871. According to Hardin's list, which included Paramore and the three black "possemen," a total of twenty-seven dangerous ne'er-do-wells were troubling the American West no longer. That represented a fair-sized cemetery.

HARDIN RETURNED TO GONZALES by January 11, 1872, the night his twenty-eight-year-old cousin Jim Clements (Hardin says it was Gip) married the soon to be fourteen-year-old Ann Caroline Tennille. George Culver Tennille, her father, would become a participant in the forthcoming Sutton-Taylor Feud.[11]

Hardin's memoirs now briefly introduced Jane Bowen, whom he would soon marry. She was born in Karnes County, Texas in 1857. She and Wes Hardin likely met before he went to Abilene at the family mercantile store a hundred yards southwest of Coon Hollow in Gonzales County. Neill Bowen, her father, was a handsome man with dark, receding hair, a mustache and goatee. He was a farmer/laborer/merchant who arrived in Texas from Florida around 1850.

If it is true that opposites attract, then Wes and Jane were made for each other. Wes was known all over East Texas as a man-slayer. However, if it were not for his and his family's forthcoming prison correspondence to her, Jane would be barely known.

One of Hardin's letters, written to Jane in January 1879, referred to their courtship:

> "I told you then and called you my own darling," Hardin wrote, "saying I did love you above all others, and should I live to come back from the mountains, that we then would no longer prolong our engagement. You dearest, looked me in the face, and said Wes, oh Wes, is there...danger of you not coming back alive. I said there is a chance, and that is the reason I propose to postpone our

Neill Bowen (left),
father of Brown Bowen
and Jane Bowen Hardin.
(Chuck Parsons Collection)
Below, Neill Bowen home.
John and Jane Hardin lived
upstairs for a brief time.
(Author's Collection.)

engagement. You said that should be no reason...and should you never get back after telling me this, life would no longer be pleasurable...."[12]

Hardin may have thought there were mountains in Kansas since he was a country boy himself and not well versed in geography. But even if he knew better, Jane did not. Jane obviously wanted a quick commitment, while Hardin hesitated. In doing so, Hardin was not above placing himself in imaginary mortal danger. Nothing like keeping the ladies quivering. Besides, this made him seem romantic and dangerous. For a young girl weaned on "penny dreadfuls"—a dreadfully written adventure story with hero and heroine, the booklet costing only a penny—Hardin would have been quite a "catch."

But for whatever her faults or degree of naivete, she was an articulate young lady. Throughout her brief lifetime she maintained a pugnacious defense of her husband.

Jane was fourteen-years-old when they married on February 29, 1872. Wes was eighteen. Methodist Minister (and Justice of the Peace) Thomas F. Rainey performed the ceremony. Their first-born arrived when she was fifteen. Judging by a photograph of Jane, she was thin but not unattractively so. By some accounts, the photo was taken on her wedding day. If so, she looked older. Her dark hair was not so much wind-blown as unkempt. Her eyes revealed a woman haunted by life.

Hardin's memoirs offered little background regarding Jane. In his autobiography he described her as his sweetheart, and once as his "darling and beloved wife." Yet, he was a consistent, absentee husband and father, a man who much preferred the company of boisterous male friends. While some writers have painted them as an adoring couple, Hardin was an indifferent husband. Except in his own mind, he was not a family man.

Jane's job was to have children, then to care for them under his tutelage. He never wrote a word about courtship, or the wedding, or who was present, or what festivities took place. He never mentioned his or her parents as attending. Hardin said only that he and his wife lived in Gonzales County. They initially resided upstairs in her father's house, a half-mile north of the family mercantile store. An outside staircase led to their quarters. Portions of a well that Hardin helped dig still remain.[13]

Jane Bowen Hardin wedding photo at left. John Wesley Hardin (right),
a photo perhaps taken on his wedding day. (R. G. McCubbin Collection)

Two months after the wedding, Hardin "bid my angel wife
goodby," and was absent a couple of weeks as he conducted undisclosed business at the King Ranch in South Texas, 175 miles
from Gonzales. During the trip, Hardin said he fired on and may
have killed two Mexican robbers. He likely meant that he had
slain two Mexicans. Should their bodies turn up, and their deaths
be traced to his handiwork, then of course they were bandits who
got what they deserved.

Upon leaving the King Ranch, Hardin remembered he had "one
of the prettiest and sweetest girls in the country as my wife." The
more he thought about her, the more he desired to express his
feelings in a more physical manner. He subsequently ruined a
$50 horse by riding it over a hundred miles with little rest. Wes
arrived home at four in the morning, and said "the sight of my
wife recompensed me for the loss of old Bob."[14]

On June 5, 1872, he left for Louisiana to sell a herd of horses
being driven there by a couple of friends, Jess and John Harper.
The Harper brothers lived in Sabine County, Texas, where their
father, Elmer Harper, was sheriff. A Billy Harper, brother to the

others, resided in Hemphill, which was in Sabine County, Big Thicket country less than ten miles from the Sabine River and the Louisiana line. Hardin arrived in advance of the herd, so he and Billy Harper gambled and raced horses to pass time.

Down at the Hemphill square, officer John Henry Hopkins Speights, better known as Sonny, had arrested a drifter named O'Connor. The twenty-six-year-old Speights, with his badge, black mustache, black hair and eyes, looked every bit the picturesque, formidable state policeman.

O'Connor packed a concealed weapon, a practice against the law in most Western communities. However, it was a law frequently violated, and therefore a violation that disbursed a nice sum of money to arresting officers, most of whom received a percentage of fines levied. That's how officers earned much of their living. Speights confiscated O'Connor's weapon, and the judge fined him twenty-five dollars. Since the drifter had no money, Speights set out to sell O'Connor's belongings, a horse and saddle blanket. As Speights auctioned the animal off from the square, a ten-year-old youngster, likely the son of O'Connor, unleased verbal abuse upon the officer. Speights would have struck the boy, but Hardin intervened. One word led to another and Hardin put a round hole in Speights's shoulder. Sonny stumbled for cover.[15]

Deciding this might be a good time to leave town, Hardin reached the stable just a couple of jumps ahead of Sheriff Harper. Hardin escaped and fled to the ranch of a friend where he waited for the Harper boys to reach Hemphill. Hardin decided against going to Louisiana and sold the herd for what the Harpers would pay. He then returned to his Uncle Barnett's place in Polk County.[16]

After hunting and fishing a few days, the now nineteen-year-old Hardin and cousin Barnett Jones visited Trinity City in Trinity County, arriving in early August 1872. Hardin hitched up his britches, securing his money belt and trousers behind a large silver belt buckle, and entered the John Gates Saloon at the corner of Caroline and Parke streets. He stuck two six-shooters into saddle bags and stashed them behind the bar. Looking around, he saw Phil Sublett, a local farmer in his early thirties who had killed George Stubblefield, a black man, during an assault back in 1867. Sublett invited Hardin to a game of tenpins, and Hardin accepted. This form of bowling had gained acceptance in Texas after the Civil War, although most games existed in small, dimly-lit, smoke-filled places and were considered social evils.

In any game with Hardin, there was always an argument regarding who won. This dispute had barely started when Hardin slapped Sublett, then jammed a bulldog revolver in his ear. A "bulldog" was a pocket gun of small caliber, suspect in accuracy except when used up close. This was the first known instance of Hardin being a three-gun man.

Bystanders intervened, tempers calmed and everybody strolled into the drinking section of the saloon where Hardin, after a while, noticed Sublett's absence. A suspicious Wes hurried to the bar, retrieved his six-shooters from the saddlebags, and glanced outside to see Sublett coming down the street screaming that he intended to kill Hardin. Hardin stepped away from the door just as Sublett missed with a shotgun blast. Hardin fired a round in return.[17]

As Hardin stood concealed in the shadows, a drunken bystander grabbed Hardin's vest and, saying the two of them could whip anyone, stumbled backwards. In doing so, he outlined Hardin between the lanterns and the street. Sublett fired a second time, and Hardin reeled. Bleeding heavily, Hardin pursued Sublett down the street and into a building where he shot Sublett through the shoulder. Sublett stumbled out the back door and kept running.

Hardin leaned on the arm of Barnett Jones and—suspecting he might be dying—asked Barnett to "take the [money] belt...which held about $2,000 in gold, to get my saddle bags, which had about $250 in silver, and give them to my wife in Gonzales County." Hardin asked Jones "to tell her that I honestly tried to avoid this trouble, but when I was shot, I ran my foe and made him pull freight for his life."[18] Hardin did not say how he had acquired this enormous amount of money. Of course, that brings up another reason why he wrote his autobiography. Hardin wanted readers to know that gambling, horse racing and horse trading, when undertaken by a man of virtue, such as himself, were successful, honorable occupations.

Barnett helped Hardin over to Dr. Carrington's office where an examination revealed two buckshot lodged between the backbone and ribs. They entered just left of the navel. Two other buckshot flattened against the silver belt buckle, and that buckle saved his life. Hardin refused opiates in order to keep his head clear. The doctor rolled him over on his stomach and with a knife and forceps extracted the two slugs.

A grand jury indicted Hardin for attempted murder. After listening to six witnesses, it concluded that John Hardin "inflicted one dangerous wound upon the body of…Philip A. Sublett in an effort to kill and murder" him. [19]

Hardin fled to Sulphur Springs, and then to Sumpter, Texas. He partially recovered in the home of Dr. Orwin Teagarden, a Virginia physician, a Texas merchant, and a long-time friend of the Hardin family.

Several posses scoured the countryside. Wes slipped from one hideout to another, arriving about the last of August in Angelina County where he stayed with Dave Harrel, a friend. Twice the State Police visited the house, suspecting Hardin's presence. Hardin and a shotgun met two of them. During the battle, Hardin took a bullet in the thigh, but shot one officer. Hardin said a coroner's jury ruled the policeman "met his death at the hands of an unknown party, from gunshot wounds."

Hardin had now killed twenty-nine men, but he also had a fresh bullet puncture of his own. Furthermore, his unhealed, festering stomach wounds from Sublett were eroding his resistance. So he sent Dave Harrel to Rusk in Cherokee County where Harrel asked Sheriff Richard B. Reagan to arrest Hardin and bring medicine. Hardin offered to surrender if the officer would split the $400 reward money.

THE FIFTY-ONE-YEAR-OLD REAGAN, a former Tennessean, owned a hotel in downtown Rusk, and operated a farm three miles from town. He worked it with convict labor leased from his own jail.[20] Law enforcement was his trade, and voters elected him sheriff of Cherokee County throughout most of the 1860s and 1870s. His popularity was a given, his fairness and courage unquestioned. With full mustache and goatee, Reagan resembled a quiet, kindly man. Four deputies accompanied the sheriff, but they remained outside the room while Reagan and Hardin conferred. "My name is Dick Reagan," the sheriff said. "I have come to arrest you as Dave Harrel said you wished to surrender."

Sheriff Richard Reagan, first of many lawmen to befriend John Wesley Hardin. (Chuck Parsons Collection)

"I told him yes," Hardin replied, but added that "a fair understanding makes long friends. I told him I did not want to be put in jail; I wanted half the reward; I wanted medical aid; I wanted protection from mob law; I wanted to go to Austin as quickly as possible and from there to [stand trial in] Gonzales."[21]

Hardin's demands were as silly as they were exaggerated and braggadocio. He was helpless, in danger of dying, and in no position to bargain for anything except abject surrender. As for that $2,000 in gold and $200 in silver that Hardin said he carried in his money belt, that was heavy metal. With that much money, a lot of men couldn't walk across the street and keep their pants up at the same time.

The young gunman obviously wrote a whopper about the surrender demands he made to Sheriff Reagan, and he probably embellished the amount of cash he claimed to be carrying. The question is why, and the answer is, in simplistic terms, that John Wesley Hardin was a rampantly insecure man. He killed people to prove his manhood, and he distorted the amount of his "spending" money for the same reason. He wanted the world to know that he was in control, that all things good came to deserving, plucky individuals like himself who prayed regularly. But coming back to the money, there could have been another reason why Hardin factually carried so much. That will be evaluated shortly.

WHILE IT IS DIFFICULT TO BELIEVE that a seriously wounded prisoner actually dictated the conditions of his arrest, Hardin said Reagan agreed to the terms and asked for Hardin's firearms. Wes pointed to one in the scabbard and the other under his pillow. As Hardin reached for the latter, a deputy standing near a window misinterpreted the move and shot Hardin in the right knee. Hardin now had four bullet holes in his body, the last two placed there by law officers.

Reagan and his deputies belatedly apologized and laid him gently in a hack with pillows and a bed quilt. They soon arrived in Rusk and arranged a private room until transferring him to the sheriff's hotel on the town square.

Dood[22] Reagan, the sheriff's son, acted as nurse, and Martha, the sheriff's wife, never tired of preparing dishes for what was now a notorious prisoner. Hardin held court for all kinds of people. Some visited for curiosity and others offered sympathy. Hardin chuckled, "I did my best to be polite to all callers."

This, of course, was the light, angelic side of Hardin. He had charm, he had manners, he had charisma, he genuinely liked people and he genuinely liked to be liked. On the other hand, the people whom Hardin killed were in many respects people like himself, the angel with the dark side.[23]

On September 22, 1872, Sheriff Dick Reagan, Deputy John Taylor and John Wesley Hardin started for Austin. Upon arrival, Travis County Sheriff George B. Zimpleman took charge. The voters had elected him during the 1860s, but military authorities removed him. When Reconstruction soldiers left during the 1870s, the voters returned him to office. Zimpleman had not made any agreements with Hardin, so he incarcerated the gunman in the rotting old jail down by the Colorado River. Judging by the

Austin Daily Democratic Statesman, the jail consisted of "a single room without air or ventilation." It had vermin, reeked with human stench and was jammed "with a suffering mass of suffocating human beings who strip themselves naked because of the intolerable heat and closeness." The newspaper said the jail's condition should "bring a blush of shame to the cheek of every citizen in our county."[24]

HARDIN QUICKLY BECAME A LEADER, the boss man of the twenty-five or so inmates. When a new prisoner entered, they shouted, "Fresh fish!" A kangaroo court proceeded with trial and judgment. If the victim did not pay fines assessed by the prisoners, Hardin said "we would shake the fresh fish" with a blanket, "tossing them nearly to the ceiling, and letting them fall."[25]

Austin friends occasionally sent food to Wes, and Hardin sometimes generously shared it with his fellow prisoners. On one occasion, however, an "overbearing devil...made a grab for some custard I was eating. I let drive at him with my boot, which was iron heeled, and sent him sprawling and bleeding to the floor."[26]

This blanket-tossing and especially the "iron-heeled boot" incident say something about Hardin which ordinarily isn't picked up. It declares that he could be niggardly, nasty and vicious, a man capable of extreme cruelty. For instance, most cowboys would have preferred solid leather boot heels, as iron heels (or iron caps) would not have improved cow work, would have been jolting to the spine, and would have been inclined to slip on smooth surfaces.

Iron heels served only the brutal purposes of saloon brawlers, of down-and-dirty fighters whose intentions were to mutilate. An iron heel was made for breaking and smashing heads, noses, teeth, ribs, fingers, knees, groin, whatever got in the way. Hardin's admission of an iron heel—and how he used it in jail—is also an admission that he could be a bruising, vicious, win-at-all-costs street brawler with his fists and feet when the six-shooter seemed inopportune or unavailable.

By now, the Texas adjutant general had arranged for Hardin to be transferred back to Gonzales where murder indictments were pending. In due time, Hardin and four state policemen reached Lockhart where Hardin's horse collapsed. He switched to a mule.

Hardin's wounds were still painful, and since the mule was frisky, one of the guards swapped his horse for the mule, and it promptly threw him.

Upon arriving in Gonzales, Hardin found a sympathetic populace. Lots of friends and relatives lived in the county. A blacksmith removed the irons. William E. Jones, an interim sheriff who had asked the attorney general for Hardin to be brought here—while admitting his jail was insecure—cautioned Hardin to be patient, as friends would release him shortly.

Through the apparent connivance of Jones, a guard slipped Hardin a saw. On or about the 19th of November, 1872, with guards acting as lookouts, Hardin cut through the iron bars on the south side and broke jail. Sheriff Jones swore the six guards on duty "must have fallen asleep." An Austin newspaper described that statement as "queer."[27]

Sheriff Jones, Manning Clements, and Nathan "Bud" McFadden—a friend—waited with horses. Jones insisted that Hardin ride "with him to the Colorado River and murder a Negro who had killed his [Jones's] brother-in-law." For whatever reason, Hardin refused to go, but Manning Clements did. Manning told Wes later that indeed he and Jones had slain a black man.[28]

The *Daily Herald* of San Antonio claimed Hardin fled as the governor offered a one thousand dollar reward. That wasn't true of course, but Sheriff Jones did make the face-saving offer of a hundred dollars reward on his own. The sheriff felt safe since he knew no one would collect.[29]

A Bullet for
Tom Haldeman

AFTER BREAKING JAIL IN GONZALES, Hardin didn't leave the county. He rode over to Coon Hollow near Elm Creek and briefly tarried with his wife, Jane. However, the comforts of home were objects Hardin only moralized about. He would rather be with the boys, and one of the boys was Jane's brother, Joshua Robert "Brown" Bowen.

Author Lewis Nordyke described Bowen as having brown eyes and light-streaked brown hair. Perhaps this is where the "Brown" originated. As a lean and wiry youth with a sallow complexion, he had a triangular-shaped head, a straight nose and straight hair parted on the left and combed back.[1] Throughout a portion of his life, at least, he sported a brown mustache and goatee.

Bowen was born in Santa Rosa County, Florida on September 27, 1849. After moving to Texas with his parents, he grew up in Karnes, Gonzales, and DeWitt counties.

For a while Brown served with the State Police, although his name does not appear on the (incomplete) muster rolls. According to the 1870 census, Bowen raised stock. By other accounts, he rustled horses and committed murder. While such characteristics were not inconsistent with being a policeman, the accusations were never proven.[2]

John MacDonald "Mac"
Billings in later years.
Mac's courtroom testimony
put a hangman's noose
around the neck of Brown
Bowen. (Marjorie Lee
Burnett Collection)

Brown Bowen, Hardin, Jim and Gip Clements, George Tennille, Rockwood Birtsell, and Thomas J. Haldeman celebrated December 17, 1872 by drinking, shooting targets, and racing horses in Nopal alongside a store operated by the tall, lanky (folks called him "Chunky") forty-year-old William MacDonald Billings, a father-in-law to Tennille. His fourteen-year-old son, John MacDonald Billings (usually called "Mac"), helped out around the business.

The twenty-four-year-old Texas-born Tom Haldeman was, by some accounts a spy for the State Police. No evidence supports this, but as an excuse for murder, someone in the group took it seriously and decided to kill him. On a chilly day, late in the afternoon, Haldeman—hopelessly drunk—wrapped himself in a blanket, stretched out under a tree, rolled over on his side and drifted off to sleep. Near dark, John "Mac" Billings passed within thirty feet of Haldeman and noticed Brown Bowen exit the store, stride over to the sleeping man, pull the cover from Haldeman's face and shoot him. Billings saw "Haldeman's head rather sink at the fire from the pistol." Back inside the building, Hardin asked, "Mac, who shot out there?"

"Mr. Bowen shot."

"What did he shoot at?" Hardin wondered.

"He shot at Mr. Haldeman," Mac responded.

William Billings asked Bowen why he had killed Haldeman. Bowen replied that he had a right to kill him. Billings asked, "what he had killed him in the presence of my son Mac for," and Bowen responded, "I did not see Mac until my finger was on the trigger, and it was too late to stop then."[3]

Haldeman's family buried him in the Old Davy Cemetery thirty-nine miles from Gonzales. Within two weeks, Sheriff Green DeWitt and Deputy Richard B. Hudson arrested Brown Bowen. A murder indictment followed in February 1873. However, Brown languished in jail only until March 26 when Wes Hardin and twelve unidentified men "rode into the town of Gonzales and delivered the county jail of all its prisoners, threatening the guard with death if he made any alarm."

Two months later, the *San Antonio Daily Express* reported "A ruffian named Bowen committed rape on a colored woman" in DeWitt County. Afterwards, "he shot and killed one of the best colored men in the county, Bob Taylor by name."

Brown Bowen was what Sheriff Green DeWitt described to Texas Attorney General William Alexander as a member of "a strong band of thieves and murderers headed by John Hardin, alias Wesley Hardin, alias Wesley Clements, who is reported to have committed sixteen different murders." The sheriff explained that he had "made no effort to arrest any of these parties because the citizens would not answer his summons,...[and] the outlaws would be released even if caught and placed in the Gonzales jail...."[4]

Brown Bowen remained in the neighborhood until August before fleeing to Florida, denying in the process he belonged to Hardin's gang. "Hardin and his party was the cause of [my] leaving the state," he said. "They threatened to kill me on sight, [and] Hardin and his party shot at me five or six times."[5] Brown accused Hardin of Haldeman's murder and of attempting to kill Bowen himself, eliminating a witness.

This temporarily ended the Bowen-Hardin-Haldeman incident. John Wesley Hardin never mentioned Haldeman's death in his memoirs, a curious oversight since the killing would have a devastating future effect upon everybody concerned. The controversy haunted the Hardins forever after. But in the meantime, following the Haldeman murder, John Hardin rode over to Karnes County—directly west of DeWitt—where Jane delivered her first child, Mary Elizabeth "Mollie" Hardin on February 6, 1873. Hardin never mentioned the birth in his autobiography. The parents named the child after John's mother.

Hardin said he planned to live in and around Karnes and Gonzales counties. There he would buy and sell cattle, as well as rope and brand mavericks. He spoke of driving livestock to Kansas. Of course, what he really had in mind involved joining the locally raging Sutton-Taylor Feud. The only question under consideration was, on whose side?

The Sutton-Taylor Feud

TEXAS VIOLENCE IS RELATIVELY easy to explain during the Reconstruction period of the late 1860s and the first half of the 1870s. While Union soldiers and black State Policemen struggled to establish law, they at best were undisciplined and untrained. Therefore, a solitary theme uniting a badly fractured populace was its shared, common hatred for Union soldiers and Texas police.

With a federal government antagonistic to the general population, and the state government often powerless, counties tried to take up the slack. But even there, life was an economic and social struggle, though people owned their own land and their own home. Clothes, food, utensils, toys, furniture, medical care and necessary equipment they either scratched for, built, grew themselves, or did without. Annual county taxes amounted to nickels and dimes. Several counties had no jails, no courthouses. They made do with rented, empty buildings often without doors or windows, and always without sufficient security. One-room log huts incarcerated dangerous criminals. Dirt floors and brush roofs facilitated escapes. Some counties dug dark, dank pits—usually called Bat Caves—under the floor and sealed them with a trap door. Criminals escaped these only by going insane.

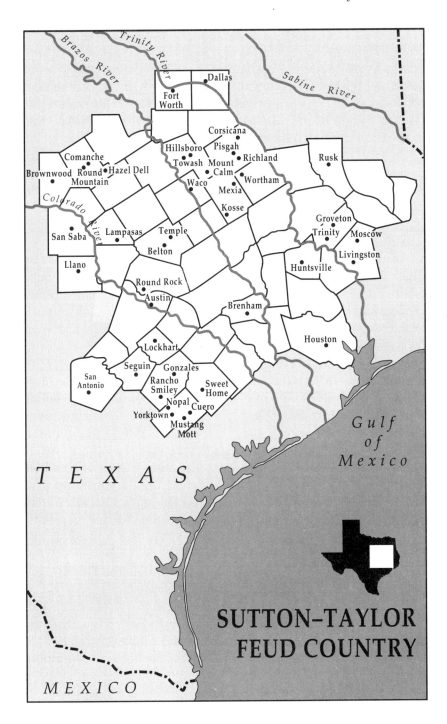

SUTTON–TAYLOR
FEUD COUNTRY

Guards, when they existed, created an enormous drain on county finances. Judges rarely assessed fines because the accused generally could not pay them, and the tribunal hesitated to order jail sentences because the county frequently had no confinement rooms available. A released criminal could thumb his nose at the law. An escaped criminal meant the whole dangerous pursuit had to be conducted all over again.

County officials, whether honest or corrupt, competent or incompetent, shared one characteristic in common: they could not control lawlessness, although a few did it better than others. As disorder escalated, families and groups struggled for power. Shotguns, six-shooters, lynch ropes, and graves became grim solutions to complex social problems.

As neighbors found no recourse in the courts against injury by other neighbors, regional feuds arose. In the far west, El Paso County engaged in a Salt War. Closer to the shadowy, piney woods, squabbles resounded with colorful titles such as Jaybird-Woodpecker, and the Regulators and the Moderators, the Feud for Miss Sue Pinckney and the Horrell-Higgins Feud.[1]

Hatred, frustration and chaos spread across Texas. An Age of Desperadoes arose which opened with racial and political murders and evolved into people killing each other just for the hell of it. Portions of Texas were at war with themselves, their residents tearing away not only at the fabric of local government, but at the core of who they were as a society.

Those people justified their brutality and absence of legalities as bringing frontier justice to a troubled region. Outrages provoked retaliations. Feudists saw themselves as the final arbitrators of crimes ordinarily judged by the State. They inflicted terroristic vengeance. They intimidated judges and juries, horsewhipped lawbreakers and other folks they didn't like, and frequently drove them from the county, or lynched or shot them. The Sutton-Taylor Feud epitomized much of this violence.[2]

T. C. Robinson, a Virginian who served in DeWitt County with Leander McNelly's Texas Rangers in mid-to-late 1874 during the Sutton-Taylor Feud, wrote humorous and informative letters to Texas newspapers, signing them "Pidge." He failed at explaining the origins of the Sutton-Taylor War, but he gave an amusing—if exaggerated—version of how it kept reproducing itself:

The people of both factions are men accustomed to righting their own wrongs, and they object decidedly to any interference, even should that interference be lawful. In any difference which may arise between two men not previously connected with the *vendetta*, each takes his place with one or the other party, and in this manner recruits are gathered in the protecting *aegis* of the band which will defend them to the death. The leaders of each party... turn the cylinder of a revolver as a rattle for the infants of this country, and give them empty cartridge cases as teething rings; they are weaned on gunpowder and brandy, and learn to shoot before they can talk.[3]

The Taylors of the Sutton-Taylor Feud were largely unrepentant Confederates. With the subsequent breakdown of law and order by a Texas people believing themselves wronged, the Taylors enforced their own canons. They ambushed a soldier now and then, snatched livestock belonging to Yankee sympathizers and killed a few stubborn Union supporters in the process. These indiscretions might have been illegal, but they were not considered sins.

In those early forlorn days, no counselors analyzed violent behavior. No one justified or explained it away as a fault of poverty, one-parent households, or a lack of entitlement programs.

Modern-day Taylors are still perplexed. They meet once a year in south-central Texas for a family reunion and use the time to discuss ancestors. They judge not by today's standards, recognizing that their kinsmen of bygone years did the best they could under circumstances of provocation, hardship and lack of communications. Today's descendants acknowledge that had they been there, as a Taylor *or* a Sutton, they might have reacted as did their grandparents and great-grandparents. They offer non-judgmental discussion and forgiveness across the board, all the while conceding the ultimate recognition that "some of those people were mean; they were just mean."[4]

WILLIAM SUTTON WAS BORN October 20, 1846, and led his first posse in 1868 at the age of twenty-one. As a Confederate veteran who supported the Union during Reconstruction, Sutton stood about six feet tall, a lean individual with an oblong face, straight nose, piercing blue eyes, fair complexion and taut lips. He combed back his light, rather curly hair, revealing a

William Sutton, leader of the Sutton faction, and his wife Laura. (Chuck Parsons Collection)

widow's peak. Friends described him as gentle of manner and quiet by nature.

He represented the "Sutton" in the Sutton-Taylor Feud, for in terms of family and the Sutton name, he stood alone. A brother, James, refused to get involved. Yet, Bill Sutton had powerful allies, specifically James Cox, Joseph Tumlinson, and Jack Helm. These four men defined the core of the Sutton Party.

James W. Cox started life about 1824, and by 1870 appeared stout, of medium height with full beard and thinning dark hair. He married twice.

Joseph Tumlinson (usually referred to as Capt. Joe) was born in Tennessee on February 16, 1811. He was the son of John Jackson Tumlinson who migrated to Texas with Stephen F. Austin and became the first *alcalde* (mayor, leader, or supervisor) of the Colorado River Colonization District. Capt. Joe grew up in a Texas

Capt. Joe Tumlinson,
the only feud leader
to die in bed.
(Sam Tumlinson
Collection)

Ranger family that historian Dan Kilgore described as "The Fighting Tumlinsons."[5] Back when everybody was still friends, Joe and Creed Taylor fought side by side during the Texas Revolution as well as the Indian Wars. They once owned adjoining tracts of land. Joe's first wife was Creed's sister, Johanna, who died in the 1830s. Creed's brother, William Riley Taylor, married Capt. Joe Tumlinson's sister, Elizabeth. Consequently, Joseph Tumlinson had blood and emotional ties with the Taylors.[6] Yet, he sided with Sutton.

BACK IN AUSTIN, UNION GENERAL Philip Sheridan assigned command of the Fifth Military District to Brevet Major-General Joseph Jones Reynolds in 1867. His Special Order No. 195 dismissed 400 Democrats from village and county offices and appointed 436 Republicans.[7] However, although Governor Elisha Pease and Reynolds seemed to think alike, they had differences. Governor Pease resigned on September 30, 1869, and Reynolds himself took charge for the next four months as military commander of Texas as well as provisional governor. In particular, he exerted closer supervision of state law enforcement. Military tribunals increased.[8] Reynolds appointed Captain Charles S. Bell

Creed Taylor. He sired a lot of fighters.
(Chuck Parsons Collection)

as a special officer for the suppression of crime, and Bell on June 1, 1869, recruited John Marshall "Jack" Helm. The forthcoming showdown between Helm and John Wesley Hardin would shake Texas.

Creed Taylor described Helm as "about five feet eight inches high, rather heavy, but well made with black hair and eyes and dark complexion. His conversation was too much about himself, and what he had done, to be fascinating. His vanity was unbounded, his egotism was immense, and his education was very limited." Helm worked as a cowboy for cattle king Abel Head "Shanghai" Pierce shortly after the Civil War. By Helm's own admission, Bell asked him "to assist in arresting desperadoes in Texas known as the Taylor Party."[9]

He told the *Victoria Advocate* that he offered protection to honest, law-abiding citizens. "To those thieves who have been depredating upon the stock interests of the country with impunity," he "had orders to arrest and bring them to justice." Helm complimented his officers "for their orderly conduct, gentlemanly bearing, and devotion to the laws of the country."[10]

Helm defended his deeds to the *San Antonio Daily Herald*, saying "no citizen can complain of the least injury at our hands. I labor for the supremacy of the law without compensation or reward; and when the robbers are brought to justice, the majesty of the law vindicated…I will be repaid…in the knowledge that I have done my duty."[11]

John Marshall "Jack" Helm's career was an example not only of how John Wesley Hardin became famous, but of how Reconstruction politics sometimes played themselves out. In October 1870, with charges of brutality and embezzlement buzzing about the embattled officer's head, Helm was suspended from the State Police. Helm denied charges regarding the wholesale execution of prisoners. In December he was dismissed although he became sheriff of DeWitt county.[12]

BY LATE 1870, JACK HELM AND BILL SUTTON were riding hard after William, Henry, Wiley and Eugene Kelly. The lawmen accused the Kellys of shooting-up a circus performance in Sweet Home (Lavaca County), Texas, a beautiful name for so much tragedy. Helm and Sutton rounded up the suspects. No one resisted.

Amanda Kelly, a daughter of Pitkin Taylor (acknowledged leader of the Sutton faction) was the wife of Henry Kelly. As such, she witnessed the brothers William and Henry Kelly leaving the road with the posse and entering a thicket. From the saddle, William cut tobacco for his pipe. Upon filling it, he stepped down, squatted and struck a match on the bottom of his boot. From atop his horse, Bill Sutton shot him through the head, and Kelly sank to the ground. Doc White, another posse member, then shot Henry off his horse. Amanda stated that "a general firing at the

Pitkin Taylor and wife Susan Cochran (Day) Taylor. There is no evidence that Pitkin, leader of the Taylor faction, ever killed anybody. Following Pitkin's death, John Wesley Hardin assumed the Taylor Party leadership. (Eddie Day Truitt Collection)

bodies...by the party then ensued, and the ground where the bodies lay and the vicinity, was so enveloped in smoke as to completely hide the men....After the firing ceased and when I was screaming and making toward the bodies, I saw the men escape in the brush."[13]

In a feud of numerous turning points, the Kelly killings were significant. The murders created such public revulsion that the Sutton Party found itself almost universally despised. As atrocity mounted upon atrocity, the *Victoria Advocate* noted that "killed while trying to escape," and "killed while resisting arrest" were "fast coming to have a melancholy and terrible significance." The *Advocate* described such deaths as "most foul, strange and unnatural."

Pitkin Taylor, lean and balding, vowed vengeance for the murder of the Kelly brothers. Bill Sutton took notice and reacted accordingly. In September 1872, Sutton and four gunmen, using a cowbell, lured Pitkin at night into his cornfield thinking he would chase away cows eating the crop. There, the Sutton Party ambushed and wounded Taylor. His daughter Amanda, the widow of Henry Kelly, nursing a small child, found her father in the field. She dragged him a short distance toward the house, returned for the child, carried him to her father, dragged her father a brief distance again, and repeated the procedure until she reached the porch. Six months later in March 1873, Pitkin died of his wounds at the age of fifty-one.

At Pitkin Taylor's funeral near Cuero, Jim Taylor lowered his father into the soft Texas soil. He grimly vowed to wash his hands in the blood of Bill Sutton.[14]

Retribution came, at least partially, on April 1, 1873, when Scrap Taylor, another of Pitkin's sons, caught William Sutton relaxing in the Banks Saloon at Cuero. A shotgun blast crashed through the window and shattered Sutton's left arm.[15]

ABOUT THIS TIME, THE SUTTON-TAYLOR FEUD and John Wesley Hardin caught up with each other. He had taken no part in the opening scenes because he was preoccupied with driving cattle to Kansas and in doing risky work by shooting rogues in Texas.

Nevertheless, the Feud carried with it strong Hardin family implications and partisanship. Hardin's wife, his in-laws, his cousins, his parents, and ultimately his brother Joe would become entwined. Fighting involved regionally famous people whom he would kill. The Feud provided Hardin with a state-wide as well as a national identity even while it represented the peak and the beginning-of-the-decline of John Wesley Hardin. The early years even without Hardin's participation, propelled him into some of the Feud's bloodiest and most electrifying moments. In large part, the Feud established not only who he was, but who and what John Wesley Hardin would become.

Exit Jim Cox
and Jack Helm

WITH RECONSTRUCTION THROUGHOUT TEXAS now in its last throbbing gasp, the Democrat Party gradually wrested control from the Republicans. On April 23, 1873, the legislature overrode Governor Davis's executive veto and abolished the detested State Police. Since the Texas Rangers would not organize until the spring of 1874, Texas went through a year essentially with no federal or military maintenance for the suppression of crime. State officials lacked authority to cross county lines to investigate lawlessness or make arrests.

Jack Helm, who sided with the Sutton faction, retained his power base as the DeWitt County sheriff. Since county budgets limited his deputies, he primarily operated through his lieutenants: Jim Cox, Capt. Joe Tumlinson, and Bill Sutton. They reputedly could field a posse of two hundred.

HARDIN'S CATTLE BUSINESS led him to seek additional markets on April 9 by following a plow furrow toward the new town of Cuero in DeWitt County. As the terminus of the Gulf, Western Texas and Pacific Railroad, Cuero in six weeks had risen from a backwoods thicket to a thriving village with a barber shop, twenty-five stores, a couple of hundred inhabitants, a pending newspaper, a church, two hotels under construction, and a proposed post office.[1]

When eighteen miles from Cuero, Hardin encountered a heavily armed rider on a gray horse. A Winchester rifle protruded from a boot, and two holstered revolvers dangled from the saddle horn. After the Civil War, sidearms and gunbelts were so heavy that gunmen on horseback wrapped their weapons around the saddle horn and let the animal shoulder the strain. Hardin suspected the stranger was either a lawman or desperado, and knew he was right when he pulled alongside the rider. The stranger immediately dismounted. Hardin did the same. Then they remounted and faced each other.

Few activities could have demonstrated the evolution of professional gun handlers more than those dismounting/mounting procedures. On the ground, if and when it became necessary to fight, each man could lunge, rear, duck, jump, drop, squat, twist, roll, charge, or run. From horseback, a rider worried about controlling his animal, retaining his seat, having nowhere to hide, and getting off a shot, all at the same time.

"Do you live around here?" the stranger asked. Hardin replied "no," that he was traveling to Cuero. The stranger then introduced himself as the sheriff of DeWitt County, and Hardin responded, "I suppose your name is Dick Hudson?"

The sheriff said he was Jack Helm. Hardin gave his name. "Are you Wesley?" Helm asked incredulously, extending his hand. Hardin declined to shake. Instead he snarled, "We are man to man and face to face on equal terms. You have said I was a murderer and a coward, and have had your deputies after me. Now arrest me if you can. I dare you to try it."

"Wesley, I am your friend," Helm sputtered. "My deputies are hunting you on their own account, and not mine."

By now Hardin had drawn his pistol. Helm pleaded for his life.

Hardin taunted him, growling "You are armed, defend yourself. You have been going round killing men long enough, and I know you belong to a legalized band of murdering cowards [who] have hung and murdered better men than yourself."

Helm called Hardin "too brave a man to shoot me." He pleaded for friendship, and asked John Wesley to "join his vigilant company." Hardin said he "declined because the people with whom he [Helm] was waging war were my friends." However, Hardin did not decline very convincingly because after discussing the matter further, the two continued to Cuero where they separated after agreeing to meet and talk again.[2]

In describing the Helm encounter in his autobiography, Hardin attempted to have it both ways. He wanted the Taylors to believe he never wavered, and he wanted the reading audience to understand that he had an opportunity to lead, or at least fight for, both sides. A key to much of Hardin's dark personality is the great lengths he went to in order to preserve the image of himself as a man of action who retained the virtues of honesty, integrity, loyalty and fair play. Actually, he had been shedding these values ever since he was fifteen years old. An engaging fact, however, is that not only did many people continue to see God's grace in him, Hardin in his own mind never doubted that it was there.

In fact, this meeting in the boondocks did happen, but not by chance, and not altogether as Hardin depicted it. It was intentional; and it was devised by both parties. The two men met in the middle of nowhere in order to keep their deliberations private. The conversation was affable. The threats were inserted into Hardin's memoirs to make the Taylors and their supporters believe that there had never been amicable relations between Hardin and Helm. Nevertheless, the false description of what was said, the ploy of an accidental meeting, is an important adjunct to the Hardin story because when studied carefully, it outlines in part Hardin's elaborate scheme to revise the history of how he became involved in the Sutton-Taylor Feud.

This episode had its origins nearly a year earlier in May 1872, when Hardin made that mysterious, unexplained "business trip" to the King Ranch in the Lower Rio Grande Valley. A rough equivalent might have been Hardin announcing a business trip to see the governor of Texas, or a trip to visit the Texas legislature so that he might address the Senate. Richard King was the largest, most legendary cattleman in Texas. His spread amounted to an empire. One did not just drop in for a visit; King asked to see you. The fact that Hardin went there at all arouses curiosity and speculation.

Hardin would not have been selling, buying or trading livestock with King. Hardin had no credentials as a cattleman. King would not have needed ranch managers, cowboys, or trail drivers. But King, in the early 1870s, did have serious, almost catastrophic problems. Richard King was being bled white by marauders operating primarily out of Mexico. The rustling and killing on his realm was beyond belief.

However, his solutions were at hand. The United States Cavalry was already riding to his rescue. The Texas Rangers were not far behind.

King wanted an audience with Hardin because, hating rustlers the way he did, he was sympathetic to the Sutton faction of the Feud. In popular parlance, at least, the Taylors were perceived by the general population as stock thieves, while the Suttons, in spite of their brutality, were perceived as fed-up vigilante/lawmen.

King knew such men as James Cox, a recognized leader of the Sutton party. While King might not have known John Wesley Hardin, he certainly knew about him. He knew John had slain Union soldiers and Mexican cowboys. Almost every cattleman and cowboy in Texas loved to repeat, and embellish, the Kansas story behind Bideno's death. Cowboys and cowmen perceived Hardin as one of them, the good guys, and since he was one of them, King anticipated that Hardin would sell his gun to the Sutton bunch.

The King Ranch, with Richard King acting as moderator, became neutral ground for a secret meeting between Jim Cox and John Wesley Hardin. That was the "business" John Wesley Hardin rode 175 miles one way just to talk about.

Evidently the discussions went well. When Hardin left the King Ranch, James Cox rode with him to San Diego, Texas. They spent the night, then visited Banquete, in Nueces County, a short distance north of the King Ranch. They stayed at least one additional day, and Hardin implies two. At this point, Hardin headed for home.[3]

Shortly after the King Ranch visit, in August 1873, Hardin had a gunfight with Phil Sublett. A wounded Hardin asked his cousin,

Barnett Jones, to deliver to his wife a money belt containing two thousand dollars in gold and over two hundred dollars in silver. If this cash actually existed, either James Cox and/or Richard King provided it.

HELM AND HARDIN MET AGAIN on April 16 at the home of Jim Cox. Hardin buttressed himself with Manning Clements and George Tennille. Clements and Tennille were related by marriage and, like Hardin, had not yet become involved in the Feud.[4]

Everybody shook hands. Cox and Helm steered Hardin into another room and offered to resolve his fugitive problems if Hardin would join them. "They would have to do a whole lot of work to get me clear of all trouble," Hardin wrote, "so I would have to do a whole lot of work for them."

Negotiations temporarily ended when Hardin stated that he, Clements, and Tennille wanted neutrality. Cox and Helm consented.[56] However, Hardin couched his neutrality in words calculated to lead the Sutton faction on in its belief that he still had their offer under serious consideration.

AFTER THE MEETING, Hardin wandered into a bar on the southwest corner of the Cuero square where he used the alias of Johnson. The name fooled no one. As Hardin won a five dollar poker pot, J. B. Morgan, an Irish stonemason, rushed over and wanted Hardin to treat him to a bottle of champagne. Hardin declined. When Morgan angrily insisted, Hardin stepped outside. In a few minutes, Morgan approached again, this time asking Hardin if he were armed. Hardin nodded. Morgan said, "Well, it's time you were defending yourself." He slipped his own pistol halfway from his pocket as Hardin jerked and fired, shooting Morgan over the left eye. Then Wes casually saddled up and rode out of town unmolested.

Texas Ranger Pidge later told the story differently, saying Hardin "killed a man in Cuero because he took his hands out of his own pockets when he (Hardin) told him not to do so. After he disposed of this willful individual,...[Hardin] went out on the prairie a short distance and peacefully went to sleep."[78]

A newspaper described the bullet as entering *under* the eye, and passing through the back of the head. Although the editor

James Cox.
(Chuck Parsons
Collection)

predicted the state would someday "put a stop to these despera-does," he admitted the killing was "believed to have been justifiable, as Morgan was the aggressor." On the basis of this, one could argue that Hardin's thirtieth victim was actually a suicide.[9]

ON APRIL 23, 1873, JACK HELM and a group of men rode through the Neill Bowen neighborhood of Gonzales County, questioning Jane Hardin regarding her husband's whereabouts and intentions. Hardin's memoirs made it sound like an ugly confrontation, but the Sutton people were impatient for a decision regarding Hardin's willingness to join their side. Hardin now made up his mind.

He sent word for the Taylors—whom he had not met—to meet him and Manning Clements at Mustang Mott, a clump of live oak west of Cuero. Late that afternoon, the Hardin party of Tennille, Clements, and himself conferred with the brothers Jim,

James Taylor, never a relative, but always a loyal Hardin friend. (R. G. McCubbin Collection)

John, and Scrap Taylor. Everyone agreed to carry their fight to a common enemy.

SOMEWHERE AROUND MAY or June, James W. Cox and John W. S. "Jake" Christman, among others, crossed between Helena and Yorktown. Cox and Christman were fifty yards in front when acrid black powder engulfed them. When it cleared, those in the rear had fled. Christman and James Cox sprawled dead. Christman, from Indiana and about forty, had family ties with the Cox family and died just because he happened to be present. Cox had nineteen buckshot in his body and a slashed throat. Some-one really disliked him.[10]

Jim and Scrap Taylor, and maybe Alf Day and Patrick Hays "Bud" Dowlearn, performed the execution. There may have been others.[11]

John Wesley Hardin never acknowledged any complicity in the Cox/Christman killings, although he squirmed in his autobiography, explaining "I have never pleaded to that [murder] case [so] I will at this time have little to say except that Jim Cox and Jake Christman met their death from the Taylor party about the 15th of May, 1873."[12]

This was Hardin's way of refusing to admit guilt for fear of prosecution. It could also have been his way of slyly implying credit for killings that others committed.

Still, it is improbable that the Taylors would have pulled off the double homicide without Hardin's presence and perhaps his participation. A shotgun murdered Cox, and a shotgun was a Hardin weapon of choice. He had used it on soldiers, and he would soon use it again during one of his most sensational killings.

WITH HARDIN NOW FIRMLY in the Taylor camp—although the word had obviously not yet reached the Sutton party—he and Jim Taylor rode into Albuquerque, Texas, a settlement on the Clear Fork of Sandies Creek in western Gonzales County.[13]

Like most lawmen and politicians, Sheriff Helm worked at other vocations to earn a living. It is not certain if he resided in Albuquerque, but he frequently visited the local blacksmith shop owned by John Bland. Helm prided himself not only on his man-killing skills, but on his talents as a tinkerer, and perhaps even a thinker. Helm had designed an agricultural implement, a cotton worm eradicator. A patent would be granted shortly before his death.[14]

Helm was a sheriff; this was his town; and the blacksmith shop—with its normal hustle and bustle—seemed a peaceful setting for civilized men to discuss propositions. From all accounts, Helm dressed in work clothing and carried nothing other than a knife he was probably sharpening for a neighbor.

Sheriff Helm had not yet learned of John Wesley Hardin's Taylor loyalties. In his autobiography, Hardin says "I went there according to agreement," the implication being that Helm wanted to continue discussing Hardin's proposed membership in the Sutton Party. Jim Taylor tagged along, according to Hardin, because Taylor had never met Jack Helm and wanted Hardin to

Artist's drawing of the Jack Helm slaying. (*The Life of John Wesley Hardin*)

introduce them. That, of course, was nonsense. Taylor tagged along with Hardin either to kill Helm or to provide support and backup for the bloodshed.

The Hardin shotgun rendered additional evidence of premeditated murder. People did not ordinarily tote heavy, bulky shotguns around unless they were hunting squirrels or human beings.

The fact that Jim Taylor had never met Helm explains how Taylor entered town incognito, separate from Hardin. He stationed himself in or near the blacksmith shop.

Suddenly, Hardin heard Helm scream, "Hands up, you son of a bitch!" Helm clutched a knife as he advanced upon James Taylor. Hardin grabbed his shotgun and "fired at Capt. Jack Helms as he [Helm] was closing with Jim Taylor." Wes then kept the crowd restrained with the menacing mouth of the other barrel. "In the meantime," Hardin wrote, "Jim Taylor had shot Helms repeatedly [with a revolver]. He fell with twelve buckshot in his breast and several six-shooter balls in his head."

"Thus did the leader of the vigilant committee, the sheriff of DeWitt, the terror of the county, whose name was a horror to all law-abiding citizens, meet his death." So wrote Hardin.[15]

THE *FAYETTE COUNTY NEW ERA* of La Grange, Texas, identified the slaying as happening on Friday, August 1, 1873. The
newspaper claimed a grocer named McCracken—the source of
the article information—was sitting alongside the blacksmith shop
chatting with Hardin and Helm. As they spoke, a stranger (Jim
Taylor) walked up behind Helm and pulled the trigger of a six-
shooter. The gun misfired. Helm heard the click, turned and
charged, only to be shot in the breast by the stranger. Hardin then
opened up with a double-barreled shotgun, wounding Helm in
the arm. Helm staggered into the shop as the stranger pursued,
shooting him repeatedly in the head. The sheriff fell dead, and
the stranger and Hardin rode away.[16]

The *San Antonio Daily Express* reported two armed men approached the sheriff, dismounted and asked if he were Jack Helm.
When Helm nodded yes, one of the men pulled a revolver which
misfired three times. Helm and Hardin raced to a nearby tree for
possession of a shotgun, and Hardin reached it first. Helm drew
his bowie knife as Hardin shot him. Jim Taylor then leisurely dispatched Helm with the six-shooter. Before leaving town, the two
slayers rode over to the blacksmith shop and waited for their
horses to be shod.[17]

Lieutenant Pidge of the Texas Rangers—later stationed in
DeWitt County—heard stories about the killing. He left no doubt
about primary responsibility. "One day in a playful mood," Pidge
wrote, "Wes gave him [Helm] a broadside, and sunk him."[18]

Although some dispute exists whether John Wesley Hardin or
Jim Taylor fired the lead that killed Jack Helm, the answer seems
conclusive. They both did it. They pulled triggers almost simultaneously. Wes Hardin had his thirty-first victim even though he
shared him with James Taylor.

Hardin dated the killing as May 17, 1873, although late July is
a better estimate. The *Dallas Times Herald* of August 2, reported
that "The notorious Jack Helm, one of Governor Davis's State
Police, was killed last week, near Seguin, by a man named
Hardin." The *San Antonio Daily Express* of July 25 noted: JACK
HELM KILLED. "In DeWitt County a desperado by the name of
Hardin, with several others of the same stripe rode up to the blacksmith shop of Jack Helm while he was engaged in his work and
riddled him with bullets."

The young Hardin took pride in his bloody work. "The news soon spread that I had killed Jack Helms," Hardin chuckled, "and I received many letters of thanks from the widows of men whom he had cruelly put to death. Many of the best citizens of Gonzales and DeWitt counties patted me on the back and told me that was the best act of my life."[19]

MEANWHILE, THE LATE PITKIN TAYLOR had come as close as anybody to commanding the Taylor Party. Following Pitkin's death, his son Jim unobtrusively slipped into the slot. However, while Jim was dangerous as well as courageous, he neither sought nor wanted the role of leader. The Taylors were never that well organized, so John Wesley Hardin inherited the position almost by default.

Contrary to published reports, and widespread perceptions, Hardin was not related to the Taylors. Some historians have noted that John Wesley Hardin took the Taylor side because his brother Jeff wed Mary Taylor. However, that did not occur until 1896 and would have played no part in the 1873 decision. Hardin became a Taylor partisan for two reasons: because he had friends who were related to the Taylors, and the Taylors had a vacancy at the top for a fast gun.

While hard proof is missing, Hardin without question organized and implemented the Cox/Christman murders. Following that, the slaying of Helm virtually catapulted the Taylor Party into the public mind as the Taylor/Hardin Party or Hardin Gang.

Too Mean to Arrest

SOUTHEAST AND SOUTH-CENTRAL TEXAS was as prone to brush as far West Texas was to desert. Tangled, sticky thickets existed everywhere. During the late evening hours, with the ground fog rising, wild animals and (some say) ghosts flitted and vanished along the narrow, slippery, meandering trails. At night, decent people preferred to remain indoors. Those who did roam under the moon tended to travel in packs and were rarely up to anything good.

The Taylor/Hardin Party, as well as the Sutton faction, ruled the darkness in much of south-central Texas. Without mentioning specific names, the *Victoria Advocate* referred to their handiwork as "Midnight Scouts On The Rampage—Mystic Riders Flitting In The Dark."

> Bands of armed men have been seen during the past week hovering around the outskirts of town under the friendly darkness. ...Several persons traveling to and fro have been stopped and interrogated....This state of affairs is a sequel to the reign of terror with which this unhappy section was afflicted some three or four years ago, over which Jack Helm and C. S. Bell were the presiding spirits. We learn that the two parties—possibly numbering fifty men each—are upon the warpath. The shooting of Wm. Sutton in Cuero some time since seems to have been the spark that rekindled the smoldering embers, and since then Helm, Cox and Christman

have fallen—the victims of revenge—whether just or not, it is not our province to determine. Their comrades...will seek to avenge their death, and thus continue the bloody carnival....This slaughtering of men on our highways, and in the very towns, is an infamous disgrace to our civilization. It should be stopped. There [are] enough law-abiding citizens, and they are ready and willing to respond to the Sheriff's call....It is the Sheriff's duty to arrest all violators of the law, and to protect the citizens....It is no excuse that there are fifty or a hundred men violating the laws—the more numerous, the greater necessity for their arrests. If this cannot be done, we had better burn the court house, abolish law, and transform the State into a seething, hating, murderous hell, and be done with it.

The Sutton-Taylor Feud continued its relentless string of useless killings as night riders resolved (and created) numerous conflicts and bad memories. Over in Navarro County where Susanna Dixon Anderson had once vowed that the baby in her body would someday avenge the death of its father—well, that was coming to pass. Alexander Hamilton "Ham" Anderson was now a man of eighteen years. He, his brother Jim Anderson, and Alec Barekman, vindictive cousins of John Wesley Hardin, were accused of waylaying the fifty-seven-year-old William Love in late May 1873. They shot Capt. Love as he took an evening ride near Richland Creek—twelve miles from Corsicana—in the vicinity where Love had slain William Anderson several years earlier. The State charged Barekman and Ham Anderson with murder, although neither ever went to trial. Barekman remained in Texas while Ham fled to Roswell, New Mexico.[1] In reality, Jim Anderson likely fired the .38 caliber bullet. The family thinks so, and Jim was the *unborn* baby in 1855 when Love murdered Anderson's father.

A FEW MILES DISTANT, after the death of Helm and Cox, only William Sutton and Capt. Joe Tumlinson remained in the Sutton Party leadership. Tumlinson had worked as a State Police officer assigned to Yorktown, Texas, in 1871.[2] Now he simply ranched and battled with the Taylors.

In mid August 1873, John Wesley Hardin learned of fifty or more gunmen gathering at the Tumlinson Ranch to slaughter the Taylor Party. So John Wesley opted for a pre-emptive assault. He

Alexander Henry "Alec" Barekman, about 1873. (Walter Clay Dixson Collection)

Joe Clements (R. G. McCubbin Collection)

and a dozen or so riders reached the Tumlinson ranch at about three o'clock in the morning. They caught Tumlinson's forces sleeping on the long porches. Hardin planned to bushwhack them, but Tumlinson's dogs created such a racket that the Taylor riflemen had no opportunity to open fire. The sleepers, unable to determine how many riflemen waited out there in the darkness, stampeded inside the house.

The siege continued for two days and one night, with nobody slain. In the meantime, as Tumlinson slipped a courier through the lines to the county seat, Hardin's forces expanded to about three dozen fighters. Before the trouble ended, roughly two hundred men altogether would be involved.

L. B. Wright, one of Governor Edmund Davis's cronies at Yorktown, Texas, wrote the governor and explained what happened next. His statement is edited for clarity:

A party of about forty men headed by Wesley Hardin, [Brown] Bowen [and others] surrounded Captain Joseph Tumlinson's house and held it for two days and nights. No person could pass in or out. They [Hardin's men] said they wanted Joe Tumlinson and several others who belonged to the [former] state police. I was in

Clinton in attendance at the District Court. When the news arrived I reported it to Judge D. D. Claiborn, and he ordered the deputy sheriff to summon a posse to relieve Tumlinson, which he did. The posse [comprised] some nine in number, and they arrived at Captain Tumlinson's. The desperadoes [Hardin's men] still had the house besieged and would not permit the [deputy's] party to pass to the house. At least two-thirds of the deputy's party joined the other party [apparently Hardin].

John Wesley Hardin insisted to Deputy Sheriff James Francis Blair that there would be no relief for Tumlinson. If Blair intended to do anything about it, he should start with Hardin. The deputy, seeing a majority of his posse joining the besiegers, responded, "Well, under the circumstances, I won't persist, especially as my men have deserted me."

Still, such stand-offs could not continue forever. Eventually a legal armed force of civilians would arrive that Hardin could not prevail against. A deal had to be struck, preferably through Blair's office, and Hardin knew it.[3]

Blair therefore negotiated with both parties and talked all concerned into riding to Clinton. Hardin's group led the procession. The posse rode in the middle, and Tumlinson brought up the rear. Upon reaching the county seat, Hardin's forces paused on one side of the village. Tumlinson occupied the other. Blair passed the word that even though both groups were well armed, no public disturbance was intended. The affair was of "a personal nature."[4]

The deputy then wrote a treaty "for the purpose of promoting peace and order and quiet in this community." Each signer promised "to abstain from any hostile acts calculated to create a breach of peace or to induce anyone to suppose that any violence is intended."

Forty-one men signed the treaty on August 12, the Sutton Party on the left side, the Taylor Party on the right. Among the signers were Joe Tumlinson (who made his mark), John Wesley Hardin, George C. Tennille, Manning, Gibson, James and Joe Clements, Jim Taylor, Alf C. Day, and P. H. Dowlearn.[5]

Wright closed out his letter thus:

All parties went to Clinton to sign an agreement not to bother one another. How long this compromise will last is a question with me as it is with Hardin and Bowen and the four Clements boys. I went to the courthouse where Judge Claiborn was holding court. Wesley Hardin was introduced to the judge [who had] all of the facts before him, and he [Hardin] and his party were permitted to leave without being molested because they were too mean to arrest.[6]

TEXAS RANGER PIDGE ALSO WROTE of the occurrences, and Pidge could not only write, he could frequently spell. In an exaggerated—at times eloquent and at times awkward—letter to the Austin *Democratic Statesman*, Pidge, six months after the event, discussed what he had heard and learned.

> Wesley Hardin and his party besieged [Joe Tumlinson] in his castle, but he hoisted his draw-bridge, and bid defiance to all creation; then Wes sent him word to remove the women and children, as he intended to bombard the fortress, demolish the stronghold, and sow the ruins with salt. Capt. Joe would not surrender, and about the time the besiegers had prepared fireballs to burn the buildings, the sheriff arrived, and a compromise was affected.
> The whole party, sheriff and all, was captured by Wes, who allowed the sheriff alone to go in and tell Captain Joe to surrender, and he [Joe] would be protected. Joe told him that was as thin as the hair on his head, as transparent as the glass on his green spectacles, and he did not want any part of it for most of the [sheriff's] posse were Taylor men. All parties, the besiegers and besieged, finally adjourned [and signed the Clinton peace treaty]. It was a beautiful compromise, well fixed up, and was warranted to last at least a month...[7]

A breathing spell followed the battle of Clinton, which was lucky for Hardin because he had wandered over to Rancho, twenty-five miles southwest of Gonzales, and drank a beer. The container held ground particles of glass—whether placed there intentionally is unknown—and Hardin swallowed those along with the beverage. The *Austin Weekly State Gazette* described him as very ill and not expected to survive. But he did.[8]

THE FRAGILE TREATY CRUMBLED. On December 30, 1873, Wiley W. Pridgen, a Taylor partisan and a brother to State Senator Bolivar Pridgen, was riddled with buckshot and revolver bullets in his store eight miles south of Cuero. Hardin called the death "feud related," but since Wiley Pridgen had earlier slain a man over a gambling incident, his own murder might have been revenge for incidents other than those involving Sutton.[9]

Each side accused the other of breaking the treaty. Skirmishing commenced in Cuero. The diary of local resident Robert J. Clowe mentioned Sutton and Taylor forces being in town, with one faction seizing control of the Gulf Hotel. A terse January 1, 1874, entry read: HARDIN HAS ARRIVED."[10]

A newspaper claimed Sutton and associates had gone to Cuero "to file an affidavit against waylayers" and "to attend the examination of Scrap Taylor, charged with the shooting of Sutton some time ago." The *Cuero Weekly Star* reported that the Taylor faction wanted to prevent any court proceedings, and "a formal war [has taken place] for two or three days in and about our town." A brief skirmish, with no one hurt, occurred near the lumber yard. The Sutton Party occupied the Gulf Hotel for two days and nights while the opposition took control of Main and Evans streets. "All of the parties were heavily armed, and the families near the scene of action thought it best to abandon their homes which some did." Although "the sheriff was powerless," according to the newspaper, the citizens tried to make peace. On Saturday, about noon, "both parties withdrew from town…[and] the matter was amicably settled."

Through it all, no killings took place. On January 3, 1874, participants for another treaty vowed "nevermore to engage in any organization against any of the signers of this agreement." Eighty-six men ratified the Treaty of Cuero, but three names were conspicuously absent: Joe Tumlinson, William Sutton and John Wesley Hardin. They did not sign because they did not regard it as necessary. Nevertheless, the signatures that did appear represented a *Who's Who* of the Sutton-Taylor Feud.[11]

Joe Hardin
and the Good Earth

JOHN WESLEY HARDIN'S BROTHER JOE, a blue-eyed, dark haired, dapper-looking young lawyer, married Arabella Adams, known as "Belle" to family but "Allie" to Joe Hardin. Both twenty-one years old, they wed in early September 1871 and moved to Comanche County, one hundred miles southwest of Fort Worth. Joe practiced law and joined the Masonic Lodge as well as the Friends of Temperance in February of 1872.

On the face of it, Joe and his brother John were as different as mules and horses. Joe sought respectability. He wore suits, joined civic organizations, and associated with people of vision, influence and power. But it didn't make him honest, just careful. His brother John carried a gun, killed people, caroused too much, often slept on the ground, and generally disdained people of vision, influence and power. The oddity is that Joe made the family proud, whereas John disgraced it; Joe supported his parents, and John borrowed their money; Joe wanted to be loved by his mother and father, John *was* loved by his mother and father. Yet, the two brothers were exceptionally fond of each other, and understood one another.

During late 1871, the Comanche commissioners court designated Joe county treasurer replacing an elected official who "had

Arabella (Adams) Hardin and her husband Joseph Gibson Hardin,
the older brother of John. Ca. 1874, perhaps in Comanche. (Harden/
Hardin/Harding Family Association Collection)

lost his mind." One of Joe's extra duties called for the solicitation
of money from taxpayers for the construction of a jail.[1] A lack of
sufficient funds killed the project. He served as postmaster between April 1872 and April of 1873.[2] On October 15, 1872, Allie
gave birth to a daughter, Dora Dean Hardin.

With Joe established in Comanche, he coaxed his parents and
brothers and sisters remaining at home into joining him. His
father, the Reverend James Hardin, however, had come on hard
times. He lived in Ellis County, a hundred miles east of Comanche,

where his personal worth appears to have been only one hundred dollars.

Preacher Hardin accepted an administrative and teaching position in Comanche at the Masonic Academy whose erratic, tangled financial problems prevented its opening until August 1874. He lived off his son, Joe.

After filing on a 160-acre homestead two miles northwest of town on a scenic hill overlooking the community, he constructed a small house and stocked the land with a few cattle. Although the elder Hardin never had a church pulpit in Comanche, he united in marriage the Reverend George Higby and Sarah J. Williams, a black couple.

The Reverend Peter W. Gravis served as Comanche's resident Methodist circuit minister. Gravis presided over the marriage of Elizabeth "Lizzie" Hardin, Joe and John's seventeen-year-old sister, to James Benton "Buck" Cobb on November 8, 1872.[3]

Joe was smooth as well as charming. Like his brother John, he had a certain eloquence, an affable personality, likable as well as believable. Unlike John he was not into man-slaying, and yet the two shared a common trait. They justified every illegal act they committed.

The Comanche courthouse, a picket-style log building, burned in 1862 and was not replaced until 1875. During Joe's tenure, county government conducted itself in space rented from businessmen. The county paid eighty dollars to lease a substantial two-story stone building on the square.[4]

Joe Hardin served as a deputy in the office of William Carnes, district clerk in 1872.[5] His duties called not only for handling court records but land titles as well. Even when he stepped aside as an appointed official, he retained access to the files. As an attorney and former county employee, he understood the archives, their strengths and weaknesses. He knew everyone on a first name basis, and with the occasional aid of local and state officials, Joe bought and sold acreage through a system of bogus titles.

A typical Hardin transaction involved the Charles Sargent land grant. Sargent served in the Republic of Texas army from October 22, 1835, until March 27, 1836, when the muskets of Mexican General Santa Anna's army massacred Sargent and the surrendered Fannin forces at Goliad. Ten years later on February 4, 1846,

Anson Jones, President of the Republic of Texas, signed a letter patent providing the heirs of Charles Sargent with 1,920 acres "in Milam County on the south prong of the Leon," property which afterwards became part of Comanche County.

In Washington County, on January 3, 1850, "James Sargent, only surviving and legal heir to Charles Sargent, Dec'd.," sold this tract of land to Barnes C. Parker for $1200. However, neither James Sargent nor Barnes C. Parker existed. Joe Hardin, in the early 1870s created this phony transaction, back-dated it by at least ten years, had it duly witnessed with invented (or bribed) officials, and then deposited it in the Comanche County records.[6] In spite of what the document says, no money changed hands during this false arrangement because the characters were figments of Hardin's imagination. Joe was shaping the Comanche world to suit purposes uniquely his own.

The non-existent Parker then appointed Joe G. Hardin as his agent and attorney-in-fact on October 15, 1872. Joe (who usually signed his name "Jo") handled all of Parker's land transactions in Comanche, Ellis and Washington counties. This meant Joe, at his discretion, could sell or lease property "owned" by Parker, and pocket the money. If the deal soured, Hardin was merely an agent, an intermediary who did not know Mr. Parker all that well anyhow. Joe was inventing what the modern world of a century later would refer to as "white collar crime."[7]

In 1872, with the assistance of Travis County attorneys James W. Maddox, J. L. Pleasants, and P. W. Wynn, Joe Hardin created a townsite called Hazle Dell, sixteen miles east of Comanche near Robinson's Mill, which had operated on Mill Branch since 1869. As agent, Joe laid out the town plat and sold several city blocks. A couple of stores arose, as did a saloon and a tenpin alley. Before long, the community had a cemetery too. Joe Hardin worked the scheme so adroitly that considerable time passed before land owners realized they lacked clear titles.[8]

During Joe Hardin's first year in Comanche (1872), the county valued his assets at $120. His effects amounted to one horse and miscellaneous property. Three years later his wealth had spiraled to $25,000. This figure included a city block in Comanche, as well as $9,000 in land outside the county. Considering Joe Hardin's capacity for misrepresentation, his true economic worth probably

Joseph Gibson
Hardin as a young
attorney. Photo
perhaps taken at
Round Rock, or
possibly Austin,
about 1870.
(R. G. McCubbin
Collection)

soared much higher. The records, scattered and convoluted, suggest his ownership of about 13,500 acres in Comanche, and 7,500
additional acres scattered through Hood, Haskell, Throckmorton,
Polk and Burnet counties. While the full record has never been
evaluated, this land seems to have been acquired in the same
fashion as the Sargent holdings.[9] His wife Allie's involvement is
also suspect. There are deed records, perhaps legitimate, where
her name appears with two "l's', but not in her handwriting. (She
signed her name with one l, Alie, whereas her husband used two
l's, Allie.) On the other hand, she appears frequently (with one l)
as a major signatory on various transactions, although none have
been evaluated for fraud. On the face of it, she was anything but
unaware of her husband's fraudulent activities. Following Joe's

death, as the nature of this swindle quickly began unraveling, several transactions wound up in court and remained several years.

Had Joe Hardin been more careful, he might have evolved into one of the legendary Western swindlers. Texas, as a province, a republic and a state, had always had shady operators who made fortunes through dishonest land development schemes. It once had so much acreage to give away—and to sell cheap—that the practice actually encouraged corruption. Joe might have become as notorious for his con-artistry as his brother John was for his fast guns.[10]

Goodby Bill Sutton

I N EARLY JANUARY 1874, John Wesley Hardin pulled out for Comanche. His wife Jane and daughter Mollie were already there. Hardin remained in Comanche until early February when City Marshal J. W. Greene attempted to arrest him for a misdemeanor. Instead the marshal placed John Denton, Stephen Cowan, Gip Clements and Ham Anderson in irons, charging them with "willfully opposing and resisting a peace officer...attempting to arrest J. W. Hardin...." The outcome is unknown, but due to the prominence of the people involved, and since no killing took place, the misdemeanor was likely "public drunkenness," or illegal gambling, or both.[1]

Hardin never seems to have been a "falling down drunk," but he drank a lot, and liquor altered his personality. Drinking gave him a sense of power. It made him more talkative, freer with money—his and other peoples—and more apt to do crazy stunts to please, or impress, an audience. Liquor could make him extremely good natured, but it could also make him mean.

Hardin acquired a race horse named Rondo and, accompanied by Jane, Mollie, James Monroe "Doc" Bockius and Gip Clements, he left Comanche and started home for Cuero by way of San Saba and Llano. In Llano, Hardin won $500 in a horse race and purchased a herd of steers. The party reached Gonzales in mid-February, and Cuero shortly afterwards. The *Cuero Weekly Star* reported that Hardin "created quite a sensation by his presence" in the community. When he left the next morning, he wore two six-shooters and carried a Spencer rifle. Yet, City Marshal R. H. Brown failed to notice any firearms. The newspaper suggested that Brown should be more observant in the future.[2]

HARDIN EVEN IN THOSE EARLY days regarded himself, as did others, as a leader among men. He flouted the law regarding weapons, as warlords have always been inclined to, and it seemed to increase his respect. As for the marshal, he was no fool. Editors could always talk tough and give advice. No one ever died from being shot to death with printer's ink.

To support a family, John Wesley Hardin primarily gambled. The Hardin memoirs suggest he earned so much money gambling that he had sufficient funds available for legitimate cattle purchases. But gambling was an iffy occupation even for one as skilled as Hardin. Gamblers lived a hand-to-mouth existence, and even considering his fearsome reputation, he could not win all the time. Gambling money alone never enabled Hardin to purchase cattle other than those sold furtively with the "owners" looking back over their shoulders. So his secondary occupation, and his front for existence, involved livestock trading. He and the Taylor and Clements boys created two herds sufficiently large for Kansas drives, and they did it while being widely suspected of cattle theft.

Nevertheless, Hardin registered a brand: ⅃Ⱶ

Hardin implied that most of his livestock were mavericks, unbranded wild cattle belonging to whoever roped them. In the nostalgia of modern times, the practice of mavericking is often romantically thought of as the finest hour of private enterprise. But cattlemen who ran the largest herds ordinarily had first rights to mavericks. Cattlemen who ran fewer head, had secondary rights. Of course, human nature being what it was, things frequently worked just the opposite. In Texas, the illegal branding of mavericks (cattle theft) remained a misdemeanor subject to a small fine (something like $20) until cattle thievery became a felony in 1873.

Mavericking also required time-consuming, arduous, danger-ous labor. Cattle drifted before the storms, and gathered near water. Tangled, heavy brush also grew near water, so roping and dragging steers to the branding fires from this environment required fierce exertions. Some cowboys were up to it, others were not. The Hardin Gang—as people tended now to refer to the Taylor portion of the Sutton-Taylor Feud participants—were more adept at gambling, horse racing and drinking than exerting the kind of sweat necessary for cow work. So while Hardin kept his branding irons hot, the evidence indicates that he purchased much of his livestock from "small-time cattlemen" who sold cheap because they needed to unload steers in a hurry.

The practice helps explain why Hardin constantly drove herds into different parts of Texas or into Louisiana to sell them. Once a herd left the state, or was two or three counties removed from the place of origin, even authentic buyers worried little about obscure brands. And Wes Hardin had an attorney brother in Comanche who furnished fraudulent bills of sale. In fact, Hardin initially visited Comanche to work out "cattle purchasing" details with Joe.[3]

Although livestock accounted for Hardin's immediate concerns, William Sutton rarely disappeared from his mind. "We had often tried to catch him," Hardin said, "but he was so wily that he always eluded us. I had made futile efforts to get him myself. I had even gone down to his home in Victoria, but did not get him." Hardin claimed the Sutton party "had violated their pledges [meaning the peace treaties] and on several occasions had turned our cattle loose."[4]

AN OPENING FOR MURDER AROSE with news that Bill Sutton's livestock would soon plod overland from Texas to Kansas. Sutton himself would sail to New Orleans from the Texas port of Indianola and travel by rail to Kansas.

At John's request, his brother Joe and cousin Alec Barekman rode over from Comanche to Indianola. Since neither knew Sutton, they made his acquaintance by pretending to be someone else. Sutton confided that he planned to sail on the steamer Clinton leaving Indianola on March 11, 1874.

Hardin passed the information on to Jim and William R. "Bill"

William R. "Bill" Taylor.
After killing Gabriel Slaughter,
Bill Taylor outlived all the
lawmen who ever chased him.
He is said to have been killed
in Oklahoma sometime
around 1895. (Eddie Day
Truitt Collection)

Taylor, second cousins to each other, and in their early twenties. They each stood about five feet ten, weighed about 160, were of dark complexion and sported straight black hair. Although Bill had an occasional hot temper, he dressed like a dandy. Friends and enemies alike said he always kept one eye out for the ladies, and the other eye out for a good horse.

For two reasons, Hardin did not join the Taylors at Indianola. He had one of the best known faces in Texas, and any hint of his presence would alert Sutton. Secondly, the Taylors, especially Jim, seething with fury since the death of his father Pitkin, insisted upon the opportunity of revenge.

The two Taylor cousins rode to Indianola on the west shore of Matagorda Bay in the Gulf of Mexico. Since Spanish times it had been the most flourishing port of entry into Texas. Six thousand people lived there in March of '74.

After purchasing a brown and a sorrel horse, fresh animals for a getaway, the Taylors tethered them at the Clinton cattle chute along Indianola's extensive wharf system. Bill Sutton, his wife and Gabriel Webster Slaughter (a grandson of former Kentucky Governor Gabriel Slaughter), had already boarded the steamer.

Slaughter was a twenty-one-year-old signer of the January 1874 peace treaty. He had planned to drive Sutton's herd up the trail. Instead he became ill before departure and opted for the easy way to Kansas, travelling with the Suttons.[5]

Around two in the afternoon of March 11, 1874, Bill Sutton, his pregnant young wife Laura, and Slaughter walked onto the boat deck. As Sutton approached the ticket booth, both Taylors commenced shooting. Sutton fell stone dead with Jim Taylor's bullets in him. Bill Taylor killed Gabe Slaughter with a shot to the face. James snatched up Sutton's Smith and Wesson revolver, and the Taylors scrambled away in good health from a maddening scene of blood, gore, two dead men and a screaming widow.

While Slaughter and Bill Sutton were laid in the Evergreen Cemetery in Victoria, Texas, the assassins opted for the perfect escape. Hardin had gathered cattle west of Cuero, sixty miles from Indianola. Joe Clements would drive them to Kansas, and the two Taylors would participate as cowboys, enjoying several months of obscurity along the trail. By the time they returned to Texas, any uproar regarding the Sutton massacre hopefully would have died down.

BUT NEW TIMES WERE COMING to Texas. Forty-three-year-old Richard Coke, an attorney and Confederate veteran, a tall man as ungainly and ungraceful as he was unpretentious, accepted the office of Texas governor in January 1874. One of Coke's first acts involved talking the state legislature into offering a $500 reward for the capture of James and William Taylor.

The widow Laura Sutton upped the ante by $1,000, declaring that her husband and Gabriel Slaughter had been slain in her presence. She said her husband fell with two Taylor bullets in his back.

Laura Sutton described Jim Taylor as "23 years [old], 165 or 170 pounds, very heavy set, 5 feet 10 inches, complexion dark, dark hair, round features, usually shaves clean about once a week, wears no whiskers, beard rather heavy, talks very little, has a low, dull tone, and very quiet in his manners."[6]

IN CUERO, LAWLESSNESS AND HUMAN SLAUGHTER had for too long disgraced the community. Residents had finally

acknowledged that they would never get satisfactory law enforcement until they deserved it. Thus arose the "Home Protection
Club." A few trembling but courageous souls, none of them
heroes, banded together for mutual protection and to support
their local lawmen. They could not have stood ten minutes against
either the Hardin or the Sutton bunch, but the fact that they stood
at all was a beginning.[7]

Meanwhile, Hardin's trail herd left for Wichita with cousin Joe
Clements in charge. The Taylor lads celebrated too long in Cuero,
and declined participation in the drive. In their elation, they felt
immune from vengeance. They were not.

Jim and Bill Taylor in particular had partied too joyously in
Cuero. Marshal Reuben H. "Rube" Brown, muscular enough to
whip any man, with a few Home Protection Club members as
backup, arrested Bill Taylor for carrying a gun, specifically Bill
Sutton's revolver. Jim Taylor had given it to him. The authorities
shipped Bill Taylor under guard to Indianola and momentary
incarceration on the steamer, Clinton.

The slaying of William Sutton did not end the Sutton-Taylor
Feud, but his death did effectively slow it down. John Wesley
Hardin now moved to the periphery of the war, turning his
attention primarily to other adventures.

Charlie Webb
Goes Down

ITH NEILL BOWEN AND JOE CLEMENTS on the trail to
Kansas, Joe Hardin, Alec Barekman, Jane Hardin and
daughter Mollie, again left Cuero for Comanche. Wes Hardin—
with Jim Taylor at his side—tarried in Cuero to raise another herd.
Joe Hardin regularly sent phony bills of sale to his brother John
in Cuero. Wes Hardin kept a stack of them around, trotting one
out whenever he made an "acquisition."[1] Everyone operated out
of his shirt pocket. Furthermore, thieves always provided bills of
sale for rustled livestock. An honest rancher building his herd
never purchased cattle with brands not his own unless he had a
written bill of sale. It didn't matter that this evidence of legiti-
macy was usually an awkwardly transcribed, smudged,
sweat-stained, torn bill of sale with an illegible signature. Many
who provided such bills of sale were long gone, usually unreach-
able. These records by law had to be filed in the courthouse, but
depending upon the time of year, the workload and the distance
from town, weeks or even months could pass between a document in hand and a notation in the county or district clerk's office.
Scrawled bills of sale on the open range gave the appearance of
legality. Appearances counted.

Hardin's cattle would be dispatched toward Kansas with trail

Sheriff John Carnes,
Comanche, about 1874.
(Fain McDaniel
Collection)

boss James Monroe "Doc" Bockius. Doc, gentlemanly in his
manner and deportment, told a newspaper editor that he had
graduated from a medical school in Philadelphia. Otherwise, he
knew a lot about herbs and as much about horses as he did people.
He stood about five-foot-six, sported a heavy walrus mustache,
and was bald and skinny. Bockius started life in Ohio about 1831,
and arrived in Gonzales County during the 1850s. He served with
the Texas Rangers as well as the Confederacy. A slouch hat and a
grungy black beard gave him a Tennessee backwoods look, but
he was a capable cowboy in his early forties, a likeable man with
a sense of humor and a sharp wit.

John Hardin and Jim Taylor headed for Comanche and a family reunion. On April 23, 1874, Bockius, several trail hands, and a
herd moseyed northwest from DeWitt County for nearly two
hundred miles toward Hamilton County. John and Joe Hardin
would be waiting nearby with another herd.[2]

Comanche proved important for Hardin. The county and
town—midway and slightly south of—Fort Worth and Abilene,
were both named for the Comanche Indians. Geographically the

region lay on the western edge of the Grand Prairie near the center of the state. Live oak and post oak trees dotted Comanche's dusty square. They shaded the log hitching racks, well and watering trough.[3]

Among a community of farmers, ranchers and small businessmen, the Georgia-born Carnes brothers (John, David and William) emerged as leaders. They arrived in Comanche about 1857.

In October 1873, at the age of thirty-nine, John Carnes won the sheriff's race and served until February 1876. Carnes knew Joe Hardin well, liked and trusted him, and accepted favors just as other officials did. He may or may not have been intimidated—or charmed—by John Wesley Hardin. If so, he would not have been the first lawman as precedents existed all over Texas.

David Carnes, younger than John Carnes by three years, owned one hundred and sixty acres in the southern part of Comanche County, but was widowed and lived in town with his parents and ten-year-old daughter. When John Wesley Hardin met him around 1872, he was operating a dry goods store.

William Carnes, about twenty-eight years old in 1873, had a wife and several children. He spent seven years as the Comanche county and district clerk.

On September 27, 1873, David and John Carnes made a deal with James Waldrip, a known cattle thief. He would convey mavericks to the Carnes brothers, all branded primarily with the Three Slashes / / /, one of the Carnes's brands. Waldrip signed a promissory note for eight thousand dollars payable to John and David Carnes in cattle.

One hundred and fifty cattle would be delivered to the Carnes brothers by October 20, 1873. One-half of the balance due, in cattle, would be met by June 10, 1874. The final cattle tally would fall due not later than June 10, 1875.[4]

Because of his rustler reputation, Waldrip ordinarily could not brand any animal without running the risk of jail or a lynch rope. Now he had a legitimate agreement to brand a certain number of maverick cattle. Left unstated, however, although certainly understood, was the stipulation that after Waldrip had met his obligation to the Carnes's, he could continue stamping / / / on additional mavericks and retain them as his own. These cattle would be Waldrip's payment for doing the work. Thus Waldrip gained ownership of his own herd, and the Carnes boys acquired several hundred cattle without sweating for it. Waldrip expected to brand cattle primarily in Brown County, next door to Comanche.

The Carnes and Waldrip herds had only paper value until the livestock were taken up the Western Trail to Kansas and sold. But Waldrip lacked the expertise, and the Carnes brothers considered themselves only marginal cattlemen. However, they all had a solution: John Wesley Hardin. John and David Carnes, plus James Waldrip, knew in the fall of 1873 that Wes Hardin planned to drive a trail herd through in early 1874.

When the first 150 head of Waldrip cattle failed to arrive at the Carnes's designated pasture in October, the brothers went to court. On November 1, 1873 they obtained a "writ of attachment sufficient to satisfy Waldrip's debt." The judge placed a hold on the Waldrip assets, but Waldrip and the Carnes's reached an undisclosed understanding by the 5th, and dismissed the attachment.[5]

On the 16th of February, Waldrip transferred the Carnes livestock to James Beard, Waldrip's associate and fellow rustler. Beard also had outstanding cattle theft indictments pending, but he seemed immune from serious prosecution.

From out of nowhere, Frank Mathewson, who spent only a fleeting period in Comanche and lacked a traceable back trail, appeared on the public record. With his partner and agent, Henry J. Ware, Mathewson, in late 1873, mortgaged cattle to Mary J. Millican, wife of James W. Millican, a rancher and one of Sheriff Carnes's deputies. When Mathewson could not meet the note, he disappeared, leaving Henry Ware to settle outstanding business affairs. The Millicans foreclosed on April 13, 1874, transferring all of the cattle—including Ware's—to Allie Hardin.[6]

Allie and Joe Hardin muddied the transaction even further by selling the Mathewson livestock to James Beard for $1,000.[7] Then Joe Hardin, acting as agent for William "Bud" Dixon, executed a bill of sale whereby James Beard resold the cattle to Dixon for "one dollar in hand and a $1,000 note."[8] Dixon, a cousin of the Hardin boys, would become an important and tragic participant in events about ready to play themselves out in Comanche.

On May 11, David and John Carnes dropped their complaint against James Waldrip.[9] One week later, on May 19, David Carnes, acting alone, "sold and delivered," without mentioning price, an unspecified number of cattle to Hardin's number one man, Bud Dixon.[10] Joe handled the paperwork.

ONE WAY OR ANOTHER, THE CATTLE of the Carnes brothers, Jim Waldrip, James Beard, Frank Mathewson, Henry Ware, Mary and James Millican, and William "Bud" Dixon, had now come under the jurisdiction of Joe Hardin who did not own any of the animals, but as agent had authority to buy, sell and trade. Joe Hardin had buried all of the cattle origins deep in a maze of clever, sophisticated paperwork. A court-of-law could spend months untangling the mess. As an agent essentially without responsibility, Joe Hardin controlled the herd and trusted it would be gone to Kansas and sold before an agent like Henry Ware tied it up in court. And John Wesley Hardin was not even mentioned as involved.

This isn't to say that no one suspected the Hardins. Ranchers in Brown County surmised exactly what was going on. In March 1874, sixteen irate cattlemen had a rancorous conference with Brown County Sheriff J. H. Gideon. They demanded a break up of the Hardin Gang. Gideon assigned Deputy Charles Webb to the job. The deputy had just recently been discharged from the Texas Rangers, having been a first lieutenant from January to March, 1874.[11]

John Hardin and Charles Webb had already met in April at Williams Ranch, a tiny settlement with a few business houses in Brown County. The ranch—which is now in Mills County and non-existent except for the cemetery—was a homesite founded by John Williams. A mob lynched a Mexican in the ranching community. Charles Webb rode over from the county seat of Brownwood to investigate, and encountered Hardin, Jim Taylor, Alec Barekman, and Bud and Tom Dixon. "They roundly cursed the deputy...and warned him to stay out of Comanche County."[12]

During the week of May 21, 1874, John Wesley Hardin moseyed over to Brown County to take possession of all the cattle entrusted to Joe. Suspecting there might be resistance—as Joe admitted the livestock were in litigation—Wes Hardin asked Comanche Sheriff John Carnes for additional muscle. Deputies Jim Millican and Bill Cunningham tagged along.

Henry Ware, described by Hardin as a bully from Canada, contested Joe's ownership of the cattle. Joe Hardin jerked his revolver, and Ware headed for the Brown County sheriff's office. The two Hardins and their cowboy gunmen departed with the livestock.

DEPUTY CHARLES WEBB, NOT KNOWING where the Brown County cattle had been secreted, but realizing that Jim Buck Waldrip and James Beard had to be involved, rode immediately to the Waldrip Ranch and arrested both men. He locked them in the Brown County jail, and charged them with cattle theft. By late that evening, with furious cattlemen converging on Brownwood, Webb transferred the two prisoners to Georgetown, Williamson County, for safer keeping. Georgetown had a secure jail, and Sheriff Sam M. Strayhorn also said the town had no vigilance committees.[13]

On that same day, the Hardin group took supper and lodged at the ranch of Jim Buck Waldrip at Logan's Gap, ten miles southwest of Comanche. A rock fence enclosure discouraged their cattle from drifting. As the men sat around the table eating, Mrs. Margaret Waldrip complained that Webb had arrested her son Jim, and had cursed and abused her. Everyone agreed that Charles Webb had done a terrible thing.

COMANCHE CELEBRATED THE LAST weekend in May with a festival, a carnival. Saloons ran full blast, and so did the race track. Hardin's stud, Rondo, won easily. His brother Joe raced Shiloh, and cousin Bud Dixon entered Dock. Hardin won three thousand dollars, fifty head of cattle, fifteen saddle horses, and a wagon or two. "I set more than one man afoot," he chuckled, "and then loaned them the horses to ride home on."[14]

Late that evening as Wes Hardin wandered from bar to bar throwing twenty dollar gold pieces on the counter and calling for drinks, Jefferson Davis Hardin, the thirteen-year-old brother of Wes, hurried over to brother Joe Hardin's stable in Comanche. He retrieved a horse and buggy for the two-mile trip to the home of his parents. Preacher Hardin and his family planned a double celebration, one for John's birthday that night (May 26), and the other for Joseph Gibson Hardin, Jr., born two days earlier to Joe and Allie on May 24, 1874.

Jefferson Davis Hardin, younger brother of John Wesley Hardin. At left is his wife Mary holding son Cleburn. Son Joseph is on his father's lap. Although Jefferson worshipped his older brother and sought to be like him, he simply lacked John's remorseless characteristics. (Jo Foster Collection)

Wes and Jim Taylor climbed into the buggy. However, when it passed Jack Wright's saloon[15] on the Comanche public square, John ordered a halt while he staggered inside. There, he bought drinks. Deputy Frank Wilson, who would be elected sheriff during the next election, locked arms with Hardin, steered him outside and pleaded, "John, the people here have treated you well; now don't drink any more but go home and avoid all trouble." Frank further warned, "You know it is a violation of the law to carry a pistol."

Hardin protested that his six-shooter was behind the bar. He opened his coat to reveal an absence of weapons, although he never displayed the hideout gun secreted under his vest.

Jim Taylor also expressed distress regarding Hardin's intoxication, although Taylor was hardly sober himself. As Hardin and his friends became more unruly, Sheriff Carnes and his deputies planned to carefully separate Hardin and Jim Taylor, get them to gambling in different saloons and during an unguarded moment, place each under arrest. However, Sheriff Carnes had a malfunctioning pistol and while the sheriff sought a gunsmith, his brother Dave Carnes looked up and growled to Hardin, "Here comes that damned Brown County sheriff."[16]

Deputy Sheriff Charles Webb wore two six-shooters. He kept his hands behind his back as he paced across the square alongside the saloon to within fifteen feet of Hardin, and paused.

In his most confrontational tone of voice, Hardin growled, "Have you any papers for my arrest?"

"I don't know you," came the soft answer.

"My name is John Wesley Hardin."

"Now I know you, but have no papers for your arrest."

"I have been informed," Hardin replied, "that the sheriff of Brown County has said that Sheriff Carnes of this county was no sheriff or he would not allow me to stay around Comanche with my murdering pals."

"I am not responsible for what the sheriff of Brown County says. I am only a deputy."

Wes asked Webb what he had behind his back. Upon being shown a cigar, Hardin relaxed. "Mr. Webb, we were just going to take a drink or a cigar; won't you join us?" he said.

"Certainly," Webb responded.

Hardin claimed that as he turned, his pal Bud Dixon shouted "Look out, Jack."[17] Wes whirled and glimpsed Webb drawing his gun. The lawman fired as Hardin lurched sideways. The bullet grazed John's left side. Hardin shot at the same instant, the slug hitting Webb in the left cheek. Webb stumbled back as his revolver roared again, aimlessly. Jim Taylor and Bud Dixon commenced firing too, their bullets perforating Webb.

Webb went down at a heavier weight. Suddenly he was dead, a quiet, thoughtful man engulfed in gunsmoke and good intentions, a deputy who never quite realized until it was too late that this was the worst possible time to visit Comanche. Hardin had notched his thirty-second victim.[18]

The *Dallas Weekly Herald* of June 6 added details:

The murder was committed last Monday in front of the saloon on the public square....

On Monday the parties rode into town and laid in wait for Webb in a saloon. He soon entered it, whereupon they engaged in a quarrel with him....They paired off, two in front to defend against him, and two at the side to do the killing. Seeing this, he retreated to the outside of the house, and they followed, again pairing off as before, and drawing their six-shooters. Seeing this, Webb drew and fired with rapid movement, but his shot went wild. Hardin now fired, followed by Dickson [Dixon], and Webb fell mortally wounded in the neck, the hand, the abdomen, and soon expired.

The *Weekly Herald* depicted the slayers as belonging to "a band of cattle thieves [who have] been operating for some time in that [Comanche/Brown] district."

The news of Webb's death ricocheted through the town. A crowd of angry residents swarmed close until an exchange of gunfire forced them back. As Sheriff John Carnes rushed up, Hardin surrendered his revolver. Within minutes a mob again approached the saloon, only to be met at gunpoint by Carnes. One of the great ironies in Hardin's life is that the law protected him even more than it chased him.

IN AN ABOUT FACE, HARDIN PULLED another weapon and covered the sheriff while he, Jim Taylor, Bud Dixon and others retreated inside the saloon. By now, someone had brought the sheriff a double-barreled shotgun. The officer stationed himself near the front door, blocking a mob threatening to break into the building and preventing those inside from escaping by that entrance.[19]

As Carnes struggled with the crowd, Hardin and his friends slipped out a side door. Hardin slashed a couple of hitching ropes and the gunmen galloped away on horses they did not own. Glancing back, Hardin saw his wife Jane and his seventeen-year-old sister, Martha Ann "Mattie" weeping in the crowd. From down the street, Hardin's father and brother left Joe's law office on the square and with shotguns hurried up the dusty road toward the saloon. "We turned and went running out of town," Hardin said, "the mob firing on us and the sheriff's party trying to protect us." Henry Ware squeezed off four rounds, and missed.[20]

Later that evening, the Hardin group and Sheriff Carnes

conferred at the home of Reverend Hardin. John's mother dressed his wound. John offered to surrender but the sheriff reportedly demurred. Considering the sheriff's attitude, and assuming Hardin told it factually, one could debate whether in allowing Hardin his freedom, Carnes was enforcing the law, safeguarding an investment, or simply recognizing that he could not protect Hardin from mob action. Wes Hardin continued to run loose as an outlaw, all the while justifying himself as an innocent victim of lawlessness.

Hardin, Taylor, Alec Barekman and Ham Anderson hid at Round Mountain, eight miles west of Comanche. At noon on the following day (May 27), Joe Hardin, with Tom and Bud Dixon, brought food and fresh horses. They had ridden fifteen miles in the opposite direction, then circled around.

Meanwhile, the body of Charles M. Webb was borne back to Brownwood and buried with full Masonic honors in Greenleaf Cemetery.

A Whale Among Little Fishes

WITH THE STATE POLICE abolished, the Texas legislature in 1874 authorized two ranger battalions, one combating the Indian menace west of Fort Worth, and the other insuring domestic tranquility. They would tangle with major Texas outlaws as well as Mexican bandits slipping north from the Rio Grande. Like the State Police, rangers had jurisdiction across county lines.

On May 30, twenty-two Comanche citizens petitioned Governor Richard Coke for assistance, complaining that their county was infested with murderers and thieves "headed by the notorious John Wesley Hardin and Jim Taylor. On the 25th day of May 1874 the said Hardin and Taylor came into the town of Comanche and wantonly murdered one Chas. Webb, the deputy sheriff of Brown County who was here peacefully and quietly attending to his private business." The citizens claimed the outlaws were in "such large numbers [that they] invariably escape before a sufficient number of citizens can be armed and brought together." John R. Waller and twenty to thirty rangers should be stationed in Comanche County and "charged with the capture of the said John Wesley Hardin and Jim Taylor." The governor should also offer "a reward commensurate with the crime of said Hardin and Taylor."[1]

Company A with fifty-five men, commanded by Captain John R. Waller, arrived at Comanche on the 27th of May, 1874.

Waller had credentials. He was fifty-seven years old, a married farmer with six children who had served in the 31st Texas Cavalry during the Civil War. Waller spent two years as sheriff of Erath County, Texas.

On May 30, he wrote his first known report to Major John B. Jones, saying "I have been in active service trying to arrest the John Wesley Hardin gang of murderers who are preying on the lives of the citizens of this county."[2]

Hardin, however, did not consider Waller so much a captain of Rangers as a captain "of a vigilante band…, [leading a] mob composed of the enemies of law and order." Hardin accused Waller of deputizing five hundred men to seek him out and lynch him.[3]

And Hardin's opinion was partly correct. Waller's sloppy record keeping, his failure to suppress lynch mobs and protect prisoners, is indicative that he cared little about the safety of manacled outlaws. Mob killings, whether by bullet or rope, were never mentioned in Waller's reports and neither regretted nor investigated.

Captain Waller sent posses to scour the countryside although not in figures of five hundred men. Still, to Hardin it must have seemed like that. Waller had set in motion the greatest manhunt in the history of Texas.

In Comanche, Waller's rangers "arrested Rev. Hardin, his wife, Mrs. J. W. Hardin, Mrs. Barekman, Mrs. Joe Hardin, Miss Hardin [evidently Mattie], Tom & Bud Dickson [Dixon], Dr. Brockes [Bockius], Jim Anderson & William Green and kept [them] under guard for a period of two weeks.…[4] Anderson and Green were cowboys who worked with Doc Bockius. The women and Reverend Hardin were not jailed, but placed under house arrest.

When Joe Hardin and the two Dixon boys returned to Comanche, the rangers detained them on May 27 to prevent their acting as spies. The town had no jail, however. Comanche authorities incarcerated Joe Hardin and the others in a two-story rock structure, in all probability the former dry goods store operated by David Carnes on the east side of the square.

On May 30, five rangers clashed in the brush "with the notorious John W. Hardin and Jim Taylor." Hardin confirmed the skirmish, writing "I would never surrender alive and Jim [Taylor] and I agreed to die together."[5]

On another occasion, the rangers chased Hardin and Taylor to the Brownwood and Comanche Road. The fugitives pulled comfortably ahead during a drizzling rain until they collided with additional rangers led by Waller himself. As Waller shouted for the outlaws to surrender, Hardin and Taylor turned and raced downhill toward their original pursuers, who were in the process of crossing a gulch. Suddenly, Hardin and Taylor wheeled and charged uphill, catching Waller off balance. In a wild melee, the two fugitives broke through, the rangers hesitating to fire for fear of hitting one another. As Hardin and Taylor raced clear, only Waller continued the chase. Hardin screamed for Jim to hold up while he (Hardin) stopped and cocked a shotgun. A handkerchief kept the powder dry. Just as Waller rode squarely into the sights, however, the wind gusted, flipped the rag around, and the hammer fell not on the caps but on the handkerchief. Waller checked his horse and returned to his men.[6] In the free-for-all, a bullet wounded Hardin's horse Frank in the hind leg.

This account jibed (relatively well) with a story printed in the *Austin Daily Democratic Statesman* on June 17. The editor reported that Hardin "and his party of seven or eight (including Jim Taylor) fought forty [rangers] all day. Last Tuesday (June 9) ten miles from Comanche on Leon Bottom he had his horse killed from under him. He is a fearless man and I [the editor] expect he will kill some more before he is taken."

In camp, Hardin could not fathom the reasoning of his sidekick cousins, Barekman and Anderson. They wearied of living in the brush, and Barekman in particular was homesick. Against Hardin's vigorous advice and warning, the overconfident and trustful Barekman and Anderson slipped off to the ranch, and safety, of William "Bill" Stone to hide. Stone, a fifty-seven-year-old Alabaman, lived in a tangled area of scrub oaks, briars and poison ivy close to Walnut and Bucksnort creeks. (In modern times, the site is near Proctor, fifteen miles northeast of Comanche.) Stone was a Freemason who sat on the Masonic Academy Board and hired the Reverend James Hardin as a teacher and manager.

Working on a tip early on the morning of June 1, Comanche

Alexander Hamilton
"Ham" Anderson (left).
(R. G. McCubbin
Collection)
Below, Joe Hardin,
Tom and William
"Bud" Dixon were
lynched from the limb
of a tree. The stump is
presently in front of
the Comanche County
Historical Museum at
Comanche. The nearby
historical marker
relates events leading
up to the deaths.
(Photo by Author)

Sheriff John Carnes and a squad of rangers located the Barekman and Anderson horses. The officers slipped deep into the brush, and what happened next is conjecture.

The *Corsicana Observer* of June 17, opened its description of the battle with dark headlines "Two More Of The Hardin Gang Gone." The newspaper reported the sheriff's party had surprised Ham Anderson and Alec Barekman while the fugitives were concealed in brush twelve miles north of Comanche. "They discovered each other about the same time, and Barekman and Anderson opened fire upon the posse, who returned it, killing both desperadoes." None of the lawmen were injured, and "the killing of these two men was purely an act of self defense, as they had evidently made up their minds to die rather than surrender." A wagon hauled the bodies to Comanche where they were buried in a common, unmarked grave at Oakwood Cemetery north of town.[7]

Captain Waller claimed twenty rangers and the posse searched for the outlaws fifteen to twenty miles from Comanche on the first, second and third of June. According to Waller, "Barekman and Anderson, two of Hardin's [gang], fired on some of my men and several citizens. My men returned the fire, killing both Barekman and Anderson." In his monthly report for May, Waller wrote that "the Notorious Ham Anderson was Killed by Private Watson of Co. A."[8]

John Henry Taylor, a young ranger serving with Waller, wrote in a letter many years later, that Barekman and Anderson had prevailed upon Stone to go into Comanche and find out what was happening. Instead, Stone talked to the lawmen about the fugitives. The rangers threw cold chuck in their saddle pockets, and rode hard for the thickets near the Stone log cabin. Late that night, by moonlight, they found tracks where two horses had gone in but not come out. The rangers spread out and cautiously entered on foot. Even so they would have missed the outlaws had not one of the horses snorted. Barekman and Anderson leaped from their pallets, fired two rounds, then died instantly from a return fusillade.[9]

AROUND MIDNIGHT ON JUNE 1, at the rock store used as a jail, a few rangers were supposedly asleep upstairs. John Wesley Hardin's brother Joe, plus several Hardin friends, relatives, and cohorts, slept in chains on the lower floor. They were detained, probably illegally, to keep them from assisting those fugitives still at large.

Over in Brownwood, a group of twenty heavily-armed prominent stockmen saddled up near the courthouse and grimly headed east toward Comanche. Upon arrival, they quietly disarmed the civilian guards, John James and county clerk J. D. Bonner. The clerk claimed that the armed horsemen resembled rangers as they rode up the street. All except the leader wore masks, and "they politely asked us to stack our guns against the wall and to turn the keys over to them. Looking into the business end of their guns, we decided to comply with their request. The posse had come for the men whom they thought were responsible for [Brown County Deputy Charles] Webb's death," he stated. After entering the building, they reappeared in a few minutes with three prisoners, all gagged and bound.

Joe Hardin, and Tom and William "Bud" Dixon, stumbled into the moonlight. The vigilantes would have preferred John Wesley Hardin also, as the two Hardins and the two Dixon boys represented the core of what the cattlemen called the "Hardin gang." Joe was not a gunman like the others, but his paper trail of theft made him liable as well as responsible. Perhaps if passions had time to cool, Joe would have been ignored like other prisoners in the jail. But blood was running hot, and vengeance, not justice, ruled the night.

The vigilantes mounted the prisoners on horses and proceeded a short distance away to a live oak tree. There they unsaddled the horses, placed the hapless men bareback on the animals, connected ropes from necks to tree limbs, permitted a brief last statement, and lashed the rumps.[10]

The *Comanche Chief* said the lynching took place two to three miles southwest of Comanche. Numerous citizens seemed unable to sleep, so by the time the party reached a suitable hanging tree, the crowd had doubled, most of them quiet and pensive. Since the two Dixons were chained together, they were lynched side-by-side from the same limb. Joe Hardin died dangling from an adjacent bough, protesting his innocence until the rope choked him off.[11] Neither Bonner's comments, nor anyone else's, referred to the absence of Sheriff Carnes. Furthermore, not the slightest hint in the county clerk's statement indicates that Bonner and Joe Hardin knew each other, or had served the same county for at least one year. They were fellow Masons. In this newspaper article, Bonner expressed not a single regret regarding Joe Hardin's death, nor did he allude to the fact that Joe Hardin had an office on the county square and had established roots in the community. Instead, Bonner coldly lumped Joe in with "the Hardin brothers, the Dixon brothers, and other tough characters who had headquartered at Comanche and Logan's Gap...." [12]

In years to come, the Bonner record of public service treated him kindly. He appears to have been honest, meticulous, careful, neat and bright. Bonner perhaps expressed no Joe Hardin regrets because he (Bonner) had realized early on that Joe Hardin was engaging in illegal practices. The two men probably were never close.

Martin V. Fleming, a thirty-six-year-old Georgian and Confederate veteran, and two black helpers cut the bodies down. They buried the young men two hundred yards to the rear of the James Hardin home. Although the Comanche Masonic Lodge No. 316 considered Joe Hardin a member in good standing, there is no reference to any funeral rituals. Instead, the secretary drew two heavy lines across the minute book and inserted a brief, unemotional notation about the lynching. The county did not display much sentiment either, although the record shows a payment of fifteen dollars for an inquest. [13]

The bodies of Joe and the Dixon brothers were later exhumed, at least what could be found. A few bones, boot heels, belt buckles, and buttons were tossed into a dry goods box and reburied at Oakwood Cemetery near Ham Anderson and Alec Barekman. [14]

NO ONE IN THE LYNCH MOB was ever identified, and none ever went to trial. Captain John Waller disregarded the lynching in his reports. He considered it a ridding of undesirables, an event unworthy of fuss or notice. For Waller, the lynching meant only that he had less work to do.

According to a newspaper account, four prisoners identified as James Anderson, James Buck Waldrip, William Green and Dr. Bockius were sleeping alongside the luckless three who were lynched. These prisoners were not threatened. [15]

Waldrip had apparently been removed from the Williamson County jail at Georgetown and taken to Comanche. The court released him shortly afterward, and he showed up next in Lampasas as a participant in the Horrell-Higgins Feud. The two parties clashed during a street fight on June 7, 1877. Waldrip was not one of the survivors.

Journalist Mollie Godbold described a Comanche in panic following the lynchings. Many townspeople believed Hardin intended to burn the town. Others feared he would kill twenty men for every one of the victims. Guards patrolled the village day and night, and bonfires illuminated the public square after dark.[16] Travelers moved about cautiously and heavily armed. Children stayed close to home.

John Wesley Hardin remained constantly on the run. He was out of touch with relatives and unaware of the deaths of his brother and the Dixon boys, or of the killing of Ham Anderson and Alec Barekman. By June 5, Wes and Jim Taylor were within six miles of Austin. They paused in cedar brakes northwest of town at the small ranch of Fancy Jim Taylor, a brother to Scrap Taylor.

Cowboys Alf Day and Charlie (the cook) rode in from Hamilton County with news that rangers had arrested Bockius and the other herdsmen. Lawmen confiscated the cattle. Only Day and the cook escaped. Day repeated what he knew about the lynching of Joe Hardin and the two Dixon boys, plus the shooting deaths of Anderson and Barekman.

Hardin, who had toyed with leaving Texas, now accepted it as his only option. Jim Taylor was ailing and wanted only to return to Gonzales. Alf Day went with him. Hardin accompanied them through Austin where they divided their money and said goodby. Then Wes returned to Fancy Jim Taylor's where he changed horses. With a paid guide named Rodgers, Hardin rode—mostly at night—toward Comanche.

When Rodgers and John reached Preacher Hardin's home about midnight, they unsaddled their horses a brief distance behind the house. After drinking at the well, they tried to contact John's father, under house arrest in town. Perhaps out of anger and frustration and grief, and out of panic at the thought of possibly being slain by neighbors if he stepped outside, he refused to risk meeting and embracing his son. "Tell him [Wes]," the father said, "that if they find out he is in the country, they will kill me. Tell him not to surrender under any circumstances."[17]

James G. left unsaid any news about John Hardin's mother. Elizabeth would give birth on August 17 to Barnett Gibson Hardin, her tenth and last child.

Hardin visited his brother's grave near two live oak trees. As he described the scene, he implied that he had already killed in reprisal. Still, he said, "my desire for revenge is not satisfied. I promise my friends and my God...[that] just as long as I can find one of them [the lynching party]...I propose to take life." John Wesley Hardin had now taken God into his confidence, and God understood that John intended to do the right thing. Obviously, they both had mutual enemies. John would slaughter them in his and God's behalf.[18]

John failed to mention Allie Hardin, Joe's widow. She left Comanche with little more in the way of possessions than she and her husband had upon arriving. On December 10, 1879, Allie remarried a professional gambler named Joseph Wood Pierce who, like Joe and Wes Hardin, survived somewhat on the edge. He was forty-five, she was thirty-one, and each brought two children into the relationship. They lived, at least for a while, at Mount Calm. She died in 1929 at Coleman County, Texas.

JOHN WESLEY HARDIN RODE AGAIN toward Gonzales. He felt guilty about abandoning his parents, writing "If it had not been for my father and the women and children, I would not have left, but [ranger Captain John R.] Waller had said that if I was seen in the country, they [the rangers] would kill father and my little brother Jeff and wind up on the women and children. No one unless he had a heart as black and bloodthirsty as Bill [sic] Waller's could ever have made such a threat, or conceived such thoughts."[19]

John saddled up, and explained to his guide Rodgers who he (Hardin) was. An astonished Rodgers bellowed, "Good God! I had no idea that you were John Wesley Hardin; all the money in the world would not have induced me knowingly to accompany you on such a trip, and here I am traveling to my grave with the notorious John Wesley Hardin at two dollars a day."

Hardin had obviously chosen the dumbest man in East Texas for a sidekick.

They pulled out for Lampasas at daylight, Hardin on a horse and Rodgers on a mule. That morning a posse slipped in behind them. Gradually the two fugitives lost the posse but did encounter horses in a field. Hardin chose an iron gray and saddled him. In the process the two men split up. When the gray gave out, Hardin stopped at the home of people named Nix where John purchased a horse. Later as he had supper with the family, Mrs. Nix—who claimed to have nursed Wes when he was a baby—stuffed the money back into Hardin's saddle pockets.

As they ate, a squad of lawmen assaulted the house. Hardin grabbed his Winchester and commenced firing through a window, leaving "one man on the ground with a bullet hole through the heart." How Hardin knew this particular fact, he did not say. Instead, he left quickly on a sorrel horse and rode to Fancy Jim's.

Hardin next appeared outside Gonzales where even the assurances of George Tennille and a few others of "their lasting friendship and devotion" did little to elevate his morale. Mobs still threatened, and John felt powerless since most of his surviving pals had taken the trail drive to Kansas with Joe Clements and Neill Bowen. Those remaining in Texas were "badly scared."

THE RANGERS AROUND COMANCHE served through June 12. Waller said he arrested twenty-two people, seven of whom were "members of John Wesley Hardin's gang of robbers." He accused them of rustling seven hundred head of cattle and thirty-three horses. He transferred the seven (J. M. Bockius, Rufus "Scrap" Taylor, Alfred "Kute" Tuggle, Thomas Bass, James White, G. W. Parkes and John Elder) to the sheriff at DeWitt County.[20]

Since the cattle theft allegations against the seven involved Gonzales and Brown counties, it is puzzling why the accused were escorted to DeWitt where no charges existed. Waller probably suspected the prisoners had the best chance of being murdered there.

Not far away, twenty men camped with Hardin at the home of his father-in-law, Neill Bowen, on Elm Creek, in Gonzales County. With this force, Hardin weighed the chances of rescuing his seven comrades, and decided not to. Hardin claimed to have received a letter from Capt. Waller on June 20th threatening that if the seven prisoners were released by force, he (Waller) "would kill my father and little brother, and probably my wife and child, whom he now held as hostages."[21]

Of course, the Waller letter was a phony plant in Hardin's autobiography. If Waller had Hardin's address, he could have delivered the message in person and at gunpoint.

Hardin had spent a lifetime touting loyalty as the highest virtue. To him, anyone deserting his comrades was a person devoid of pluck and honor. Now, with an opportunity to rescue his friends, Hardin never budged from his hideout. The excuse that rangers would kill his family was the ultimate cop-out.

With a full jail, officers housed the seven accused rustlers in the DeWitt County Courthouse. The rangers remained thirty-six hours, then turned the shackled men over to Sheriff William J. Weisiger and twenty deputies.

On Sunday night of June 21, at about 1:00 A.M., a mob approached the courthouse. The guards capitulated. Rufus P. "Scrap" Taylor, Jim White and Alfred "Kute" Tuggle, described by the *Cuero Weekly Star* "as the accomplices of John Wesley Hardin" were removed by a group of masked men and lynched near the Clinton graveyard. Lynch mobs preferred hanging trees near cemeteries as it made removal and burial less stressful for the families.

The *San Antonio Herald* claimed thirty-five men comprised the lynch mob, and one of the victims continually protested his innocence. The corpses remained suspended until the next morning when their relatives cut them down and interred them. Bockius survived because a friend named Joseph Sunday secreted him away from the others, and nobody noticed.

Newspapers identified the mob as the Sutton Party. The victims were cattle thieves and alleged accomplices in the slaying of Webb. Rumor also had it that those lynched had been involved in "the steamboat killings," the deaths of Bill Sutton and Gabe Slaughter. None of the accusations, except cattle theft, were true.

Early the next morning, the surviving prisoners went before Justice O. K. Tuton. He released them when no one appeared to press charges.[22]

POSSES STILL SWARMED around the countryside, and another Hardin partisan and cousin was about to fall. George Culver Tennille had a wife and six children, two of whom married into the Clements family. He looked like a Mormon bishop with his straight nose, stern eyes and beard shaved from the chin up. Although Tennille had always supported Hardin and the Taylors, he seems also to have worked quietly to bring an end to the fighting. George was considering refuge in Mexico when a posse led by Sheriff Green DeWitt caught up with the forty-nine-year-old sometimes outlaw and sometimes peacemaker on July 8, 1874. Tennille made a fight of it and they shot him dead near the edge of a corn field fifteen miles from Gonzales.[23]

Tennille's wife, Amanda, remained a widow for ten years and in 1884 married James Bockius. Doc Bockius became a medical consultant and postmaster for Gonzales County and died in 1909 at the age of seventy-eight.

With John Wesley Hardin fleeing Comanche, everyone assumed he would return to DeWitt and Gonzales counties. Since the Sutton-Taylor Feud still simmered with all-around new, if not flashy, leadership, Captain Leander McNelly—a thirty-year-old former Virginian who fought for Texas during the Civil War—recruited a forty-five-man force of rangers to bring peace to Dewitt County. Governor Richard Coke described it as "making friends."[24]

The *Daily Democratic Statesman* of Austin described Clinton as a "seat of war," a message made apparent on August 6 when Joe Tumlinson's forces attacked four rangers escorting John Milam Taylor from Yorktown to Clinton. Private John Chalk was wounded and three ranger horses disabled before Tumlinson's men apologized, saying they had mistaken the rangers for the Hardin/Taylor Party. McNelly's teeth-gritting response to the ambush, and to his enforced policy of "making friends," was to ask Adjutant General William Steele for Winchester rifles, saying Tumlinson's forces outnumbered him and "if I am compelled to fight I don't want to get whipped." Those twelve words spoke volumes regarding the sad state of law and order in south-central Texas.[25]

The *San Antonio Express* of August 23 snapped "Is it not passingly strange, incomprehensibly strange, that the Governor

At left, Rufus P. "Scrap" Taylor. (Eddie Day Truitt Collection)
Center, James Monroe "Doc" Bockius a few years after the feud wars
had passed him by, and (right) George Culver Tennille. A man of peace,
he tried to outrun the feuds, and failed. (Chuck Parsons Collection)

The Gonzales County Duderstadt Ranch near the turn of the century.
Left to right are Doc Bockius (against tree), Fred Duderstadt, Tom Gory,
Mrs. Bockius (George Tennille's widow), John Duderstadt, Mrs. Fred
Duderstadt, and Charlie Campbell. (E. D. Spellman Collection)

of a great State like Texas should allow a handful of desperadoes to hold a whole county in terror, to take helpless prisoners out of jail and hang them, and to hold possession of a county seat, and disperse the courts at their pleasure, for a period of several months altogether?"

McNelly reported that "a perfect reign of terror existed [as] armed bands of men were making predatory excursions through the country, overawing the law-abiding citizens, while the civil authorities were unable, or unwilling to enforce the laws framed for their protection. The lives of peaceful citizens who had given no offense to either party were in jeopardy, as neutrals were considered obnoxious to both factions." The ranger captain believed both parties could field over a hundred men if necessary although the Taylors had "no regularly organized force."[26]

While John Wesley Hardin sought ways just to keep a low profile and survive, this left the rascally Joe Tumlinson as the only high profile villain still active. McNelly said the roguish Capt. Joe had "seventy-five well-armed men who have no interest but in obeying his orders; he is a man who has always righted his own wrongs and he tells me that the only way for this country to have peace is to allow him to kill off the Taylor Party." McNelly growled that "I feel entirely able to whip Tumlinson with the men I have if it must be a fight but will need more [as] fifty men cannot overawe these people; they have been in the habit of overriding the officers of the law for so long that it will require more force than I have."

Ranger Pidge, in McNelly's command, still using exaggeration for effect, and still writing letters to the newspapers, said in his jestful way, that "Tumlinson goes about like Robinson Crusoe with a gun on each shoulder and two Smith & Wesson's in his belt. He has the frosts of sixty winters on his head, and green spectacles on his nose, and, it is said, can see with his naked eye father than any hawk this side of the Rio Grande." Pidge considered Tumlinson a picturesque, colorful, nearly over-the-hill scoundrel.[27]

Pidge commented again—still in as much banter as seriousness—that he had been approached by a prominent newspaper editor for a history of the DeWitt County War (Sutton-Taylor Feud). The ranger responded that he could tell tales that would "make the hair stand on anybody's head except Capt. Joe's," but he was declining to write *Brigands of the Brush: or the Desperadoes of DeWitt* because of expenses involved, portions of that being the expense to his health. "Some of the men whom I would have liked to interview were murdered," he said, "and some are in Mexico; some killed and some in Kansas, some hanged and some in hell."

"The history of Wes Hardin alone would fill the newspaper for six months," Pidge quipped. He "can make Catherine-wheels of a pair of six-shooters, and drop a man with each barrel."[28]

Pidge alluded to an alarm bell placed in Cuero "on account of the playfulness of John Wesley Hardin and some of his confreres [comrades] who sometimes rode into stores and amused themselves by shooting out the lights. No one knows where Wes is at present, and I hope never to know, for Capt. McNelly seems to be impressed with the idea that I am suffering because I cannot get at him; but…if I never see him, I will try to survive it. His commands could not have been more implicitly obeyed had he been the Sultan of Turkey. When he told them [the Clinton and Cuero residents] to get to their holes they got, and those who didn't stood a good chance of being carried to them. Wes was a whale among little fishes, and [is] more dreaded than any desperado in the state of Texas."[29]

The literate ranger said John Wesley Hardin "kills men just to see them kick." On one occasion "he charged Cuero alone with a yell of 'rats to your holes.' Such a shutting up of shops had not been seen since the panic. He is said to have killed thirty men and is a dead shot."[30]

Pidge explained how he (Pidge) and several rangers believed they had once trapped Hardin. "We drew near the silent house," the letter stated, "the ghostly-looking moss trailing from the trees swept across my head, making me think of Wes reaching for my scalp. We dismounted and cautiously approached the building, which was as silent as an Austin hotel in August." At that moment, forty-nine dogs came barreling out, and all was chaos. Hardin was not there.[31]

Pidge, with his grounding in Greek, Roman, French, German and English literature, tended to see his mortals as part human and part God, partly flawed and partly angelic. His writings might not have added much authenticity to the life and career of

John Wesley Hardin, but they certainly gilded the legend. By publishing his letters in the Austin *Daily Democratic Statesman,* Pidge expanded upon the regional, national and even international figure of Hardin. He spread the name and fame of John Wesley Hardin, and in the process contributed to the image of a Wes Hardin as a romantic desperado.

But Pidge never saw Hardin, and neither did Captain Leander McNelly. In Hardin's absence, the lawmen marked time, presiding over a modicum of peace in DeWitt and nearby counties. When they finally pulled out in late November 1874, reassigned to different duties along the Mexican border, they were a seasoned, different group of warrior rangers. They did not have to "make friends" along the Rio Grande; they simply shot the bad guys and stacked bodies in the town plazas. Along the international line, McNelly was in his element.[32]

AS FOR CAPTAIN JOE TUMLINSON, with his wars behind him, it was time to go. He became ill, got religion, was baptized and died in bed on November 23, 1874. The salty, unflinching sixty-three-year-old frontiersman went to his final rest with full Masonic honors at Yorktown.

Texas in the meantime commenced a general housecleaning of its outlaws and renegades. Bill Taylor, involved in the William Sutton assassination, and jailed on a ship at Indianola, Texas, swam free on September 15, 1875, when a hurricane destroyed Indianola forever. His freedom was only momentary, however, as he went on trial at Texana, Jackson County, Texas, where in May of 1878 a jury acquitted him of slaying Sutton. Within a couple of years he had dropped from sight. So did his reputation as a desperado.

As for Reuben H. Brown, the Cuero marshal who arrested Taylor and who assumed leadership of the Sutton Party after Bill Sutton's death, he took a seat in the crowded Merchant's Exchange Saloon in Cuero on November 17, 1875. As he dealt monte, three to five men shouldered their way inside, fired a fusillade of hot lead into Brown, then dragged him outside and shot him again. A black man, Thomas Freeman, took a couple of misdirected bullets and died on the spot too. James Taylor was the immediate suspect. James Taylor was always an immediate suspect.[33]

JIM TAYLOR AND SEVERAL PARTISANS rode into Clinton on December 27, 1875, by some accounts to burn the courthouse, by other accounts to surrender a friend for trial. After placing their horses in Martin King's stable, they wandered up the street, unaware that informers had crossed the Guadalupe River and alerted law officers. A posse slipped into town, locked the outlaw horses inside the stable, and forced the Taylor faction into a running fight. When it ended, James C. Taylor and two friends, Mace Arnold and A. R. Hendricks were dead. As a touch of irony, Hendricks had been a ranger with Leander McNelly.[34] Today all three gunmen—Taylor, Arnold and Hendricks—lie within a few feet of each other in the Taylor-Bennett Cemetery near Cuero.

The Sutton-Taylor Feud sputtered for years afterward although its principle characters were mostly dead or hiding. John Wesley Hardin was part of the latter.[35]

Capturing the Grand Mogul

A S LATE AS JUNE 17, 1874, the Texas Rangers suspected John Wesley Hardin still considered Comanche home. Ranger W. J. Maltby wrote Major John B. Jones from Brownwood, and said the local people are still "severely threatened by the notorious outlaw John Hardin and a band of desperadoes that he has enlisted under his banner." Maltby believed Hardin was still in the county and "seeking the lives of the best citizens." For the next three years, newspapers frequently reported Hardin activity in Texas when he actually was in Alabama and Florida.[1]

Hardin considered vanishing into Mexico as well as Great Britain, but a Hardin on the run needed funds. Joe Clements and Neill Bowen were in Kansas where their cattle remained unsold, awaiting a favorable market. A desperate John Wesley dispatched his younger brother Jefferson to Kansas with instructions to sell regardless of price. Jeff returned with five hundred dollars. Neill Bowen followed shortly thereafter, and he and Hardin settled accounts. Hardin said he had considerable money when he left the state.[2]

Brenham, Texas, City Marshal Harry Swain, a relative of Jane, took her and daughter Mollie to New Orleans by boat. Hardin rode horseback across the land route, traveling under the alias of

John Wesley Hardin
(alias John Swain)
in 1875. Photo likely
taken in Florida or
Alabama. Wes Hardin
looks exactly like what
he was: a gambler. (R. G.
McCubbin Collection)

Walker. From New Orleans he went to Cedar Keys, Florida, then
on to Gainsville near the geographic center of the state. Hardin
wrote Jane on September 8, 1874, complaining that he had problems paying his board, and it was good that he was living alone.

Nevertheless, he purchased Samuel H. Burnett's Gainsville
Saloon. On opening day Bill McCulloch and Frank Harper, two
Texas stockmen, strolled in. Everybody recognized each other
although the cattlemen promised never to reveal Hardin's new
identity or hiding place. By now John Wesley Hardin had become
John H. Swain, adopting the last name of Jane's relatives.

As usual with Hardin, events happened fast. A city marshal
named Wilson argued with black men in front of the saloon, and
during the resultant struggle, Wilson deputized Hardin for assistance. Hardin knocked down one man and shot another. Those
still on their feet went to jail.

Shortly afterwards, a black man named Eli attempted to rape a
white woman, and was jailed. At midnight, several masked men,
including Hardin, came calling. They burned the jail, cremating Eli.[3]

Jane Hardin and
daughter Mollie,
about 1875.
Photo probably
taken in Alabama.
(Harden/Hardin/
Harding Family
Association Collection)

Hardin sold his saloon during early 1875. He, Jane and Mollie relocated a few miles south in Micanopy, Florida where the Hardin, alias Swain, family re-entered the saloon business. Due to a need to keep moving, in July 1875 the Hardins turned up at Jacksonville, remaining a year on the northeast coast of Florida, just south of the Georgia line. Hardin characterized Jacksonville as "a resort for people from the North who go down there to make money."[4] Jacksonville even then dominated the social and commercial world of Florida, its wide streets shaded by huge live oaks, its commercial houses thriving. Here Hardin contracted to furnish 150 head of beef to the butchering firm of Haddock & Company.

Haddock died before the steers arrived, and his company refused to accept the animals. This left little financial maneuvering for Hardin, so he forsook the saloon business and entered the butchering trade. Slaughtering cattle may not have enriched the family but between that and the gambling tables, Swain earned a satisfactory living. On August 3, 1875, his only son, John Wesley Hardin, Jr. was born in the Hardin/Swain home at 127 Pine Street, Jacksonville, Florida.

THROUGHOUT HIS CAREER, John Wesley Hardin cultivated peace officers. Killing them was understandable, but he also recognized the value of having them as friends. In spite of his constant assertions that Hickok intended to murder him, Hardin and Hickok had a respectful relationship. The Cherokee County, Texas Sheriff Richard B. "Dick" Reagan befriended Hardin, the Gonzales County Sheriff William E. Jones had allowed, even encouraged, his jail break. Sheriff Jack Helm had allegedly been Hardin's friend until Hardin killed him, and Comanche County Sheriff John Carnes had shielded Hardin from lynch mobs.

The city marshal of Brenham, Harry Swain, was related to Hardin's wife, and thus did favors for Hardin. Gus Kenedy, a Jacksonville city policeman, became one of Hardin's closest Florida associates. Some of Hardin's Florida mail reached him through the Nassau County Sheriff, Malcolm McMillan, another relative of Jane Hardin through the Bowen side of the family.

Sheriff Malcolm McMillan warned Hardin that Pinkerton operatives were asking questions.

ON JANUARY 20, 1875, THE TEXAS LEGISLATURE, in a joint resolution, offered "a reward of four thousand dollars for the apprehension and delivery of the body of the notorious murderer, John Wesley Hardin,...[to the] jail house door of Travis County."[5] A general consensus among legislators regarding the number of men Hardin had slain placed the figure at twenty-seven. Some legislators believed four thousand dollars was too much for any desperado, regardless of reputation. On the other hand, since the resolution meant "dead or alive," a couple of representatives argued that neither Hardin "nor anyone else, should be shot down without trial." No doubt Hardin would have agreed.

Comanche Senator John D. Stephens pushed the resolution so vigorously that Hardin allegedly threatened his life, a threat supposedly routing the senator into concealment until Hardin's absence from the state had been confirmed. Anyway, the resolution passed sixty-nine to six, and the reward made John Wesley Hardin the highest-priced desperado in the annals of Texas.[6]

This kind of money would certainly entice Pinkerton operatives, just as it would beguile Texas Rangers. This kind of money meant Texans had grown weary of law breakers and would pay to see them dead or in jail. This kind of money explained why Hardin stayed constantly on the run. This kind of money had influence.

"I REMAINED IN JACKSONVILLE until I was forced to leave by detectives," Hardin exclaimed. "I escaped before they could get papers from the governor."[7]

Hardin sent Jane, Mollie and John Jr. to Aufaula, Alabama. He and Jacksonville city policeman Gus Kenedy—who apparently quit his job so that he could ride with Hardin—planned to rendezvous with them in New Orleans. However, somewhere around the Georgia/Florida line, Hardin and Kenedy killed two alleged Pinkerton detectives during a shootout.[8]

As for why Pinkertons would pursue Hardin, one answer is that the Pinkertons were the largest, best known and most prestigious private investigative firm in the world. They sought Hardin for the reward. Various Pinkerton bounty hunters were "stringers" or part-timers, people ordinarily unlisted as regular employees.

Following the possible Pinkerton killings, John Wesley Hardin retired to Pollard, Alabama, three miles north of the Florida line. Here he joined Jane and the children. They considered fleeing to Tuxpan, Mexico, a coastal village between Tampico and Vera Cruz, but that scheme went awry because of the risk of yellow fever in New Orleans. The family therefore settled briefly at Pascagoula, Mississippi, on the Gulf Coast while Hardin commuted to Mobile, Alabama for gambling purposes.

An irony is that with Hardin on the run, his family paid the price. They did without, hid, lied in his behalf while he, a fugitive from justice, imprisoned them in a circle of grief while he caroused in the saloons and wagering houses.

DURING THE 1876 PRESIDENTIAL elections, Republican Rutherford B. Hayes fought an intense, bitter battle against

John Wesley Hardin, Jr.
and Mollie. Photo likely
taken in Gonzales County,
Texas, ca. early 1880s.
(R. G. McCubbin Collection)

Samuel J. Tilden. Strong sectional emotions flourished, and an election brawl started in a Mobile gambling establishment and boiled over into the streets. Hardin implied that he and Kenedy killed two men. They tossed their weapons into back yards and gave police their most innocent look when arrested in a coffee house. Kenedy and Hardin spent several days in jail before the State dismissed charges.[9]

The Alabama *Mobile Register* of May 3, 1877, said "Gus Kenedy and J. H. Swayne were arrested for disorderly conduct on Tuesday night last, and fined $5." The newspaper mentioned no deaths but did write that "Sergeant Ryan, of the police force, while in discharge of his duty, was shot in the arm by one of three parties whom he and Officer Spencer [ejected from] a house." A day later, the *Register* referred to "charges of malicious mischief" against Swain and Kenedy, summarizing that part of their fine required them to be "kicked out of town." The police confiscated a deck of "swindling cards," their backs marked so that crooked dealers could easily determine the faces. Hardin might have been a legend in Texas, but in Alabama he was little more than a routine card shark.[10]

From his base in Pollard, Hardin and Shep Hardy, a forty-year-old married laborer from Florida, entered the logging business along the Styx River. The enterprise failed because Hardin could not chop wood and gamble at the same time. Hardin's letters to Jane in mid 1877, document a man spending more and more time away from his family. She and the children lived with her brother Brown Bowen as Hardin struggled to send her twenty dollars. Even confidence men had their bad days.[11]

THE TENUOUS BROTHER-IN-LAW relationship between John Wesley Hardin and Brown Bowen continued to unravel. After killing Tom Haldeman in Texas, Bowen fled to Kansas in 1873 and thereafter appeared in Florida and Alabama where he may have had brothers and sisters, and certainly aunts and uncles. Bowen married Mary Catherine Mayo, a lady ten years his junior.[12] Although a son was born in 1876, the event failed to moderate the nature or reputation of Brown Bowen. Bowen was a multi-murderer, a rapist, a whiner, an individual of neither pluck nor manhood, a sly man of non-existent virtue who happened to be the brother of Jane Hardin. This reluctantly made him family to John Wesley Hardin. Hardin failed to realize the danger of just being near Brown Bowen. David Haldeman, the father of Tom Haldeman, relentlessly goaded Texas Governor Richard Hubbard into offering a reward of suitable significance for Bowen, that Bowen be forcibly returned to Texas and tried for murder. Haldeman even located Brown Bowen in Alabama, and demanded that the authorities do their duty. The elder Haldeman's undeviating campaign for justice would have far-reaching Hardin (and Bowen) consequences. That desire for vengeance triggered the first step in a protracted road back to Texas for both Bowen and Hardin.[13]

OVER IN AUSTIN, the government had not forgotten Hardin although it was trying to disregard Bowen. The State put a $500 reward out for Brown Bowen, an interesting sum but still insufficient for much Texas Ranger or out-of-state heed. But Hardin had a bounty of $4,000 dead or alive, and once the State turned its attention toward him, there was no turning back. Governor Richard Hubbard might have weighed three hundred pounds, but those were relentless pounds when it came to apprehending the desperado. He made his wishes known to the red-headed, North Carolina born J. Lee Hall who took command of the Special Forces of Texas Rangers from Leander McNelly in January 1877.

Hall promoted Sergeant John Barclay Armstrong to lieutenant, and the unit returned to DeWitt County where Armstrong made additional Sutton-Taylor Feud arrests. Of course, some of that ardor momentarily faded in May 1877, when in Goliad, he carelessly shot himself in the groin. Nevertheless, the ranger recovered quickly. In April 1877, Armstrong apprehended the number two desperado in Texas, King Fisher. Following that, Armstrong became obsessed with capturing John Wesley Hardin and pocketing the four thousand dollars.

In those more relaxed days before the turn of the century, state lines meant little to law officers in quest of wanted men with bounties on their head. The Texas Rangers habitually chased Texas outlaws into Mexico, New Mexico, Arizona and even California. The length and duration of the pursuit usually depended upon the amount of reward money involved. Many individuals became sheriffs, marshals and Texas Rangers because of this extra income, a pecuniary inducement to the job.

Rangers Hall and Armstrong suspected Hardin had his wife and children with him. They understood the exceptionally strong bonds of family, knowing that contact would undoubtedly be made between families still living in Texas and families who had fled.

Hall and Armstrong retained John Riley Duncan, better known as Jack Duncan. A Kentucky-born policeman, Duncan was a jovial, good-natured man with black hair and eyes. He worked as a city detective in Dallas, and was the best sleuth in the state, a man occasionally operating as a Pinkerton stringer.[14] In the spring of 1877, Governor Hubbard appointed Duncan as a special ranger assigned to Lieutenant John B. Armstrong. Their job involved tracking down and either capturing or killing John Wesley Hardin.[15]

Lt. John Barclay
Armstrong,
Texas Ranger.
(Chuck Parsons
Collection)

The twenty-six-year-old Duncan, using the alias of Mr.
Williams, slipped into Gonzales county disguised as a merchant.
Mr. Williams approached Brown's father, Neill Bowen, and expressed an interest in renting a storehouse. The two men became
friends long enough for Duncan to intercept a Pollard, Alabama,
letter from Brown Bowen to his father. Brown closed by mentioning that his sister sent love to all. That sister could only be Jane
Hardin, and where she was, there would John Wesley Hardin
likely be.

In order to get out of Gonzales County without arousing suspicion that he was a spy, Duncan wired code words to Texas
Ranger John B. Armstrong: "Come get your horse." Within a day
or so, the rangers arrived and, playing along with the ruse, pretended to arrest Duncan. They released and congratulated him
as soon as all were safely out of sight.

Hall was busy with other cases, so Armstrong acquired train
tickets and requested that warrants be forwarded for (both) John
Wesley Hardin and John Swain to Montgomery, Alabama. The
lawmen reached Montgomery on June 20, 1877.

Duncan, falling back on his sleuth trade, moseyed over to Pollard as a transient, then south a mile or so to Whiting (locally known as Junction) where Hardin and Bowen lived. He casually inquired about a man named Swain, and learned that Swain had left for Pensacola, Florida to gamble. Subsequent inquiries led them to William D. Chipley, a superintendent of the Pensacola Railroad who lived in Pensacola and disliked both Brown Bowen and John Swain.

According to the *Pensacola Gazette*, an altercation between Chipley and Bowen occurred at the Pensacola station and hotel. An intoxicated Bowen chased a black man around the terminal and through the hotel dining room. The black man escaped as Superintendent Chipley passed by while going to his office. Bowen cornered Chipley, screaming "Why didn't you stop that nigger for me?" An astonished Chipley responded, "I have nothing to do with your nigger." An angry Bowen then pointed a cocked six-shooter at Chipley who jammed his hand between the firing pin and the frame. He jerked the gun from Bowen's hand and beat him over the head with it. The confrontation ended with Bowen swearing he would kill Chipley.

An odd aspect of this affair is that another newspaper, the *Atlanta Constitution* published essentially the same story, only it named Swain as the offending thug. Judging from his background, Bowen was the more logical assailant. Hardin certainly had his prejudices, but Bowen was the more cruel and vindictive.[16]

After conversing by wire with Duncan and Armstrong, Chipley steamed north by train to meet them in Whiting. Since Armstrong still awaited Texas warrants for Hardin and Swain, Chipley brought a Pensacola judge as well as the Escambia County, Florida, Sheriff William H. Hutchinson. The sheriff was a twenty-seven-year-old Alabaman, a Confederate veteran, a former logger now in his first term as a lawman.

The Pensacola authorities sought assurances that the Texas Rangers would also arrest Brown Bowen. Armstrong affirmed that, so everybody headed south to Pensacola from Whiting. In Florida, the lawmen learned that Brown Bowen had left (or perhaps was never with) the Hardin party. Hardin himself planned a return to Pollard on the afternoon train. Since everyone agreed that the best opportunity, and least dangerous time, to make an

William D. Chipley. He disliked
Hardin, but he hated Brown Bowen.
(Chuck Parsons Collection)

William Henry Hutchinson, Florida
sheriff. (Chuck Parsons Collection)

apprehension would be in the railroad car, Sheriff Hutchinson
deputized several residents. He stationed deputies around the
depot in case Hardin/Swain should elude officers on board. The
date was August 23, 1877.

As anticipated, John Wesley Hardin and his gambling associates Shep Hardy, Neal Campbell and twenty-one-year-old Jim
Mann, entered the smoking car where Hardin sat alongside the
aisle relaxing with his pipe. Armstrong positioned himself in the
express car next to the smoker as Sheriff Hutchinson and a deputy
nonchalantly strolled through, throwing off drunks and undesirables while mentally evaluating Hardin and his friends. Up front,
the engineer had been told to move out when someone yanked
the bell cord according to a pre-arranged code.

Exactly what happened next depends upon who recalled the
incident. The agreed-upon facts seem to be these: Hardin was
leaning back with both arms raised overhead and clutching the
back of the seat as if stretching. Sheriff Hutchinson and the muscular Florida Deputy A. J. Perdue re-entered the car from behind

The capture of John Wesley Hardin in Pensacola, Florida.
(*The Life of John Wesley Hardin*)

Hardin and grabbed him. Perhaps a better description would be that both men tumbled upon him. A wild cursing, screaming, kicking, struggle followed.

Armstrong (carrying a revolver and still suffering from his self-inflicted groin wound), limped down the aisle toward the bundle of fiercely grappling men. He ignored the uproar, paused over the melee, hesitated while waiting for an opening, and swung the heavy six-shooter, bringing it to rest with a resounding whack upon Hardin's head. The alias Mr. Swain slumped senseless. In fact, he lay unconscious so long that Armstrong feared he had killed him. The officers slapped on the leg irons, but could not find the handcuffs. So they bound Hardin with rope, and lashed him to his seat.

As passengers stampeded from the car, Jim Mann, sitting opposite Hardin, probably thought he and the others were beset upon by madmen. He jumped up and fired a wild round or two, but was slain by deputy Martin Sullivan.[17] Mann was not wanted for anything, and would have been released had he not panicked. Someone yanked the bell cord, and the train lurched forward as

Passenger train interior in use at the time of John Wesley Hardin's capture. (Chuck Parsons Collection)

one of the lawmen found a six-shooter dangling inside Hardin's trousers, a suspender strap through the trigger guard. It was a fine hiding place, but not much could be said for it regarding a fast draw. Had Hardin been able to reach it, chances are he would have shot only himself. He stated in a letter to Jane that "I had no show [opportunity] to get my pistol," and "Jane I expect that it is a good thing they caught me the way they did for they had 40 men withe the Shariffe and Deputie of pensicolia. So you see I would have been a corps."[18] Hardin signed the letter "J. H. Swain."

The train stopped within a short distance, and Armstrong explained to Sheriff Hutchinson and deputy Perdue the true identity of John Swain. He paid them $500 for their assistance. Hutchinson left the train and returned home, while Perdue went all the way to Whiting in the hope of arresting Brown Bowen. But Bowen was not to be located. From the Whiting station, where Hardy and Campbell were released, Wes sent money with them to his wife who apparently needed it since their third and last child, Jane "Jennie" Hardin, was only a month old.

At Whiting, Hardin hoped for a quick release since he knew the rangers lacked warrants. He wrote, "my friends at Pollard, eight miles away, had formed a rescuing party with the sheriff at their head and expected to legally release me when the train came through...[and] stopped several minutes. But unfortunately the train passed through without stopping...."[19]

Armstrong telegraphed Texas Adjutant General William H. Steele that a desperately fighting Hardin had been captured after some lively shooting. "This is Hardin's home [Whiting] and his friends are trying to rally men to release him," Armstrong stated. "Have some good citizens with [me] & we will make it interesting."[20]

Armstrong also wired telegrams to the press. Newspapers from New York to Chicago, and Tennessee to New Orleans, ran the story. The ranger had a strong sense of personal publicity.

The train chugged along, traveling slowly, periodically pausing to take on water. Hardin occasionally stepped outside for air, always in chains, much to the relief of the other passengers since John was wildly profane. Once outdoors, he sulked and frequently refused to climb back aboard. So the lawmen carried him on.[21]

At Decatur, Alabama, Hardin briefly saw, and described, his one golden opportunity to escape. The opening was cold and calculating, but all too fleeting even for John Wesley Hardin:

> I knew my only hope was to escape. My guards were kind to me but they were not most vigilant. By promising to be quiet, I had caused them to relax somewhat. When we got to Decatur, we had to stop and change cars for Memphis. They took me to a hotel, got a room, and sent for our meals. Jack [Duncan] and Armstrong were now getting intimate with me, and when dinner came I suggested the necessity of removing my cuffs and they agreed to do so. Armstrong unlocked the jewelry [manacles] and started to turn around, exposing his six-shooter to me, when Jack jerked him around and pulled his pistol at the same time. "Look out," he said, "John will kill us and escape." Of course, I laughed at him and ridiculed the idea. It was really the very chance I was looking for, but Jack had taken the play away just before it got ripe. I intended to jerk Armstrong's pistol, kill Jack Duncan or make him throw up his hands. I could have made him unlock my shackles, or get the key from his dead body and do it myself. I could then have easily made my escape. That time never came again.[22]

TEXAS RANGER DETECTIVE JACK DUNCAN questioned Hardin, asking "And now, John, did you know that two men were sent out this way for you once before?" Hardin replied, "Yes, I know that." The detective continued, "And do you know that those men never came back to Texas?" Hardin emotionally responded, "Yes, I know that, and I know by God, they never will come back."[23]

The *Atlanta Constitution* suspected Hardin had killed two people in the Southeast. Within a week after Hardin's capture, the *Constitution* reported that "John Swayne [Swain] is a gambler and spends much time in Pensacola. He had killed one or two men here, as also has his brother-in-law Bowen...."[24]

At Montgomery, Alabama, a worried Armstrong sent a flurry of telegrams insisting upon his warrants to Adjutant General Steele as well as Governor Hubbard. "What is the matter?" he cried. Fortunately, although Alabama Judge John B. Fuller waffled, he still refused to release Hardin because the authorities had charged him with the murder of Charles Webb. The *Austin Statesman* of August 29, 1877, reported the timely arrival of warrants, saying the paper work "enabled Lieut. Armstrong and Detective Duncan to start on their way, rejoicing with the Grand Mogul of Texas desperadoes."[25]

I am a
Human Being

JOHN WROTE JANE, INSISTING he had been captured by foul means in Pensacola, that his gambling friend Jimmy Mann had been murdered, but that the officers were treating him well. He urged her to be cautious in her letters, as they would be read by others, and he reminded her of good times, saying "You have ever been true." Most of all, he stated with relief that Armstrong and Duncan had assured him, "I will not be mobbed."

Jane and her youngest child of six weeks had meanwhile made it to Montgomery, Alabama. A local newspaper quoted her as anxious to return to Texas, and described her as "conversing like a person of much more than ordinary nerve and courage. She boasts of being able to shoot and manage a horse as well as most men, and says that things will be extremely lively for Armstrong and Duncan, and also for some others who had a hand in the capture of Hardin. In personal appearance Mrs. Hardin (or Swain, the name they assumed since they left Texas), is quite good looking and apparently 21 or 22 years of age. She seems to be well educated and speaks fluently, expressing her feelings with much force."[1]

The Hardin story from this time until his arrival in Austin was like an ancient history replay, a Caesar returning in triumph. The young gunman could not even leave Montgomery, Alabama

The Travis County Jail at Austin during the period of Hardin's
incarceration. Travis County Courthouse at right.
(Archives Division — Texas State Library)

Congress Avenue, Austin, Texas, during the 1880s. Capitol Building at
the end of the street. (Archives Division — Texas State Library)

without running a gauntlet of curiosity seekers. "A large crowd of persons eager to see him was assembled and took, perhaps, their last look at the wonder," reported the *Montgomery Advertiser and Mail* on August 26, 1877.

It mattered not that this Grand Mogul was a manacled prisoner, a murderer going home to justice. As word flashed ahead, people gathered along the tracks for a glimpse of the desperado. In Memphis, where Hardin spent the night in jail, a jailer warned Duncan about a missing case knife. During a Hardin search, no one found it, but on the train for Texarkana, Duncan noticed it up Hardin's sleeve. The detective jerked it loose and tossed it out the train window. Hardin broke down and sobbed, claiming he needed it for defense should a mob attempt to lynch him. Armstrong offered assurances that if necessary, the lawmen would provide him with a six-shooter.[2]

Hardin wrote that a man named Roe traveled from Memphis to Texarkana, and "gallant officers…brought him into the sleeper where I was trying to rest. Why, he [Roe] said, 'there is nothing bad in your face. Your life has been misrepresented to me. Here is $50. Take it from a sympathizer.'"[3]

Crowds gathered at Little Rock. At Texarkana, special police muscled back the multitudes, but the throngs were no more infatuated than the lawmen. The officers handed him empty revolvers, and Duncan said Hardin "could take one in each hand and swing them around his forefinger and keep one of them going off [clicking] all the time."[4] Hardin had been doing this ever since he was a kid. He was not only a killer, he was a born entertainer.

On August 28, 1877, the train arrived in Austin, but Hardin was not on it. It stopped just outside the city, the rangers hustling Hardin into a hack with curtained windows. With heavily armed lawmen surrounding the vehicle, Hardin reached the Travis County jail as throngs of spectators refused to part for the we-ried lawmen. With only one way in, they formed a wedge, lifted Hardin off his feet and bodily carried him through the gates and into what the *Galveston News* called "the largest and best county prison in Texas." The *News* also interviewed Hardin, describing him as "mild featured and mild mannered," light complexion with "mild blue eyes" and pleasant talk. The newspaper portrayed him as wanting to go to trial as "I am sick and tired of fleeing and would not go away if I could." He claimed to be innocent, and asked authorities "to protect him against mobs for it is mob violence alone that he fears."[5]

Armstrong and Duncan now signed off on their man, and drew the four-thousand-dollar reward. At about the same time, Florida Sheriff W. H. Hutchinson sent a telegram to the *Dallas Herald* on September 7, 1877, saying, "I captured and forwarded John Wesley Hardin, the noted Texas outlaw. Please telegraph me amount of authoritative reward offered."

Hutchinson, still residing in Pensacola, protested that media accounts regarding Hardin's capture were "at variance with the actual arrest." However, Hutchinson offered little additional facts or insight. He complained that "I received a paltry $500...for assisting in the capture." And Hardin snapped at him, saying, "I have killed twenty-seven men, and Hutch, you came near being the twenty-eighth."[6]

The newspaper replied that Hutchinson was out of luck, the money had already been drawn. Armstrong had taken his share, whatever it amounted to, and in 1882 used it to purchase the fifty-thousand-acre Armstrong Ranch in Willacy County. He died at Armstrong, Texas on May 1, 1913.[7]

Hutchinson probably needed the money for his defense. An Escambia County grand jury, during its fall 1877 term, indicted the sheriff for "kidnapping another person to wit—one John W. Hardin with intent to cause him to be sent out of the State of Florida against his will." The case never went to trial, and Hutchinson was re-elected.[8]

ON SEPTEMBER 18, 1877, Sheriff F. E. Wilson of Comanche County, with several deputies, arrived in Austin to escort John Wesley Hardin to Comanche for trial. The *Fort Worth Democrat* said the removal of John Wesley Hardin from the Austin prison should be done under the strictest surveillance, and with a strong guard of tried and trusty men."[9] Wilson requested an escort of rangers, so the governor assigned thirty men of Company E led by Lieutenant N. O. Reynolds. Sergeant James Gillett, one of the thirty, would go on to fame with his marvelous book *Six Years With the Texas Rangers*. Gillett called Hardin "the most desperate criminal in Texas," and wrote that on the day Hardin left Austin, "between one and two thousand people gathered about the Travis County jail to see this notorious desperado." Gillett and ranger Henry Thomas escorted Hardin out of the prison, describing him as "heavily shackled and handcuffed," a prisoner who "walked very slowly between us."[10]

The *Daily Democratic Statesman* noted that "A very large crowd of people gathered to see this knight of the six-shooter as he passed from the jail to the carriage waiting for him. When Hardin appeared upon the stone steps he seemed nervous and looked about as if to observe who was there, and if possible to rest his eyes upon a familiar face. In a moment he became complacent and pleasant, conversing freely with the sheriff and guard who occupied the vehicle with him."

Some twenty or more rangers filed behind Hardin along the Georgetown road as onlookers sought a clear view. In Lampasas, a newspaper said "more people rushed to see him than if he had been a rhinoceros...."[11]

During nights and periods of rest, the rangers kept Hardin in an "enclosure," a description of which was never provided. The *Victoria Advocate* explained that, "Such formidable precautions have been taken, so that an attempt at rescue will not be made by the miserable cut-throats called his friends."

THOSE RANGERS WHO WISHED TO TALK with Hardin—and most of them were curious and anxious—laid aside their weapons before entering the enclosure. Several had long conversations with the prisoner, finding him entertaining and witty. With the rangers gathered around, Hardin took an unloaded six-shooter and astonished everyone with his dexterity as he performed the "double roll" and the "single roll," both forward and backwards.[12]

A ranger calling himself Mervyn wrote to the *Galveston News*. His letter described the four-day trip from Austin to Comanche:

> Hardin deported himself with the utmost decorum, evincing no restlessness, though his patience was sorely tried by the gaping crowds who gathered at the noon and evening camps to stare him in the face, with a sense of curiosity that knows no sense of delicacy. He was quite communicative, talking freely of his

terrible adventures, expressing regrets for what he termed his errors, and hopes for the future. He is what the ladies would call a blonde: about five feet ten inches high, wears his whiskers in the French style, and is fairly educated in English in the common school branches. He has been wounded in several places, and suffered with one old bullet wound on the trip hither.

This same letter mentioned a commonly held view that Hardin spent restless nights because of "appalling dreams" whereby he sprang like a madman from his bed "to grapple with phantom foes or to cower whimpering on the floor." But "I have guarded him at midnight," Mervyn wrote, and "John Wesley Hardin is the gentlest sleeper of them all."[13]

A correspondent in Comanche reported that Hardin arrived at ten o'clock on a Monday morning. "The news spread like lightning," the reporter stated, "and in a few seconds everybody had left their employment to get a glimpse of him. Crowds gathered along the streets." The man had become a legend in his own time.[14]

Upon reaching Comanche, Hardin was so heavily shackled that he could not walk, so the rangers toted him into a jail not nearly as spacious as the one in Austin. This was simply a small stone building with oak lining around the inside walls. An iron cage squatted in the middle. Throughout the trial, although Hardin never lost his fear, the rangers never left him, and the mobs never seriously threatened.

THE TWO-DAY TRIAL STARTED on Friday, September 28, within a week after Hardin's arrival. Perhaps not so oddly, County Attorney John D. Stephens, the state senator who pushed through the four-thousand-dollar reward for Hardin's dead or alive body, continued as Hardin's chief nemesis. District Attorney N. R. Lindsey handled the prosecution opening and closing statements, plus interrogations. Attorneys S. C. Buck, and S. P. Burns of Brownwood, assisted the prosecution. Hardin retained several attorneys, all of whom had fine reputations as capable lawyers and honest men: Samuel Henry Renick of Waco, Thomas Lewis Nugent of Stephenville, W. S. J. Adams and G. R. Hart, both of Comanche, plus Abner Lipscomb of Brenham.[15] The lawyers and their client appeared before the 12th Judicial District Court of Comanche, the Honorable James Richard Fleming, a local pillar of the Methodist Church, presiding. Judge Fleming was a Stephens law partner in Comanche.[16]

Not a man on the jury had doubts about his ability to render justice, although most had moved into the county after the death of Webb, not that their previous absence made any difference. They all knew Hardin was guilty.

The indictment charged John Wesley Hardin and James Taylor with the murder of the Brown County Deputy Sheriff, Charles Webb. Taylor had since been slain, so authorities amended the arraignment. Even then, the charge did not indicate when or where Webb died. However, the appeals court would not consider this oversight sufficient grounds for a mistrial.

The *Weatherford Exponent* of October 13, 1877, mentioned charges of cattle stealing also outstanding against Hardin. However, he wasn't additionally being tried for that, the newspaper dryly stating that the offense was so common in Texas that rustling in itself "would not add further notoriety" to the prisoner's name.

Hardin never asked for a change of venue, although he later claimed he did. Jury selection took a half-day, and after that one witness after another described what he knew about Hardin's activities on the day of Webb's death. According to one newspaper reporter, "Hardin presented an indifferent, fearless countenance while the above testimony was being given...."

The *Weatherford Exponent* provided a more detailed picture of Hardin:

> In personal appearance, Hardin does not impress you as a desperado. He is of medium height, rather heavy build, and round shouldered—with a slight rolling swagger in his gait. He appeared in court dressed in a nice blue-gray suit, blue cravat, rings on his fingers, a mustache and goatee, and pomatum [sic] on his hair. At a distance he might easily be mistaken for a country dandy—the lead spirit at county singings and social gatherings. When smiling, he had a very pleasant expression. His features in repose are not by any means repulsive, but a closer and more careful inspection convinces you there is a lurking devil within, delighting more in tragedy than in comedy. There is a bull-dog determination and courage about the mouth. The eyes are bold and steady in their gaze, sometimes giving forth a flashing expression of ferocity that shows the tiger within is easily excited and dangerous when aroused. His demeanor throughout the trial was free and easy,

often smiling and chatting with his counsel; but after his conviction, his features looked somewhat heavy and haggard. Though a reckless desperado, Hardin is not a mean, avaricious or morbidly blood-thirsty man. He is by nature a bold and reckless man, but has not a bad disposition. He owes his ruin chiefly to whiskey and unsavory associations.

The original trial testimony was not preserved, but arguments lasted into the night on Friday and until late the following day. As for Judge J. R. Fleming he "presided at the trial with marked ability, impartiality and firmness, and the charge of the court on the law was thorough and exhaustive, embracing some twenty-four sections." The State introduced eight to ten witnesses, the defense two. None were identified. Some mentioned twenty or thirty shots being fired almost like a volley. Hardin and his companions fired all but two of those rounds.

While the all male jury debated, the *Exponent* said "the courtroom presented a weird and interesting scene. It was densely packed with men deeply anxious to know the verdict, yet the utmost order and quiet was maintained. The Rangers and Sheriffs guarded the doors and promenaded the aisles, the flaring light of the candles gleaming upon their pistols and leading to a scene resembling a warlike appearance. At each click of the door of the jury room, hundreds of heads turned, breathless with attention. At eleven o'clock [after nearly three hours of debating], the jury returned a verdict of murder in the second degree, assessing the punishment at confinement in the penitentiary at hard labor for twenty-five years."

The defendant's counsel gave notice of appeal and the prisoner was remanded to jail, no one but the guard being permitted to leave the court room until the prisoner had crossed the square and neared the entrance to the building. "If the verdict had been one of acquittal, Hardin would have been hung by a mob, the thirty rangers notwithstanding." Hardin hid his disappointment as best he could in the courtroom, but wept bitterly in his cell.[17]

The appeals process summarized the witness statements, thus offering additional insight:

> William Cunningham testified that, a few days before the homicide [Webb's], he was at Waldrip's ranch, about ten miles west of Comanche, having been employed by Joe G. Hardin,...to go

there and get some cattle. There he met John Wesley Hardin, Joe G. Hardin, and six cousins of theirs—Alex Barekman, Ham Anderson, James Taylor, James Anderson, Bud Dixon, and Tom Dixon. About two weeks previous to this occasion, witness was at the same ranch, when Charles Webb, the deceased, arrested a son of old Mrs. Waldrip. While witness and the above-named parties were at supper, Mrs. Waldrip told the crowd that Webb had arrested her son and mistreated her, and if she could she would kill him. Joe G. Hardin replied, "We will do away with him for you when we get him to the right place."

G. W. Talbot testified that he was trying to collect a livery-stable bill from John Wesley Hardin, and found him in the Carnes & Wilson Saloon, fifty feet west of Wright's Saloon. Before Talbot could speak with Hardin, however, John Hardin and Jim Taylor went out the back door, sat on a log and became crying drunks. They were still weeping upon re-entering the saloon, at which time Hardin bought Talbot a drink, then stepped to the front door and noticed Charles Webb walking along the east side of the public square. Turning to Taylor, Hardin said, "Did you ever see anything coming up finer in your life?" Hardin and Taylor then stepped outside the building and walked toward Wright's Saloon.

James Carnes, Jr., [another brother of the Carnes boys] testified that he was standing on the east side of the [Jack Wright] saloon, and noticed Webb coming around the north-east corner of the building. John Wesley Hardin remarked to his companion, "There comes that damn Brown County sheriff, now." Webb came on as if he intended to pass Hardin and enter a side door of the saloon. Just as he was about to pass Hardin the latter stopped him and asked him if he was not the sheriff of Brown County.

Webb replied, "No, I am the deputy sheriff."

Hardin then asked him if he had papers for him. Webb answered that he did not know him. Hardin said, "I am that damned desperado, John Wesley Hardin, as people call me; now you know me." Webb replied that he had no papers for him.

Hardin then asked Webb what he had in his hand, and Webb answered that he had a cigar, and showed it. Hardin then said to Webb, "I have heard that you have said that John Carnes had not done his duty, and was no sheriff."

Webb replied that he had made no such remark; that so far as he knew, Mr. Carnes did discharge his duty.

Hardin then said, "Your people in Brown County say that John Carnes was no sheriff and no man."

Webb answered that he knew nothing about it, and was not responsible for what the people of Brown County said.

Mr. Thurmond, a lawyer, was standing in the street at a short distance, and called to Webb, saying, "Charley, come here." Hardin turned toward Thurmond and said "I am attending to Charley now."

Webb started to move toward Thurmond, and Hardin said to him, "You can't go off from me" or "You ain't going off from me in that way."

Webb then stepped back and said, "No, God damn you, I am not afraid of you," and drew his pistol and fired as soon as he got it out of its scabbard, and before he got it presented.

Hardin, James Taylor and Dixon all fired at Webb, Hardin being in front of him, Taylor to his left, and Dixon to his right. Webb had his back to the saloon, and was pretty close to it. Webb fell at the first crack of Hardin's and Taylor's pistols. Witness saw Hardin fire two shots at him, and after the firing ceased saw Webb lying in the saloon, dead.

On his cross-examination this witness stated that Hardin and Webb fired very close together. But he could not say that the former had his hand on his pistol when the latter fired. When Webb fell, he laid his pistol on his knee and fired again.

David[18] Carnes...gave a very similar account down to the shooting. But he said, "They all then drew their pistols, and all fired at once, or nearly so. If there was any difference, Webb fired first. This witness knew Hardin previously. In talking to Webb, Hardin spoke in a loud tone, excited and angry. Webb was very cool and collected, and spoke in a very low tone. Webb was struck in the head, through the abdomen, and on his hand."[19]

Oddly, the official record made no mention of possible lawman involvement in the murder, or of any acts of cowardice on their part. The *Weatherford Exponent* of October 13, 1877, spoke its mind, however, saying "cattle stealing and murder were of a daily occurrence [in Comanche] and the offenders paraded the streets in open defiance of the law. At the time Webb was killed, the sheriff and deputy sheriff of the county were standing by and, it is said, had writs for Hardin in their pockets, yet neither prevented the murder, nor detained the murderers. The exasperated citizens therefore rose in self-defense and took the execution of the law into their own hands."

The Appeals Court examination described Webb as "a quiet, peaceable man, a brave and efficient officer," whereas "the appellant, John Wesley Hardin, has succeeded in achieving a remarkable and wide-spread reputation of sanguinary deeds. For years…he and his 'gang' were the terror of whole communities in different sections of western Texas, and the law long proved impotent to arrest their career, or afford protection to those who had incurred their easily earned animosity."

The record failed to state if John Wesley Hardin took the stand. He himself wrote the *Austin Gazette*, expressing confidence that the appeals court would overturn his conviction. "It is true the state of Texas has spent many dollars to convict me; but for a few dollars would the state of Texas rob me of my rights and privileges?"

In his shame, his frustration and his rage, he cried out, "I have been compared to the beasts of the forest; but, my dear readers, I am a human being, a native of the great state of Texas, and all I ask is law and justice, which I hope I will yet get."[20]

In the years since, Hardin biographers have sometimes stated that he went to prison for a killing that was probably self defense. The appeals court considered that issue too, and concluded that Hardin could not provoke an assault, that he could not enter into a conspiracy to kill someone and then claim self-defense as an excuse. It would make no difference even if Webb had fired first.[21]

The *Weatherford Exponent* saw it roughly the same way, writing "the doctrines of conspiracy and self-defense were the prominent law features of the case. The State attempted but failed to prove a conspiracy between Hardin and his gang to murder Webb, but the position, action and character of the parties…will convince most men that it was their [the Hardin party's] intention beforehand to [kill Webb]."

Had there been no conspiracy issue in the death of Webb, the verdict almost certainly would have been acquittal on the grounds of self defense. So it was not the act of killing Webb that sent John Wesley Hardin to prison. The jury believed Hardin provoked the fight, and that conclusion was sufficient for second degree murder. However, had there not been elements of self defense on Hardin's part, the jury might have found for first degree murder, and John Wesley Hardin would have gotten the rope.

Hardin maintained for the remainder of his life that Charles Webb had come over from Brown County to kill him, believing that Hardin "was drinking and at a disadvantage." He argued that he was tried "in a town in which three years before my own brother and cousins had met an awful death at the hands of a mob. Who…would like to be tried under these circumstances? On that jury that tried me sat six men whom I knew to be directly implicated in my own brother's death."[22]

Back in the Austin jail where he awaited the result of his appeal, Hardin encountered a couple of relatives. Manning Clements was awaiting trial on a charge of murder, and so was Brown Bowen after being arrested in Florida.

Of lesser note, the Texas outlaw John Ringo, fresh from the Mason County War of Texas, roomed nearby. Ringo would exit from this prison to Tombstone, Arizona, and begin his march toward national recognition as one of the West's premier gunfighters. In July 1879, Hardin wrote a now-free Manning Clements, saying he understood Ringo had been killed, and would Clements send him the details.[23]

State Prison

JOHN WESLEY HARDIN SPENT A YEAR in the Travis County Jail awaiting the appeal results, and he had much to think about, including a family now torn asunder. His wife Jane, ailing and too poverty stricken to return to Texas, did not leave Alabama until February 1878, and even then she and the three children initially lived with John's mother, Elizabeth. Hardin's father, James Gibson Hardin, had "died a praying" at his home in Red River County, Texas of unknown, but natural causes in August 1876 while John Wesley was on the run in Florida.

Now his mother, writing to her son in the Austin jail, urged him to be prayerful, to look toward the Heavenly Father for the light. She expressed a willingness to talk with her son's lawyers, insisting she "had a true statement of the killing of Webb written by your Pa." This assertion would explain how "we were all treated and how your poor Pa was destroyed,...dying before he could publish it." According to Preacher Hardin, "there was a plot made to kill you the very day Webb was killed." Since John's attorneys had already used this same rationalization before the Comanche jury, there is no evidence that his father's statement ever came in contact with the judge or the jury.[1]

Nevertheless, during this period in the Austin bastille, Hardin's spirits remained high, and he received visitors as if he were a

Joshua Robert "Brown" Bowen.
Photo likely taken in Alabama
or Florida, ca. early 1870s.
(Chuck Parsons Collection)

potentate instead of a prisoner. A Texas Ranger, who identified himself only as "Total Wreck," visited with the gunman and "found him to be a great talker." Hardin praised Texas Ranger John Armstrong as "a Texan of the old school, and said he had never been treated better by anyone in his life."[2] Lawmen just couldn't help but like Hardin.

BROWN BOWEN HAD JOINED HARDIN in the Travis County jail after being arrested at Pensacola, Florida on September 17, 1877, thanks to William Dudley Chipley who refused to let Texas get away with ignoring Bowen. Brown came by train to Austin, then transferred to Gonzales and stood trial on October 18 for the murder of Thomas J. Haldeman. After deliberating for one day, the jury found Bowen guilty of murder in the first degree, and sentenced him to hang. Bowen rose to hear the verdict, standing "pale, yet calm and collected, not a muscle quivering, quietly twirling his mustache. His hair was neatly combed and brushed back from his forehead, his brows were knitted together, and his glance was firm and unwavering."[3] Bowen had testified that John Wesley Hardin actually committed the crime, that Hardin had admitted his guilt in front of four witnesses in Florida.

The appeals court rebutted that Bowen had an opportunity to get depositions from the Florida parties, but did not. John Wesley Hardin was on standby in the Austin jail, and Bowen had never sought his testimony for cross-examination. The eight witnesses who did appear offered "evidence abundantly sufficient to sustain the verdict,…[that the crime was a] cold-blooded, deliberate, premeditated, and cruel murder committed by the defendant."[4]

While an appeals court studied the Bowen case, brothers-in-law Brown and Hardin got along relatively well. According to the newspapers, they were in the "best of spirits." However, on March 26, 1878, an angry Hardin wrote Jane that he was sorry to see her brother Bowen get the death penalty, but "he has tried to lay his foul and disgraceful crimes on me…."

Judge Everett Lewis officially sentenced Brown Bowen to hang in Gonzales, Texas, on Friday, May 17, 1878.

On April 13, the *Gonzales Inquirer* published a headline reading, *A Doomed Man Pleads His Innocence*. Brown Bowen again accused John Wesley Hardin of killing Thomas Haldeman because Haldeman spied for the Sutton faction. "I did everything I could to keep Hardin from killing him," cried Bowen. Brown claimed Hardin and Gip Clements purchased whiskey, oysters, sardines and crackers inside the Billings grocery, then Hardin called Bowen over and said, "I will show you how to kill a man." After the shooting, Hardin conferred quietly with Mac Billings, the fourteen-year-old boy whose eye-witness testimony regarding the shooting placed the noose around Brown Bowen's neck.[5]

Hardin responded to an article in the *Daily Democratic Statesman* saying he understood Brown Bowen had "stated before his God" that he (Bowen) was to be hung for another man's crime. Hardin pointed out that Bowen "was not convicted on circumstantial evidence" but by his own confession "as well as positive proof of an eye witness whose testimony was unimpeachable." Hardin growled that his load "was heavy enough without carrying Brown Bowen's." He then terminated the newspaper interview by apologizing for throwing the blame back on Bowen, but argued that "self-preservation is the first law of nature."

On May 15, two days before he died, Brown Bowen sent a final message to Hardin via the newspapers.

> On Friday, 17th of May, I have to pay the penalty of law for your crime. John, you know I am innocent of this deed. I ask you to clear my name for my children's sake. John, you know you have to appear before a God who knows all, and can you stand before that great tribunal and look on your God and say, 'I did not kill Haldeman.' You know you will have to say, 'I, John Hardin, did it, and allowed Brown Bowen to be punished for it.' If you do [not make a statement, my death] will be another of the dreadful murders which you will have to answer for.[6]

Before the execution, Brown's father Neill (who was also John Wesley Hardin's father-in-law), and Bowen's sister Martha visited Hardin in his Austin cell. Hardin wrote Jane about their discussion, saying he did not fault Jane's father and sister for trying to save Brown Bowen, but that "her pa wanted to know if there was a statement I could make that could save Brown." Hardin said no.

Apparently the two misunderstood him, for the next morning they reappeared at the facility and said they anticipated a confession from Hardin. When none was forthcoming, Martha sent him a note, pleading "You told me you would make a true statement about my brother. Oh God, why didn't you? Oh my God, my poor brother has to be hung. Oh my God, do something for him on my account."

"Let every tub stand on its own bottom," Hardin angrily wrote Jane. "For your sake I would do anything honorable and I know that you would not ask me to do anything dishonorable [but] I cannot be made a scapegoat of. A true statement will do your brother no good and a false one I cannot make. I forgive poor Brown for his false and unfounded reports and may God forgive him."[7]

The Bowen difficulty placed heavy strains on Hardin. While still confined in the Travis County Jail in Austin, his attitude and temper gave an indication of things to come. On May 10, Hardin nearly killed an elderly inmate waiter because Hardin had waited too long for his meal. The *Daily Democratic Statesman* grumbled that "This rash and uncalled for act is evidence that Hardin is not

William Longley
in handcuffs,
and his captors,
Bill Burroughs
and Milton A. Mast.
(Chuck Parsons
Collection)

lamb-like in his disposition, but capable of doing great harm over a trivial matter."[8]

The State hanged Brown Bowen on May 17, 1878 at the Gonzales jail, the same structure John Wesley Hardin had broken out of six years earlier. Four thousand witnesses saw Bowen step from the jail stairway out onto the platform. With the rope around his neck and the white hood over his head, Bowen called for a halt until he could write a letter to his wife. The hood and rope were removed, and Bowen scribbled a note advising her to keep their child away from bad company. The noose and hood went back on, and Bowen once more interrupted the proceedings, imploring Chaplain Seale to pray with him. This time the hood came off but the noose stayed on. As he and the preacher petitioned the Lord together, Bowen expressed anxiety that the trap door might open before he was ready.

Finally, even Bowen could not delay the event any longer, and the end came with him dropping seven feet and living (although unconscious) for four minutes. A statement released by the *Gonzales Inquirer* said "he knew all had sinned and all must suffer from sin. So far as the crime…was concerned, he did not fear the future. In the eyes of his Maker he was free from that sin. Guilty parties had sworn his life away, and their crime was the coldest, most brutal murder—a sin not easily to be forgiven."[9]

AS IF THE EXTRAORDINARY OCCURRENCES involving Brown Bowen and Wes Hardin were not enough during Hardin's stay in the Austin jail, another tempest—not quite as controversial but certainly as incredible—awaited in the wings.

This one involved the Texas outlaw William Preston Longley. Some accounts credit Bill Longley with killing thirty-two men, and those who knew Longley—or knew of him—seldom questioned it. As a murderous loner, he ranged from Salt Lake City, Utah, to St. Joseph, Missouri, and on to Wyoming—where he broke out of prison—before he returned to Texas and continued his bloody career.

Longley was a little taller and darker than Hardin, and nearly two years older. According to historian Doug Ellison, "both men would travel far and kill often,"[10] as they shared parallel careers. The law captured Longley in DeSoto Parish, Louisiana, on June 6, 1877 (two months prior to Hardin's capture in Florida), and tried him for an 1875 Giddings, Texas, murder of a boyhood friend, Wilson Anderson. The judge sentenced Longley to hang on October 11, 1878 at Giddings in Lee County. As Longley waited in the Galveston jail for news of his appeal, some fascinating newspaper correspondence occurred.

It started with Hardin languishing in the Austin jail and answering specific questions for the *Galveston News*. He denied ever breaking jail, said he never had anything to do with horse thieves and robbers, and had never associated with individuals who "were not men of honor." He denied knowing Bill Longley, and insisted that Longley and others had laid their crimes on him.[11]

Here was the innocent Hardin at his best, a desperado who had spent a lifetime avoiding violent deeds as well as harmful personalities and companions. And where was his thanks?

On October 29, the *Galveston News* printed Longley's response in the form of a letter to Sheriff Milton Mast. Longley commented on Hardin's boast that he would never be captured alive, snorting there "never was a man so fast but that he found a man just a little bit faster." As for men of honor, Longley wondered where those gentlemen friends of Hardin's might be now. "They certainly are not in jail where the honorable John Wesley is." Unlike himself and Hardin, Longley said, those honorable men "do not inhale the gentle breezes that flow through prison windows."

Longley defended Webb as a brave man, and accused Hardin of taking every cowardly advantage in killing Webb. The tall outlaw said it was "death by the law of Hardin for any man to say he was not afraid of Wesley Hardin." Speaking of himself, Longley wrote that he "had no help in my meanness when it came to killing a man," but with regards to the matter of honor, "neither Hardin nor myself are overburdened."

Displaying a bit of humor, Longley noted that "Wes Hardin says the people of Texas need not be afraid to turn him loose. I am like him about that. They need not be afraid to turn me loose either, for you may bet your sweet life that I would get fast and far away from Texas."

Longley closed by asking "don't you think it is a one-sided thing to kill me for my sins and give Hardin only twenty-five years in prison? But I guess he would say it is none of my business what they have done with him."

The *Nacogdoches News* also printed a letter with a comment about Longley's "considerable jealousy of John Wesley Hardin, both on account of the assumed superiority of the latter as a high-toned murderer, and that Hardin gets but twenty-five years while Longley is booked for that bourne from whence no traveler returns...."

The newspapers now ceased carrying the Hardin-Longley correspondence, perhaps because the two men resolved their hatreds. On February 23, 1878, John Wesley wrote his Uncle Robert E. Hardin, his closing remarks saying:

> I got the best letter the other day. It was from Bill Longley of Gv [Galveston]. He says...he sympathizes with me. Besides, he says, there is hope for me, but as for himself that he will die game. [The letter] is well-composed.[12]

IN EARLY JUNE 1878, JOHN WESLEY HARDIN learned his appeal had been denied. He denounced the appeals judge, insisting that the judge blamed the Comanche jury for not finding Hardin guilty of murder in the "1st degree." In his anger, frustration and self pity, Hardin swore to Jane that as the Jews had "set loose the guilty Barabbas and crucified Christ," so public opinion had done the same to him as it had Jesus. It was a convoluted way of thinking, but Hardin was now a convoluted felon.[13]

On the 20th of September, 1878, Lieutenant N. O. Reynolds and twenty rangers arrived to escort Hardin back to Comanche for his official sentencing. Major John B. Jones, commander of the Frontier Battalion, cautioned Reynolds about mobs threatening the life of Hardin, and wrote "I shall be much surprised to hear that Hardin or any other prisoner has been taken from you either by force or strategy."

The *National Police Gazette* of September 21, also referred to the notorious John Wesley Hardin as heading for Comanche to "receive his ridiculous sentence of twenty-five years. A heavy guard of state troops will accompany him to prevent lynching."

Hardin stepped outside the jail handcuffed and shackled to enter a two-horse wagon driven by a ranger. A newspaper described him as "unusually cheerful," a man who "laughed and talked with those around him."

His wife Jane had arrived from Gonzales County, and conversed aside with him for a few minutes. The same newspaper described her as "much affected at first [but she]…became more composed. She is a prepossessing lady of rather slight figure, and above the medium height, showing traces of care and sorrow upon her face."[14]

This should be of little wonder. Hardin had never been more than a part-time, detached husband and father. He had spent his married life gambling and running. In her brief time left, in poor health she grappled with raising and feeding three children. Her own kin turned their backs, and her husband's family barely assisted.

ON SEPTEMBER 28, HARDIN appeared a second time before Judge Fleming. When asked if he had any remarks before sentence was passed, Hardin made a lengthy statement, arguing that he had never threatened any Comanche citizen and protested again that he was incapable of homicide. Webb had gone down in self defense. Judge Fleming then made the sentence official, sending Hardin to twenty-five years imprisonment at hard labor within the stone walls of the state penitentiary. However, Fleming softened his tone and promised that if Hardin profited by moral instruction in prison, he Judge Fleming, at some future time, would "use his influence in procuring him a pardon."[15]

Now that the appeals court had upheld the verdict *and* the sentence, Hardin reversed his own opinion, "deciding that Judge Fleming's views were strictly correct. Any man guilty of the same act of which he had been proven guilty, ought to go to the penitentiary for at least twenty-five years." Hardin apologized for his own "stupid construction of the law," and departed for Huntsville.

The *Victoria Advocate* wryly noted that "It is likely Hardin's limited legal knowledge is entirely responsible for his career—had he known that killing was illegal, he might have done less of it."[16]

WITH FOUR PRISONERS, INCLUDING HARDIN, shackled by two's in a wagon, Hardin started toward Huntsville. The trip was a replay of his last few journeys. In Fort Worth, a procession of rangers, described as "armed to the teeth with breech-loading Winchesters, six-shooters, etc.," rode into the St. Louis wagon yard on Weatherford Street next to the hide house. Hardin climbed out of the wagon and shook hands for over an hour before guards eased him through the crowd.

After things quieted, Hardin sat down—Indian fashion—against the hide house, his left leg shackled to Nat Mackey, another murderer heading for Huntsville. A *Democrat* reporter found Hardin there. Squatting himself on a pallet of old coats and pants, he warmly shook the desperado's hand. Hardin, who had been described as "considerably bleached" during his confinement in the Austin jail, was now depicted as a "natural brunette type, tanned from his long journey in the sun." The reporter claimed Hardin made him "feel as comfortable and easy as though he had been sent to interview a minister of the gospel, instead of a man who rumors and reports have it, has killed a regiment."

"Wesley is what any lady would describe as being a fine-looking fellow," the reporter continued. "His worn and shabby clothes did not detract a jot or tittle from his rather handsome face. He had a fine well-developed forehead, and large brilliant, piercing, dove-colored eyes [warm gray with a slight purplish or pinkish tint], coupled with an equal amount of shrewdness and intelligence. Dark brown hair and mustache and chin whiskers, beneath which are a pretty set of white teeth, completes the pen picture of our hero's face. He stands about five feet nine inches, and weighs about one hundred and sixty pounds."[17]

As guards and prisoners took the Fort Worth train to Huntsville, clusters of curious people lined the track. Upon reaching the prison on October 5 (six days before Longley was hanged in Giddings), Hardin said convicts paused to gaze and wonder as he trudged through the gate. Then the officials bathed him, noted the scars and marks on his body, shaved him smooth and cut his hair. He now had his own stripes, was Convict #7109 and assigned initially to the wheelwright shop. The *Houston Item* announced Hardin's arrival at the penitentiary, and congratulated him "upon his escape from having to perform upon a perpendicular tight rope."[18]

A prison Certificate of Conduct listed him as arriving at twenty-six years of age, standing five-foot-nine, and weighing 160 pounds. The paper described his habits as "temperate," his education "common," and his occupation "laborer." He gave his residence as Gonzales County. Another prison file described him as having dark hair, hazel eyes and a fair complexion. It itemized wound scars on his right knee, left thigh, left side, right hip, right elbow, right shoulder, and back. Oddly, the sheet listed only seven wounds. There had to be at least ten. A prison doctor recorded his health as "fair." (When Hardin left the prison fifteen years later, it was still "fair." The sheets, except for the one mentioning scars, provided no details.[19])

HARDIN ENTERED THE PRISON AT HUNTSVILLE with escape on his mind, and noted that the armory was but seventy-five yards from the wheelwright shop. To reach it required tunneling under the superintendent's office as well as the carpenter shop. When the guards stacked their weapons and went to supper, Hardin and his confederates would break into the armory, grab

the guns and seize control of the penitentiary. All prisoners except "rape fiends" would be released. Incredibly Hardin said he
confided his escape plans to seventy-five lifers and long-term
prisoners. By November 20th they had completed the tunnel. At
this point, several convicts squealed, and Hardin had difficulty
understanding why. He could not believe prisoners would do
that. The authorities seized ten people, including Hardin. They
put a ball and chain on his ankle, tossed him into solitary and fed
him bread and water.

A letter to Jane on December 28, 1878, confirmed the break
attempt, Hardin saying that Jane might have read in the newspapers of how "I undertook to capture their [prison] armory with
50 other convicts." He claimed to be within two hours of success
when "the alarm was given by a convict or convicts," who identified Hardin as the leader. Hardin was "punished for the break,
spending five days in a dark cell. Still, the guards and convicts
treated him well and he had all the candles, extra grub, tobacco
and bedding he needed.[20]

John Hardin had charmed the guards just as he had charmed
lawmen. He was a state-wide legend. Hardin had charisma, he
could be likable. People preferred to forget the evil.

No sooner did he get released from solitary than Hardin and a
fellow prisoner named John Williams duplicated keys to each cell
on their row. On some dark night they planned to open the cells
one by one until reaching the prison gate. Hardin had a key to
that too. Anyway, John Williams talked, and one afternoon twenty
officers removed John Wesley Hardin from his cell, stripped him,
roped his hands and legs, and spread-eagled him on a concrete
floor. The *San Antonio Daily Express* of January 25, 1879, reported
that he "received thirty-nine lashes" across his back. With his sides
and back quivering and bleeding, Hardin walked through the
snow to an adjacent building where he was thrown into another
solitary cell and left three days without food or drink. After nearly
a week, with a high fever and unable to walk, Hardin transferred
to another cell for thirty days.[21]

On January 26, 1879, he wrote his wife, saying "I have not done
a day's work in 6 weeks since the break. My health has not been
good. I will be able to go to work in a few days. I have thus far
borne my troubles here the best I could and take all for the best

believing it is God's will or it would not be so. Don't bother about my punishment for I am doing as well as a man could do under the circumstances."[22]

The harsh discipline finally got John's attention, for on February 9, 1879, he wrote his wife, saying, "Jane dearest, I do not think they [the prison authorities] will ever have grounds to complain [about me] again, for my motto from this time on is to strictly obey all orders and do right. Let who will do wrong. The Sup says he will give me a fair trial, which if he does, & I hope [so], he never will regret it."

Still, John could not stay out of trouble. Hardin and a few others bribed a guard named Long. The *Austin Statesman* reported that four convicts tried to escape by way of the roof, but were caught. When the authorities searched Long's belongings, they found correspondence between him and the friends of John Wesley Hardin.[23]

All four convicts spent additional time in solitary. Hardin was flogged again, "but not so cruelly as before."

Hardin's Certificate of Prison Conduct made no mention of any attempted escapes, but it referred to eleven misconduct charges, and itemized six: "Mutinous conduct, conspiring to incite impudence—throwing food on floor—laziness—gambling—trying to incite convicts to impudence." The dates range from January 1879 to May 26, 1893. There is no reference to punishments.[24]

This could be explained. Hardin's last years show him as a model prisoner. He had charm and magnetism, and knew prison assistant superintendent Ben McCulloch from his trail driving days. It is credible to suspect that prison authorities believed Hardin had indeed reformed. They were not above "doctoring" the record to confirm fairly good behavior to the outside world.

The gunman's last known escape plan called for smuggling revolvers into the prison. As the plot jelled, Hardin at long last realized the unreliability of convicts. He withdrew from the scheme and gained some satisfaction when the plan failed and the plotters were rounded up. The authorities flogged all except Hardin.[25]

Interestingly, the *Express* shortly afterwards published a startling note that:

A gentleman who has just returned from a trip to the Huntsville penitentiary states that John Wesley Hardin, the notorious desperado now within its walls, has acknowledged the killing of Haldeman, for which deed Brown [Bowen] was hung at Gonzales about a year ago. It will be remembered that Brown charged the crime to Hardin upon the gallows, and call[ed upon] God to witness that he told the truth. He maintained his innocence to the last.[26]

Hardin vigorously denied the allegation in a follow-up letter to the *Gonzales Inquirer*. He challenged the *Daily Express* to reveal the name of the "gentleman" who has heard the so-called confession. "Please ask the press to give me a rest unless they publish the truth," Hardin wrote.[27]

ON THE FIRST OF FEBRUARY 1879, Hardin started work in the carpenter shop, but transferred out in June to the boot and shoe plant. By his own account, he became an outstanding fitter and cutter.[28]

Hardin worked in the shoe shop until the fall of 1883 when the shotgun wounds in the stomach administered by Phil Sublett in 1872 abscessed. He had long suffered from various wounds, including the one inflicted by Webb. Hardin wrote Jane in 1877, saying "I had a severe attack in my side but received good attention and [the pain] did not last long."[29] John Wesley said prison officials denied him a bed in the hospital, so he lay in his cell for eight months until recovering. Even then he refused to work until a bread and water diet brought a return of reason. After that, he made quilts in the tailor shop.[30]

The *Laredo Times* of September 12, 1884, stated "the health of the notorious John Wesley Hardin is very bad, and he is not expected to survive. He has served out five of his twenty-five year sentence."

Apparently John's well-being did not improve much, for on August 26, 1885, Hardin wrote Ben McCulloch, the assistant warden, with a desperate plea for medical assistance:

I once more earnestly appeal to you for [medical aid as] this disease or malady or whatever you may call it unfits me for any use. It seems that my life is threatened every moment and the final assault is likely to be made at any time. I have for two years patiently bore all with Christian fortitude. I don't know whether I have Bright's Disease, cancer or heart disease or whatever else it is, but it gives me much pain beyond description...I am wasting away of this disease and have suffered for two years....I have no disposition to complain unnecessarily. I may be beyond the point where a cure is possible but I hope not. I do believe with common sense treatment my condition could be greatly improved. That I have an internal disorder no one can deny and that my heart, lungs, liver and kidneys are affected I have little doubt. Please see Major Goree [the prison superintendent] and tell him that I have become incapacitated and ask for humane treatment or at least a place where I can bear my pain & suffering unmolested. I have been trying to work [but] I can do very little. I do not wish to be worked to death nor punished to death for my immobility. The court passed sentence on me for 25 yrs in the penn and unless you see that I am treated in a different manner I fear I shall not be able to serve out the 25 yrs. To make a long story short, I am sick, I am suffering death by degrees and ask you to take cognisance of the fact. I make this plain unvarnished statement to you hoping you will be favorably disposed.[31]

Apparently McCulloch saw to it that Hardin received medical attention, and the gunman improved.

But Hardin was learning even inside prison. In the fall of 1881, the *Burnet Bulletin* and the *Longview Democrat* noted that "The once notorious outlaw, a mere boy, dreaded by the State as a murderer, is now superintendent of the prison Sunday School in the state penitentiary at Huntsville. It is said by those who have visited the prison that John Wesley Hardin conducts the service in a very credible manner."[32]

Hardin became president and secretary of the debating team. On one occasion he wrote Jane, proudly exclaiming that he and a prisoner known as John S., had debated the merits of Women's Rights. The other felon believed women deserved the same rights as men, whereupon Hardin maintained just the opposite. Hardin said the judges, after observing his oratorical skills, "decided in my favor."[33]

He studied history, theology and the classics. In 1885, he wrote prison superintendent Thomas J. Goree for advice regarding civil and criminal law. The superintendent turned the letter over to Col. A. T. McKinney of the Huntsville Bar. McKinney responded with a long list of legal books.

On February 1, 1889 Hardin wrote to the "Lawmakers of Texas

Assembled at Austin." He suggested five specific prison reforms, especially in homicide cases, and a revision in the length and conditions of imprisonment. Hardin signed the petition first, and numerous convicts followed with their signatures.[34]

Perhaps part of Hardin's turnabout stemmed from his fifty-nine-year-old mother's failing health and death by natural causes in Ellis County on June 6, 1885. Throughout the years she had stoutly supported her son, praying for him, writing him faithfully, insisting to those who would listen that he was a victim and never the victimizer.

Jane Hardin and her three children had stayed with his mother throughout the early, difficult years of his incarceration. With very little money—and part of what they had, they sent to John—the two women formed an uneasy compact. By the early 1880s, the alliance unraveled. Jane and the children moved out, the reason appears to have been something Elizabeth Hardin said. John Hardin's subsequent letters insisted upon reconciliation as he urged each to forgive the other. He only partially succeeded, and their relationship up until his mother's death remained strained.

Hardin could write two letters a month, and receive mail only on Sunday. So he wrote in tiny scrawls, composing his letters with margins on the front and back. He then filled in the margins on the side as well as the ones at the top and bottom.

As for the subject matter, there are times in the Hardin letters when one is forced to wonder if he was consuming too much alcohol from the prison infirmary. Consider this 1888 missive to Jane:

> I belong to myself and God for all of my acts. I am responsible to myself and to my God for his laws are right. It has been said of me before I reached my majority, that I had vanquished E. J. Davis's [Reconstruction Governor of Texas] police from the Red River to the Rio Grande, from Matamoros to Sabine Pass, that I had defeated the diabolical agents and U.S. soldiers in many contests, and that I had invaded a foreign state [Kansas] and released from prison a dear, true friend [Manning Clements, his cousin], whose custodian was Wild Bill the Notorious, the redoubtable Bill Hickok of Abilene of whom no braver man ever drew a breath. As to the truth or falsity of these assertions, I have nothing to say, except that I have ever been ready to stand trial on any or all of these charges....[35]

Jane Hardin (left), 1880s. (R. G. McCubbin Collection) At right, Elizabeth "Mollie" Hardin. Mollie was the oldest daughter of John Wesley Hardin, and the one through which most of the present-day Hardin descendants stem. (Jo Foster Collection)

Rare was the letter that failed to mention, repeatedly, in detail and sometimes hysterically, that his slaying of Webb had been self-defense. Other messages were instructive, cautioning the receiver to trust God, to pray, to seek forgiveness, to turn the other cheek. Some letters were straightforward requests for the recipient to help free him from prison. These also included assurances that Webb's death had been justifiable. Not that anyone asked.

Pretentiousness surfaced in John's affected habit of closing with "Adieu, John Wesley Hardin." He sometimes used "Adieu" even when signing off to his mother and wife.

By the mid through the late 1880s, Hardin's letters to Jane were more on the rambling order of ranting and pompousness than reasonable statements. Here is how one letter to Jane opened:

> I greet you my beloved with a soft sweet good morning, my dear, and through you I desire to salute and embrace each of our dear precious children. Jane there is an old proverb which says "let every tub stand upon its own bottom." In this short but

Jane "Jennie" Hardin, (left), the youngest child. At right, John Wesley Hardin, Jr., early 1900s. (Harden/Hardin/Harding Family Association)

beautiful sentence I compare profound knowledge and it seems to me that it contains the very appeal of truth of justice and its wisdom cannot be questioned for it measures to everyone justice according to truth. Solomon has said "the fear of the Lord is the beginning of wisdom." The statutes of the Lord are right. It is not my purpose to pose before you today in an ostentatious manner as a hero or a philosopher or a scholar, far be it from me, but as in my true form but still as a man who in the past has had the fortitude of heart to fight all foes from whence or where they came....

Although many letters to her contained expressions of devotion and longing, particularly those written during the beginning of his term, plus repeated references of her faithfulness, towards the end they rarely were love letters so much as dictatorial tracts. As he settled into his prison sentence and realized (which took a while), that he had no chance of being released within two or three years, he often did not write for months, explaining that he "would have written long ago but I thought you had enough to think of at the present."[36] He derived comfort from Jane while it is difficult to understand how she could have drawn solace from him. He rarely if ever met—or understood—her emotional needs. The senselessness and frequent hysteria of his letters might strike reasonable persons as frightening, and while there may be a basis for none of her letters being saved, a studied conclusion leads one to suspect that—understandably—she rarely wrote.

Now and then Hardin asked Jane to read between the lines. He once apologized for a long period between letters, quietly commenting, "it was not on account of any unfaithfulness on my part," but that he wished to spare her some "disgraceful correspondence and something I cannot mention now." He closed by writing, "I hope it needs no more explanation."[37]

Hardin "probably" was referring to a series of homosexual acts involving him in prison. The behavior humiliated and disgraced him. Yet, though disgusted, he participated. He could not talk about it, could not defend it, and therefore could not write about it. At least a year went by without any letters to Jane. She probably learned of the practice through other sources: letters, comments by released prisoners, rumors. Even when she questioned him, he responded reluctantly, his letter revealing self-hate, a revulsion about discussing the subject, whatever it was.

On another occasion she apparently accused Hardin of deserting her and the children, evidently in Alabama. He responded by writing, "God forbid that I ever should desert loved ones. Circumstances may separate me from loved ones. Positions may keep me from writing to those I love dearer than life. Though separated, divided and surrounded by almost insurmountable difficulties, yet I say for a truth that I have never forsaken you for one moment in my heart. God knows that many a tear I have shed for you and my children. Silently in my cell to say nothing of those in public."[38]

HARDIN CAUTIONED JANE to "watch the children carefully, encourage them in healthful sports, make their home as pleasant as possible, don't scold them or grumble at them in order to govern them but rather rule them with kind words backed by reason and love." He asked his son John, not to be quarrelsome, "but to be kind and obliging to everyone, not to drink whiskey or go with rowdies, do not gamble but make an honest living for your ma and your sisters...."[39]

But this kind of letter was exceptional. On July 14, 1889, he wrote his daughter Jennie a long and bitterly wild letter protesting his unjust imprisonment for the slaying of Charles Webb, pointing out how his brother Joe and the Dixons were "insulted, silenced, and inhumanely treated by a midnight ribald mob who…tore them from the embrace of loving families. Amid the frantic screams of sisters and loved ones, they were led by a halter barefoot through the streets of Comanche to a temporary scaffold in the shape of an oak tree and there by the light of the moon swung into eternity."

Other Hardin letters were pontificating, sometimes frenzied, and often nutty. He wrote as if he were God instructing people not in the Ten Commandments, but in the Commandments of Religious Babble written by John Wesley Hardin himself.

John's correspondence, especially to his family, in the end were not so much tracts directed to others, as mirrors held up to himself. His letters were a way of maintaining sanity in the insane world of the state prison, or reassuring himself that he was not like the other prisoners, that he was unjustly convicted, and that goodness and integrity still flourished in the world because he saw so much of it in himself.

IN EARLY 1892 HARDIN SENSED imminent emancipation from his long imprisonment. He had started the process back in 1879 when he asked Manning Clements at least twice to circulate petitions for his release. In January 1888, Hardin sent a note to J. G. Smith, Assistant Superintendent of the Huntsville Prison:

> Please be kind enough to inform me when my time will be up providing my conduct remains excellent as I wish to make application for pardon and everybody wants to know just when I will be turned loose. I have been asked a hundred times in the last month, "John when are you going out," not only by convicts but by men with work clothes on. Of course, you are aware that my relatives are anxious to know. So please give me the information now. Obediently and respectfully, John W. Hardin.

A response scrawled across Hardin's note, replied:

> You continue to behave yourself, and you will go out at the proper time. J. G. Smith, Asst. Supt.[40]

Governor
James S. Hogg
started the ball
rolling for
Hardin's release
from prison.

The proper time apparently arrived with the election of
Governor James S. Hogg in January 1891. Hugh Fitzgerald said
of Hogg that "he was for the underdog when the underdog had a
grievance." And John Wesley Hardin had felt like an underdog
for fourteen years.

By now, Hardin's attorney, W. S. Fly of Gonzales, fretted over
those other indictments scattered around Texas. Hardin could hit
the street tomorrow with a pardon, be immediately re-arrested
for ancient crimes, tried, and be back in the Huntsville penitentiary within six weeks. So Fly checked around and confirmed that
only the James Morgan killing in DeWitt County had relevance.

Why this case posed a threat when all other indictments had
been dropped, or were no longer outstanding, is unfathomable.
Hardin shot Morgan in 1873, and most officials considered it justifiable homicide. However, four years later in 1877, the county
abruptly indicted Hardin and steadfastly refused to quash it.
Hardin, and the newspapers of 1873, claimed Morgan went down
with a single bullet in the head. The indictment declared Hardin
shot Morgan in the neck and breast, inflicting "several mortal
wounds."[41]

Governor
Richard Hubbard.
(Archives Division,
Texas State Library)

That murder arraignment had to be resolved, so Hardin agreed to voluntarily return to DeWitt County. There the *Cuero Star* found him "cheerful, communicative and anxious to go to trial. He is of sprightly intellect," the newspaper said, "and has read law systematically for the past four years. He will likely practice this profession upon his liberation."[42]

Hardin's counsel wanted him to plead justifiable homicide, but Hardin prevailed and pled guilty to manslaughter. Attorney W. S. Fly, in "the most affecting scene ever witnessed in a court room," addressed the jury "in a very feeling manner." Hardin's presentation "brought tears to the eyes of nearly every one present." To cap off the performances, Jane Hardin, whom Hardin had not seen in twelve years, made an unexpected entrance and gave a tearful statement to the court. Hardin accepted a two-year manslaughter sentence on January 1, 1892. It would run concurrently with his present term. The prison assigned him a new number, No. 7712.[43]

On January 6, 1892, Hardin asked W. S. Fly to lead the charge for freedom, and Fly briskly responded that "I can get a thousand men in Gonzales County to sign an application to the Gov. for a full pardon. I believe you will justify my action by living a quiet and useful life. I have faith in your integrity and manhood and I do not believe it is misplaced."[44] Fly sent petitions to several counties, and found potent support for Hardin's release.

Hardin also wrote his boyhood friend, Attorney William B. Teagarden. Teagarden, with urging by Fly, obtained strong Hardin patronage letters from friends of the governor.

Petitions arrived from practically every county in East Texas, all containing dozens of male signatures. Judges, politicians and prominent business and professional men signed, as did twenty-six sheriffs attending a lawman's convention. Letters from private individuals gushed into Governor Hogg's office, all supportive.

In this respect, Hardin's rebellion during the early years turned out to work in his behalf. After beating his head repeatedly against the system, and coming up a loser, he reformed. He taught Sunday School, he studied law, he became a model prisoner. He had changed, paid the price, and believed he deserved to be released.

JANE DIED AT THE AGE OF THIRTY-FIVE on November 6, 1892, at Mound Creek (Sedan), Texas, probably of consumption. The Reverend J. B. Hardwicke, a pastor of the Baptist Church, said that to earn a living for herself and children, "she peddled laces and other articles of ladies wearing apparel," which was how she happened to call at the good pastor's residence. He described her as "both a lady and a Christian."[45]

John went on with life although he wrote to James Ben "Buck" Cobb, his brother-in-law, saying "He [John Wesley Hardin] who knew her best loved her most, at least with all his heart and no one knew better than she and no one knew better than he that his love was reciprocated."[46]

Although historians have generally taken John Wesley Hardin at his word, and treated the Wes-Jane relationship as one of sublime tragedy, of an undying love story cut short by fate, the truth is that this man and this woman hardly knew each other. They were kids when they met. Although married twenty years, John Wesley Hardin spent over fifteen of those either under arrest or in prison. During the remaining five, Hardin frittered them away in saloons, in gambling halls, at the race track, and in driving cattle and scrambling from the law. In short, he was never home. He spent as much time sleeping on the ground as in his own bed. He was a non-husband by choice, not by destiny and certainly not by chance or injustice. For a man who wrote his autobiography, there is very little evidence that he gave Jane or his children much thought except during incarceration, and even that attention was sporadic and more indicative of self love than sharing love. Killing people was the serious part of Hardin's life; being a responsible citizen, father and husband was not an option Hardin wasted minutes on except during periods of reflective intoxication or extreme prison boredom.

HARDIN SUBMITTED HIS REQUEST for a pardon on January 1, 1893. In a long, carefully worded statement he went over the 1874 Comanche events, how he had never plotted to kill Webb, and mentioning how mobs had taken the life of his brother and cousins. Hardin said a troop of rangers had to protect him in Comanche, and in an atmosphere like that, the State refused a change of venue. The account closed with Hardin citing chapter and verse from numerous law books, declaring himself justified in killing Webb, arguing that at worst it was manslaughter and not murder in the second degree. This too was vintage Hardin: fifteen years in prison, desperate to be free, and yet refusing to back down one inch from previous stands. He remained to the end as he had always thought of himself, "a warrior born of battle, a man who belongs to no man or set of men."[47] If he lived by rules, they would be his own.

He closed by asking Hogg to "grant me a pardon," saying that "my highest hopes, object, aim and ambition is to yet lead a life of usefulness of peace in the path of rectitude and righteousness."[48]

Mail poured into Hogg's office pointing out that Hardin now was the only supporter of three homeless children, all of whom needed their father. J. B. Cobb wrote the governor a tearful letter, saying Hardin's "only boy is expected to die."

> I found his two sisters working over their dying brother, soon to be left without father, mother or brother. Gov. Hogg please give them back their father as it is in your power do so. Mrs. J. W. Hardin died at my house. She worked and toiled for thirteen years to try to raise and educate her children. Her last words was Good Lord guard and protect my dear children for they have no mother or father to care for them now.[49]

The whole state seemed to applaud a pardon for Hardin. Only an occasional individual or newspaper expressed dismay, as did the editor of the *Gonzales Inquirer*:

> With surprise I have read sympathetic articles on behalf of John Wesley Hardin. [I was astonished] at the almost unanimous sympathy his speech created in the court room during his last trial. [I was astounded by] the fact that this man was once the terror of Cuero, DeWitt county, and West Texas, and large rewards were offered for his capture. But all seems to be forgotten, perhaps through his speech, gentlemanly appearance and declaring to be a reformed man. Nothing is more detrimental to a town than these fighting characters who terrorize whole counties, where panic-stricken businessmen close their stores to avoid difficulties. Honest hard working farmers stay away from towns and places of danger. We are well aware that a dead victim will never come to life again, no matter how much the perpetrator, after servitude perhaps, is condoned by the once terrorized and trembling citizen. I was a small schoolboy during John Wesley Hardin's best days in DeWitt county, but can remember well the deep seated dread and fear of this once famous outlaw. Your correspondent has got nothing personally against Hardin, he only wishes to express his surprise.[50]

The *Inquirer* had a legitimate point, but the populace had mellowed. It hoped Hardin had too.

The *Cuero Star* responded that the true object of punishment was to change the criminal. "After he has been transformed into a useful citizen, further punishment would be cruelty," the newspaper believed. The *Star* referred to penitentiary officials as "men of large experience with human nature in general and the criminal classes in particular." They had "pronounced Hardin a thoroughly reformed man," and the *Star* was willing to accept their decision.[51]

JOHN WESLEY HARDIN WALKED OUT of Huntsville a free man on February 17, 1894. The *San Antonio Daily Express* summed it up best: "For the first five years of his incarceration he was stubborn, sullen and vicious. It required five years of all kinds of prison torture to subdue him. He finally settled down...and during the past ten years he has been an exemplary prisoner."[52]

Wes Hardin had spent fifteen years, eight months and twelve days behind bars. After all that, the State released a forty-year-old-widower who had three children waiting for him, none of whom knew what he looked like.

Tell Wes to be a Good Man

JOHN WESLEY HARDIN REACHED Gonzales on February 19, 1894, two days after leaving Huntsville. John Wesley Hardin, Jr., picked him up at the train station and took him home to the neighborhood of Smiley Lake, twenty-five miles south of Gonzales. For whatever reason, Hardin arrived quite sick. Sheriff Richard M. Glover advised the press that John was too ill for interviews, but he would be in town next week and speak for publication.[1]

Hardin had not been home twenty-four hours, and already the local sheriff had signed on as his spokesman. As the Gonzales County chief lawman, Glover had strongly endorsed Hardin's release from prison. He had even intervened with Tom Bell, the sheriff of Hill County, who also supported Hardin's release, but resurrected the 1870 Benjamin Bradley murder indictment. Hardin had shot Bradley down in the street on a frigid night following a poker game that went sour. Now, years later, Bell planned to hold that obscure indictment over Hardin's head until John lived up to hopes and expectations.

Out of the goodness of his heart, Glover prevailed upon Bell to get the charges dropped. Bell thereupon wrote Glover, saying, "The case against John Wesley Hardin was dismissed," and no

Fred Duderstadt.
He kept the Hardin
children during the
John Wesley Hardin
prison years. (R. G.
McCubbin Collection)

other indictments exist in Hill County against him. "Tell Wes to be a good man, and keep out of trouble," Bell said.[2]

Hardin's children had resided with Fred Duderstadt, John's cow-punching buddy of Abilene days. Jane Hardin, after falling out with John's mother, lived most of her remaining years at the Duderstadt Ranch. She helped around the house for room and board, as most of her Bowen family had returned to the Florida/ Alabama region by the early 1880s.[3] While she actually died at the home of her brother-in-law, Buck Cobb, she went there only when she needed intensive care. The three children likely remained at Duderstadt's. Mary Elizabeth "Mollie" was twenty-one, John Wesley Hardin, Jr., eighteen, and Jane "Jennie" Hardin, sixteen years old. They grew up with the Duderstadt children.

After spending a brief week or two at Duderstadt's, John Wesley Hardin and the three children moved to Gonzales. However, the youngsters never warmed up to their father. They were grown and missed their friends. Mollie was especially restless as she and Charles Billings had delayed their marriage due to her father's request.

On March 16, 1894, six weeks after Hardin's release, at the urging primarily of Judge W. W. Fly, Governor Hogg granted John Wesley Hardin a full pardon, restoring his citizenship.[4] In sending Hardin the papers, Fly exhibited a curious sympathy and fascination with the former desperado. Like a father, he cautioned Wes to "turn your back upon a past with all its suffering and sorrow and fix your eyes upon the future. Make yourself an honorable and useful member of society. The hand of every true man will be extended to assist you in your upward course and I trust that the name of Hardin will be associated with the performance of deeds that will ennoble your family and be a blessing to humanity."

"You ought to read Victor Hugo's masterpiece, *Les Miserables*," Fly went on. "It paints in graphic terms the life of one who had tasted the bitterest dregs of life's cup, but his Christian manhood rose above it almost like a god and he left behind him a path luminous with good deeds."

On July 21, 1894, in the District Court of Gonzales County, a committee of attorneys examined and found Hardin acceptable and capable in his knowledge of law. The judiciary therefore licensed Hardin to practice in any of the state's district and lower courts. A man who had once been Texas's most noted fugitive, "now declared that his future life would be one of peace."[5]

CORRESPONDENCE AND NEWSPAPER HINTS EXIST of one or two murder cases that Hardin handled, plus the usual civil entanglements relating to arguments, brawls, family and business disputes that entwined locals briefly in the court system. Few residents had money, so they paid with barter. Hardin failed to keep Ramon Aguero out of jail for whatever he had done, but Aguero respected his attorney sufficiently to be grateful for his representation. Aguero instructed his wife to give Hardin the family wagon and two mares in compensation for attorney fees.

La Opinion Del Pueblo (a short-lived Gonzales newspaper), thanked Hardin with an editorial for his successful efforts on behalf of the Mexican-American community. The account provided no details other than Hardin representing six Mexicans who on October 6 had protected themselves and their families. They went to jail. In court, Hardin defended the group with such eloquence and spirit that the judge released three men and bonded the others out, their charges to be judged later.[6]

Cases like this might have made Hardin feel good in his heart, but they did little to inflate his bank account. Creditors constantly dunned Hardin for payments on law books, as well as debts accumulated at the local dry goods store.[7]

THE ELECTION SEASON OF 1894 STARTED quietly enough. Robert R. Coleman announced for sheriff at a gathering of the People's (Populist) Party during the week of March 8, pointing out he had served as a keeper of the jail and a deputy under Sheriff Richard M. Glover. The incumbent, Dick Glover, thanked his supporters and backed his deputy, Coleman.

A week later, William E. Jones, a former sheriff of 1871-72 vintage, announced as a candidate of the Democratic Party. My "qualifications and ability for such an office has been... unquestioned by all," he proudly boasted.[8]

When Jones asked Hardin for a written endorsement, Hardin not only refused, he advised Coleman of the discussion. Furthermore, he told Coleman of past Hardin/Jones indiscretions, and Coleman spread the word.

On October 11, Jones published a letter accusing Coleman of lying, of claiming that Jones "had turned Wes Hardin out of jail...to kill a Negro, [and] that I had accepted bribes to tamper with juries." Jones challenged Coleman to "turn on the lights, state FACTS."[9]

On the following day, John Wesley Hardin responded in the Gonzales *Drag Net* to "Bill Jones and his parasites." These "henchmen" were saying "all manner of hard and ugly things" about Hardin, all because John had accused Jones of "misleading, humbugging and deceiving the people of Gonzales County."

Hardin claimed Sheriff Jones had aided his escape from the Gonzales jail many years earlier. Furthermore, Hardin asserted he had once witnessed the sheriff beating a Negro prisoner. Having now revealed the Bill Jones "perfidy," Hardin wrote, "I dismiss and turn him over to you and the democratic party to deal with as you wish, not as he deserves."[10]

HARDIN GAVE HIS BLESSINGS to Coleman not because he knew or even liked the candidate but because he deeply respected Coleman's steadfast backer: Sheriff Richard M. Glover. The incumbent had proven his friendship and loyalty toward Hardin when he (Glover), with nothing to gain, talked Sheriff Bell into voiding the Bradley indictment in Hill County.

Considering Hardin's punitive relationship with black people in days past, why would he now take the moral high road and constantly emphasize Jones's brutality toward blacks? The answer lay in black votes. Blacks votes could elect the next sheriff.

Less than a week before the campaign ended, Jones published a letter decrying the notoriety given "to a convicted felon and publicly proved liar." He described Hardin as a man having "no character to lose," saying "Hardin's statements of the circumstances and methods by which he escaped from jail have been so varied and devious that it is like following the trail of a serpent to scotch him. Like most liars he tells a different tale every time...."[11]

When Jones won the November 6, 1894 sheriff's race by eight votes, Hardin closed his law office in Gonzales, left his children with Duderstadt (the children had been there most of the time anyway), and moved west toward Kerrville in the Hill Country. His twenty-year-old brother James (formerly Barnett) Gipson Hardin, known as Gip, taught school in nearby Junction.[12]

Meanwhile, over in DeWitt County, his daughter Mollie married Charles Billings on December 16, 1894. There is no indication that Hardin attended the wedding, or was invited.

TWO ADDITIONAL EVENTS ALSO LURED HARDIN WEST: one was a call for assistance from a cousin by marriage, Jim Miller, and the other was a letter written by a very young lady.

This very young lady's father, Captain Leonard L. Lewis, was an Englishman, a Union Army officer and a horse trader recently from Clay County, Illinois. Capt. Len, as he preferred to be called, married the Kimble County widow Mary Elizabeth "Bettie" Boyce Anderson. Lewis had ambitious dreams of turning northeastern Kimble County into a trade center rivaling Junction, Texas, a few miles south. He purchased a half-section, staked out forty lots and a public square. Capt. Len planned a modern community called "Bettie Lewis," for his wife, and this town would become the seat of "Schreiner," a new county. However, sufficient funds could not be raised for a survey, and the new county died aborning. Furthermore, the post office would not accept "Bettie Lewis," so Capt. Len renamed his town "London," after the city of his birth. He became postmaster and the local hotel owner.[13].

Carolyn "Callie" Lewis, was born in Burnet, Texas, on July 23, 1879, the fifth of six Lewis children. She had spirited manners, expressed herself intensely, was tall (about five foot eight), lean, with long, light brown hair, and blue eyes. She was essentially a beautiful woman.

In some respects, Callie resembled Jane. Both were teenagers when John courted them. Jane was mature and young, and John Hardin was reckless and young. Now, years later, Hardin was middle-aged and stumbling, and Callie was young and wild. In modern-day parlance, she would be a rock band groupie; in 1895 she was a desperado groupie. She had a young girl's attraction and fascination for older men who took what they wanted, who swept girls off their feet and off the farm. She was not ready for Hardin, but she thought she was.

How she and Hardin became acquainted is unknown, although a good bet is that they met at her father's hotel. She wrote John on October 30, 1894:

> Mr. Hardin:
> I guess you will be a little bit surprised to receive a note from me. Either that or think me cheeky to address you first but you told me if I wanted to see you to let you know so I will tell you that I expect you [for] New Year's. Come and I will be glad to see you.
> > Your friend,
> > Callie Lewis

On January 1, Hardin apologized for missing the New Year's party because of "bruises he received in a runaway the evening I left you." Evidently he had asked her to marry him. He referred to her as "dear," and said "You know my proposition so please let me hear from you at your earliest...."[14]

Callie answered promptly, writing "You spoke in your letter about the proposition you made. I will say that I don't like to

Callie Lewis, second wife of John Wesley Hardin. The marriage lasted less than a week, but neither Callie or Hardin ever sought a divorce or annulment. (Bobby McNellis Collection)

answer such questions by letter. I would rather see you yourself. Come as soon as you can."[15]

Apparently Hardin healed in a hurry for the couple married at London, Texas on January 9, 1895. She was fifteen and one-half, and acted every bit of it; John Wesley Hardin was forty-one, and feeling every day of it.

Hardin had lost nearly sixteen years of his youth in the state prison. He must have thought his adolescence was simply dormant until recalled; he did not realize until now that it was gone forever. Furthermore, the headstrong, tempestuous nature of Callie, which had originally charmed and fascinated Hardin, was starting to irritate him.

The wedding party planned to go from London to Junction, and take the stage to Kerrville. All that's known for certain is that they married in London, and got as far as Junction. Whether they went on to Kerrville is questionable. Stories abound that Callie refused to live with Hardin because of the age differences. Jeff Hardin, a member of the wedding party, made a jesting remark about his older brother marrying a child, and that set her off. Callie's mother reinforced that point of view when she wrote Hardin, saying "I believe that if you had not met up with your brother and sister when you started off, that you and Callie would have been living together now, but of course you know more about that than I do."[16]

Other stories indicate that Hardin won Callie in a poker game, that her father paid his gambling debt by offering his daughter in marriage.[17] But that hardly seems likely since the elder Lewis's own letters reveal a spoiled Callie, a young lady knowing her own mind and unresponsive to parental influences. Captain Lewis not only approved of the marriage, he reveled in it, likely figuring that an older man could support and keep his daughter under control. He also apparently reveled in the prospect of a famous son-in-law.

Within hours of the marriage, or certainly within a week or two of the vows, John Wesley Hardin returned Callie to her parents. An exchange of letters commenced. Hardin hoped Leonard and Bettie Lewis would intercede in his behalf, that they would reason with their rebellious daughter. He showed remarkable patience.

The father-in-law wrote Hardin on January 16, assuring him that "if you have got a friend in the United States, it is Capt. Len L. Lewis." He called Hardin "a thoroughbred gentleman for the treatment you gave Callie at Junction City, and I will never so long as we both may live forget you for that kindness. Callie in my belief will be all right in a short time," he said, "and my sincere wish for her is to be with you at an early date which I have all reason to believe will come to pass. You are never off Callie's mind day or night."

Bettie Lewis wrote Hardin on March 4, saying Callie was washing clothes and seemed down-hearted. She had gone to a dance with a man, but otherwise stayed home most of the time. Mrs. Lewis mentioned that Callie needed clothing, the implication being that Hardin should send money. The letter ended on a positive note that someday he and Callie would "be living happy together."

Captain Lewis also wrote on March 4 to "Dear son and friend," saying he had received John's letter, and that "Callie is just as you left her. She is full of hell—we keep her at home but the devil is in her. What and how she will come out is more than I can tell."

On March 23, Lewis wrote again, mentioning that he had received Hardin's letter, but was "waiting to see if there was any change in Callie. I see no change in her. She seems just as you left her. You said in your letter that you wanted me to be plain in the matter. I don't think she will [ever] become satisfied with you…[so] we might as well let the matter sleep."[18]

The marriage ended there. In 1906, Leonard and Bettie moved to McCulloch County, then homesteaded in Montana. Captain Len died on a train in 1923, and was buried in Soldiers Cemetery, Arkansas City, Kansas.

As for Hardin and Callie, the couple may have exchanged correspondence afterwards, but they never lived together and probably never saw each other again. No divorce or annulment papers have been located. In 1898, the widow Callie Lewis Hardin wed a country physician, Dr. Perry Allen Baze. He was nearer her own age. They had one son, Seth, before she divorced her husband for adultery in 1915. She worked briefly as a hotel hostess in Mexico City, then returned to San Antonio. Finally she joined the Presbyterian Church and settled in Mason, Texas, near her three great-grandchildren. Callie died of congestive heart failure in Mason at the age of eighty-four on September 30, 1963. Interment took place in Mission Burial Park at San Antonio. She never spoke of John Wesley Hardin.

JUST A FEW MILES DISTANT FROM JUNCTION in what was then called Pecos City, James Brown Miller had a need for the talents of John Wesley Hardin. Miller was one of nine children, being born in Arkansas in 1861. His family moved to Texas. By 1884, Jim Miller had slain his brother-in-law, John Coop. A jury gave Miller life, but lawyers reversed the judgment on appeal. Miller never went back to trial.

Instead Jim Miller showed up in McCulloch County where Mannen "Manning" Clements hired him as a cowboy. Here he met his future wife, Sarah Frances "Sally" Clements, the daughter of Manning.

Manning, who had spent a brief time in the Austin jail with his cousin John Wesley Hardin, was acquitted at his murder trial. He became one of the few relatives to visit Hardin in prison, to show genuine concern, and to do what he could in assisting Jane and the children. However, Manning's time on earth ended abruptly when Joe Townsend, a deputy sheriff in Ballinger, shot him dead in a saloon on March 27, 1887. Manning's son, Emanuel "Mannie" Clements, Jr., was nineteen.

Someone ambushed Townsend shortly afterwards, shooting off his arm and sending him into retirement. Suspicion focused on Jim Miller, but nobody was ever indicted.

Sally Clements and Miller married in McCulloch County on February 15, 1888. This union made shirt-tail relatives out of John Wesley Hardin and James Miller, two of the most complex, murderous men in the American Southwest. Jim, with his wife Sally, and her mother and brother Mannie, visited Pecos shortly thereafter.

Miller was an immaculate dresser sporting a black frock coat, white shirt with stiff collar, a stick pin and diamond ring. The manners of this soft spoken, polite man were impeccable, and it is said that he went to church, never smoked, never swore, and seldom drank. Folks who prayed with him, called him "Deacon Jim." Those who knew him better called him "Killin Jim."

In Pecos, Miller met the Reeves County Sheriff George A. "Bud" Frazer, a man twenty-seven years old, a former Texas Ranger born in Fort Stockton, Texas. Frazer appointed Jim Miller as a deputy, then dismissed him when Miller killed a Mexican prisoner. Miller campaigned against his boss in the elections of 1892, but was easily defeated. Unfazed, Miller applied for the job of city marshal, and got it. He appointed his brother-in-law Mannie Clements as his night deputy.

On May 22, 1893, Con Gibson—an itinerant saloon patron—warned Frazer that Miller, Mannie Clements and Martin Q. Hardin (no provable relation to John Wesley Hardin, although they referred to each other as cousins),[19] planned to kill him. The sheriff wired for Texas Ranger Capt. John R. Hughes, and Hughes arrested Miller, Clements and Martin Hardin. Indictments of September 7, 1893, charged the three with "unlawfully conspiring...to kill and murder G. A. Frazer." When the case transferred to El Paso, Con Gibson, the primary prosecution witness, fled to Eddy, New Mexico. There, John Denson, a gunman and a cousin of

James Brown "Killin Jim" Miller. He and Hardin were relatives through marriage but both had killing records that still remain virtually unequaled throughout the American West. (R. G. McCubbin Collection)

Miller and Hardin, caught Gibson in a saloon and shot him dead. The State at El Paso had no case, and Miller, Clements and M. Q. Hardin walked free.[20]

Frazer ran for re-election in 1894, and lost. On December 26th, he and Miller met in the street. Miller wore a metal breast-plate under a heavy black frock coat. After a couple of bullets hit Miller in the chest and knocked him down, Frazer walked away, assuming he left a dead man behind. Someone hauled Miller away for convalescing.

Over in Kerrville, John Wesley Hardin, anxious to move on and recognizing that he and Callie Lewis were through, wrote Miller a sympathetic letter offering legal assistance. Miller's wife Sally responded on January 26, 1895. She said her husband was still recovering from his recent wounds, but Hardin should hear from him soon. "Where will you be in a few weeks, say three weeks?," she asked. "We want you by that time sure."[21]

In March, Hardin arrived in Pecos, and filed charges of attempted

James Miller telegram to John Wesley Hardin. (R. G. McCubbin Collection)

Telegram from Miller to his wife, Sallie. (John McNellis Collection) murder against Bud Frazer. The former sheriff obtained a change of venue to El Paso. Hardin and Miller followed.

The Frazer trial concluded at El Paso in mid April with a hung jury, four for acquittal and eight for guilty. Whether or not Miller ever saw his cousin John Wesley Hardin after that is doubtful. He paid Hardin with an engraved pocket watch and a .38 caliber self-cocking Colt.

The next trial of Frazer took place in Colorado City, Texas, where a jury acquitted the defendant on May 20, 1896. Killin Jim then bided his time and sent Bud Frazer into eternity on September 14, 1896, when he caught the ex-sheriff relaxing at poker in a Toyah, Texas, saloon. Death came instantly following a shotgun blast. A jury acquitted Miller, and he went on to other assassination plots, his string of murders running out on April 19, 1909, when Ada, Oklahoma, vigilantes removed him from jail and lynched him from a barn rafter.

El Paso

IN 1895, THESE GUNMEN WERE RESIDENTS of El Paso—
George Scarborough, Jeff Milton, Martin M'Rose, the John
Selmans (Sr. & Jr.), Tom Fennessey and the curly-wolf of them all:
John Wesley Hardin.

THE WESTERN FRONTIER had vanished everywhere except at
isolated communities such as El Paso. Bordertowns attracted the
best and the worst, acting as magnets for ruffians one step ahead
of the sheriff.

El Paso in 1895 had 13,000 people, twice as many as Ciudad
Juarez, Chihuahua, its Mexican neighbor across the Rio Grande.
El Paso Street served as the commercial center of town, extending from Pioneer Plaza to the Rio Grande. Most of the other streets
simply branched off. A few well-to-do residents moved north of
the Southern Pacific tracks into Piety Hills, as locals called it, but
that area showed few signs of spectacular growth.

With the arrival of the railroads in 1881, El Paso had become
"Americanized," shifting from an adobe community to one of
brick and occasionally wood. Only 20 percent of the population
had Hispanic surnames, which meant El Paso was an island of
Anglo-Americans due to the railroad hubs and Fort Bliss, plus a
strong influx of miners, gamblers, prostitutes, professional people
and health-seekers.

El Paso street scene, 1880s, before the arrival of John Wesley Hardin. Hardin's law office would have been opposite the four-story building on the right. (Aultman Collection, El Paso Public Library)

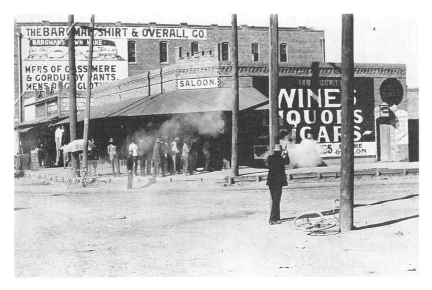

A gunfight occurring in El Paso after the turn of the century. Participants unknown. (Aultman Collection, El Paso Public Library)

John Selman and his son, John Selman, Jr. Photo
likely taken in Fort Davis, Texas, during the late
1870s. Prostitutes in El Paso had access to this
picture. They marked a big X on Selman's crotch.
(R. G. McCubbin Collection)

And so it was that El Paso's two conflicting political and moral
forces collided with no hope of reconciliation. One was the long
established liquor, prostitution and gambling interests. The other
lumped together as the Reform Movement, frequently paraded
by torchlight through dusty streets to the refrain of "Onward
Christian Soldiers." They demanded nothing less than the abol-
ishment of the sinful, lustful, advocates of the devil, as represented
on earth by liquor, prostitution and gambling.

ONE OF THE LATTER DEVOTEES was John Henry Selman, who left Arkansas to settle in Texas. He married, deserted the Confederacy, and wandered over to Fort Griffin, Texas, where at times he played the part of a vigilante and at other times, the person the vigilantes sought to hang.

As a deputy, Selman allied himself to the Shackelford County sheriff, John Larn. As lawmen they enforced ordinances, rustled cattle and did whatever was needed to steal a dollar. Their association ended in June 1878 when the vigilantes locked Larn in his own jail and shot him to death. Selman headed for a safer locale.

He thereafter drifted into Lincoln County, New Mexico, where he organized cutthroats called "Selman's Scouts." Throughout 1878 and 1879, they plundered and raped until the countryside rose up in anger and disgust, and decimated the gang. Selman was again on the run, appearing next in Fort Davis, Texas, where he caught the Mexican Black Smallpox. Since his wife had died, he and his two boys, William "Bud" Selman and John Selman, Jr. disappeared into Mexico. There old John married a woman named Niconora Zarate in San Pablo.

In 1888, John Selman migrated to El Paso where he and his sons briefly worked at the smelter. On November 8, 1892, during general elections, Selman campaigned as a Democrat for the position of El Paso constable, and the Democrats swept the city. Selman was about five ten, rather skinny, with dark but graying hair, and a prominent nose with mustache underneath. His holstered six-shooter hung in front and away from the coat so that everyone could see it, the belt sagging somewhat, the trigger guard high and open to accommodate a fast draw. A tin star adorned the left side of the chest, and the requisite heavy, gold watch chain dangled across the vest.[1]

The thirty-two-year-old Niconora died in El Paso on October 9, 1892. Less than a year later, on August 23, 1893, the fifty-four-year-old Selman, now known as "Old John" or "Uncle John," married the sixteen-year-old Romula Granadino, a ward of Selman's first deputy, W. H. Wheat. The two Selman boys continued close relations with their father, but they moved into another house.

Selman had always been good with a gun, as attested to by a half-dozen or more graves behind him. Two more still loomed ahead. The third would be his own.

The next Selman killing involved an ex-Texas Ranger named Baz Outlaw, a pugnacious young man of average height who learned cowboy and gun-handling skills in turbulent Kimble County, Texas during the 1880s. He could be gentle when sober but dangerous when drinking…and drinking was the fundamental reason he no longer rode with the rangers. Outlaw had recently taken employment as a United States deputy marshal earning his living predominately by serving legal papers under the general supervision of West Texas Marshal, Richard C. "Dick" Ware.

Outlaw rode into El Paso on April 5, 1894, to act as a court witness. After drunkenly wandering up Utah (later Mesa Street), he encountered John Selman and Englishman and buffalo hunter, Frank Collinson. Together, they strayed over to Tillie Howard's Parlor House because Baz wanted to see "Ruby."

Upon entering the parlor, Selman and Collinson seated themselves while Outlaw stumbled off to the toilet. A few minutes later, a shot thundered through the house, and Selman jested, "I guess Baz dropped his gun."

When trouble occurred in the brothels, madams rushed outside and called the police by blowing a whistle. Tillie dashed toward the back yard with Outlaw in pursuit, blowing hard even before she cleared the rear door. They struggled in the yard for possession of the whistle. Joe McKidrict, a Texas Ranger in town testifying before a grand jury, heard the commotion, vaulted the fence, separated the two, heard Tillie's story, and chastised Outlaw.

John Selman had by now reached the back porch as Outlaw screamed at McKidrict, "Do you want some too." With that, he shot the ranger point-blank in the head, then fired again as he fell.

Selman drew and jumped off the porch, he and Outlaw firing simultaneously from close range. The constable's bullet whacked Outlaw over the heart, whereas Outlaw missed Selman, but the gunpowder spray blinded the constable. While Selman hollered and sightlessly stumbled about, Outlaw reeled backwards toward the adobe wall where he propped himself up and fired twice more. Both bullets struck Selman in the right leg. One round severed an artery.

Chief of Police Jeff Milton and United States Deputy Marshal George Scarborough during their El Paso years, early to mid-1890s. In those days, a large part of an officer's income stemmed from the incarceration of military deserters. (Author's Collection)

As Selman crawled off to bleed, Outlaw tumbled over the wall and staggered up Utah Street where Ranger Frank McMahan, hurrying to the scene of the shooting, half-carried and half-dragged him inside the Barnum Show Saloon at the corner of Overland and Utah. Onlookers stretched him out on the bar. A doctor shook his head, so saloon patrons toted the ex-ranger to a prostitute's bed in the backroom where he expired four hours later, screaming, "Where are my friends?" One bystander described Outlaw as the only man he had ever seen who died in mortal terror.[2]

Outlaw was buried in El Paso. Selman hurried by carriage to the office of Dr. Alward White, who patched him up. From that time on, John Selman lacked clear vision, and walked with a cane. On October 30, 1894, the State tried him for murder. However, the district attorney requested a directed verdict of acquittal, and Judge Charles N. Buckler obliged.[3]

Ely Poole,
Cicero Scarborough
and his brother
George Scarborough,
Jones County, Texas,
where George was
sheriff. Ely and
Cicero were deputies
under George.
(R. G. McCubbin
Collection)

THE CITY OF EL PASO SWORE Jefferson Davis Milton in as police chief on August 10, 1894. Jeff Milton, born on November 7, 1861, a son of Florida Governor John Milton, spent much of his life as a lawman, serving at one period or another as a sheriff, a Texas Ranger, police chief, customs officer, and a United States marshal. Milton was chubby, dark with jet-black eyes, well-combed hair, and bushy mustache. He was a conductor for the Southern Pacific when El Paso Mayor Robert F. "Bob" Johnson wired the thirty-two-year-old Jeff Milton at St. Louis and offered him the police chief's position. Milton accepted, and later that year, at the instigation of John Selman, Jeff Milton hired the twenty-one-year-old John Selman, Jr., as a policeman.[4] The police officer would generally be called "Young John" to differentiate between him and his father, "Old John."

GEORGE SCARBOROUGH PROVIDED another link in a chain that would soon envelop John Wesley Hardin. He was born in Louisiana in 1859 and became a man of medium height with

Martin M'Rose
and Tom Fennessey,
in a photo likely
taken in Juarez,
Chihuahua,
around 1894.
(Author's
Collection)

straight sandy hair, pale blue eyes, and the traditional bushy mustache. After becoming sheriff of Jones County, Texas, and killing A. J. Williams, he lost the next election and was appointed a deputy marshal for West Texas by Dick Ware. Scarborough reached El Paso during late June, 1893.

Scarborough married Mary Frances McMahan, and fathered several children. Her brother, Frank M. McMahan, also moved to El Paso, and joined the Texas Rangers in nearby Ysleta. While retaining his ranger status, he too signed on as a deputy U.S. marshal.[5]

This left only Martin M'Rose, his wife and his nefarious friends as the final El Paso players involved in the Hardin drama. Martin M'Rose migrated out of Saint Hedwig, a Silesian settlement east of San Antonio where the family spelled the name Mroz. El Paso and New Mexico newspapers used M'Rose, Morose, and Monrose. Martin and his wife Beulah consistently wrote it as M'Rose, making the heritage look Irish or Scottish instead of Polish, but nevertheless that spelling tradition will be continued here.

Constable
John Selman
in an El Paso photo
probably taken
before his gunfight
with Baz Outlaw
(note absence
of cane).
(R. G. McCubbin
collection)

He spoke with a Polish accent, and was an intelligent, stocky, dark blond, blue-eyed, nice-looking man probably in his twenties. As a youngster he became a cowboy in southeastern New Mexico. He also acquired an addiction for horses, cattle and hogs belonging to other people.

M'Rose hung around Seven Rivers, New Mexico, although he was no stranger to the Eddy County seat of Eddy (now Carlsbad), and the sin town of Phenix. The latter sprouted on the doorstep of Eddy, a transient village of brothels and saloons made possible when Eddy refused to legitimize liquor and wild women.

While M'Rose had some standing as a badman, whether or

Beulah M'Rose
and son Albert.
Photo may have
been taken in
El Paso or Phenix,
New Mexico, during
the early 1890s.
(C. L. Sonnichsen
Collection)

not he deserved it is debatable. He himself hinted, and even bragged about various killings, but no confirmation is on record.

Tom Fennessey and Vic Queen were two of M'Rose's closest New Mexico friends. Fennessey campaigned for Eddy county clerk in 1890, and won. He was a hard drinker and a tough, trail-driving cowboy who killed a man at Seven Rivers. Vic Queen was a medium-size, lean man with a square head, dark hair and mustache. Like M'Rose, he tilted toward blustery speech.

In 1894 or early 1895, M'Rose met and married the twenty or twenty-one-year-old blue-eyed blonde, historically known as Helen Beulah. As a prostitute working West Texas and southeastern New Mexico, she reportedly wed Martin at the sheriff's whorehouse at Eddy, New Mexico. While she has consistently been described as an "outstanding beauty," the one known photograph reveals an attractive but plain woman, thin, somewhat washed-out and showing the strains of her occupation. She had a five-year-old son named Albert, presumably fathered by someone other than Martin since the two adults did not likely meet that long ago. Helen Beulah M'Rose was intelligent, fairly-well educated, conniving, and inclined toward disorderliness. Her maiden name, and where she came from, are as obscure as whatever eventually happened to her.

Just Return
What I Lost

ON MARCH 30, 1895, THE *EL PASO HERALD* announced a stranger's presence in the city, and referred to him as "one of the most noted characters in Texas."

A week later, the *El Paso Times*, in a rather ominous article, mentioned that several Pecos people, including John Wesley Hardin, were in town, heavily armed, and in attendance at the Frazer trial. They "will no doubt be taught," the *Times* growled, "that El Paso has her own peace officers. The day for man killers in this town has passed."[1]

Having said that, the *El Paso Times* was more effusive a week later:

> Among the many leading citizens of Pecos City now in El Paso is John Wesley Hardin, Esq., a leading member of the Pecos City bar. In his younger days, Mr. Hardin was as wild as the broad western plains upon which he was raised. But he was a generous, brave-hearted youth and got into no small amount of trouble for the sake of his friends. He soon gained a reputation for being quick tempered and a dead shot. In those days when one man insulted another, one of the two died then and there. Young Hardin, having a reputation for being a man who never took water, was picked out by every bad man who wanted to make a reputation, and there is where the "bad men" made a mistake. The young westerner still survives many warm and tragic encounters. Forty-one years

has steadied the impetuous cowboy down to a quiet, dignified, peaceable man of business. Mr. Hardin is a modest gentleman of pleasant address, but underneath the modest dignity is a firmness that never yields except to reason and the law. He is a man who makes friends of all who come in close contact.[2]

Without any doubt, Hardin paid for the *Times* advertisement, which was what it was. It announced Hardin's presence in the Pass city, modestly pointed out how, throughout his lifetime, he had opposed evil, in the process shouldering the burdens of friends and fellow men. He still fought against injustice, wherever it might be found. Nowadays, he did his scrapping the civilized way, in the courtroom. His last unpretentious line noted that he was just one of the guys, approachable either for a drink, or to discuss legal matters.

WHILE HARDIN REVELED IN HIS PUBLICITY, Martin M'Rose sold his ranch eighteen miles from Eddy, and came to El Paso with several thousand dollars in cash, his wife Beulah, and his pal Vic Queen. They fled into Juarez, Chihuahua, as New Mexico officers accused them of rustling livestock. On March 26, Mexican authorities jailed Vic Queen.

M'Rose slipped away from the city as every lawman in the El Paso region—after getting current figures ($250 reward) on their man—searched for him in two countries. Beauregard Lee, a Santa Fe Railroad detective, saw Beulah purchase a train ticket in Juarez for Magdalena, Sonora. Since he was out of his jurisdiction, Lee talked Juarez Chief of Police Haro into accompanying him on the train. They rode a few seats behind Mrs. M'Rose.

As Martin M'Rose greeted his wife in Sonora on April 6, Lee stuck a six-shooter under the outlaw's chin while Haro handcuffed him. Beulah reached for a revolver in her blouse, but a passenger wrenched it away. A search of Beulah turned up a bankroll of eighteen hundred and eighty dollars, which the Mexican officers confiscated.

With Martin in cuffs, and perhaps Beulah too, the party returned to Juarez where the officers locked Martin in the same jail with Vic Queen. They released Mrs. M'Rose.

She retained attorney John Wesley Hardin to represent her husband and to get her money returned from the Juarez officers.

JOHN W. HARDIN Esq.

ATTORNEY AT LAW

OFFICE:
200½ El Paso
Wells Fargo Bldg.

PRACTICE IN
ALL COURTS

John Wesley Hardin's El Paso business card.
(R. G. McCubbin Collection)

El Paso Wells Fargo Building during the 1890s at El Paso and San Antonio streets. Hardin's law office was on the second floor, immediately to right of center telephone pole. (State National Bank Collection)

Hardin had a second floor Wells Fargo Building office at the southeast corner of San Antonio and El Paso streets. Justice of the Peace Walter D. Howe rented the corner office next door.

Hardin retained a Mexican lawyer, and also talked the American consul in Juarez into intervening on his client's behalf. Between the three of them, they forced Mexican officials to refund Beulah's money. She now had between two and three thousand dollars, plus other funds previously socked away.

New Mexico lawmen started extradition proceedings against the outlaws. The process continued until early May when Mexican authorities declared that extradition would not be granted. Hardin and the Mexican lawyer had spread sufficient money around, and M'Rose and Queen were now being considered for Mexican citizenship.[3]

The Mexican Supreme Court ordered the release of M'Rose and Queen, having found no evidence of cattle rustling sufficient for conviction in Mexico. The outlaws remained in Juarez while awaiting "naturalization papers."[4]

By this time, Hardin and Beulah had become much more than client and attorney. Although she remained primarily in Juarez to be near her husband, Hardin became her personal as well as her legal advisor. One of the things he advised her against was spending additional money on her husband. She therefore shut down the flow of income to Martin, and when "he and his friends threatened and abused her," she moved to El Paso. Perhaps by coincidence, she took rooms in the Herndon Lodging House of Annie Williams on East Overland Street. Hardin had rooms there too. Within a week they shared the same bed, evidently to save on expenses.

Beulah had M'Rose's money in cash and drafts, and Martin believed Hardin baffled and confused her with legalese as the lawyer prevailed upon her to keep the M'Rose funds. She refused to talk or meet with her husband after his release from jail, leaving Martin without a cent and wondering what happened.[5]

The *Eddy Current* said "M'Rose may now walk the soil of Mexico a free man, but the business has cost him dear. When he went to Juarez he possessed $3,400 in American certificates of deposit and drafts. When he was turned loose, he was a 'busted commodity.' His woman is said to have flown with a better looking man and refuses to have anything to do with Martin."[6]

On April 21, Martin's friends, Andrew Jackson Lightfoot, Tom Fennessey (accused of embezzling $731.31 in Eddy County funds, and no longer county clerk),[7] and Queen, among others, cornered Hardin on a Juarez street and "grew saucy in their talk." Hardin had sense enough to realize he was outgunned, but the newspaper said "the little Sabbath day collision did not sit well on his good-natured stomach."[8]

On the following evening, Hardin returned to Juarez, accompanied by his cousin, Mannie Clements. They met Jeff Milton and George Scarborough in the street, and all of them strolled into Dieter's and Saur's Saloon for refreshments. There in a back room of this Juarez cantina they encountered Tom Fennessey, Sam Kaufman, Lightfoot, and two others, all sitting around a table arguing with Beulah M'Rose about money, and about her relationship with Hardin. Martin was absent.

The latecomers took a seat and verbally sparred with the New Mexico contingent until Fennessey sarcastically asked Hardin if he, as M'Rose's attorney, had any late developments regarding the case. Hardin and Fennessey both jumped up. Hardin stepped forward, slapped Fennessey and jammed a gun into his belly. Chief Milton grabbed the revolver, wrenched it from Hardin's grasp, and returned it only when the gunman agreed to stash it away, which he did. Then Hardin marched over to Andrew Jackson Lightfoot, a thirty-one-year-old itinerant Texas cowboy who did not altogether realize he was hanging out with bad company, and "gave him a slap in the face that could have been heard for a block." Milton now put his back to the door, and drew a weapon. Everyone in the room "agreed that the matter should be dropped."[9]

ON MAY 1, A NEW MAYOR, Robert "Poker Bob" Campbell, took office and immediately swore in Ed M. Fink—a former policeman fired by Milton—as the new police chief. Poker Bob believed in lax enforcement of city gambling and prostitution ordinances.

As for the dismissed Milton, he made do by picking up fees as a United States deputy marshal in El Paso. The State also appointed Milton as a Special Texas Ranger.

Meanwhile, since few people dropped by his office for legal

consultations—he had failed to renew his law license—John Wesley Hardin spent more and more time at the gambling tables. Crowds gathered as Hardin obviously was the best show in town.

On May 1, 1895, after losing steadily at poker in the Acme Saloon, Hardin reached across the green cloth, scooped up the pot and walked off. No one said a word.[10]

On the following night, encouraged by yesterday's success, Hardin crossed El Paso Street from his office and entered the Gem Saloon. The ornateness of the polished bar—set off by massive mirrors and buxom ladies decorating the wall—contrasted sharply with the prize fights that often occurred there. Since wagers were technically illegal, saloon patrons did their drinking downstairs and their gambling upstairs. A police officer—walking past the front door—could honestly report that he had glanced inside and witnessed no games.

Between midnight and one o'clock in the morning, Hardin grew weary of dealer Phil Baker's crap game. John was losing, and when Baker jested about the gunman's bad luck, Hardin drew a self-cocking .41 caliber Colt, walked around the table, gave the dealer a serious smell of the hole in the barrel, and snapped, "Since you are trying to be cute, just hand over the money I lost here." As patrons and onlookers thundered out of the line of fire and over against the wall, the dealer stammered, "Yes sir, I'll give you anything you want." After he counted out ninety-five dollars, Hardin stopped him, softly saying, "That's all I want, just what I lost and no more." He stuck the money in his pocket, shoved the weapon back under his vest, and started downstairs, all the while humming a few bars of "Annie Laurie."

In describing the Gem event, the *El Paso Times* again referred to Hardin only as a stranger in town, a visitor to the city. While the omission of Hardin's name has often been cited as an expression of the town's fear, that was unlikely. Newspaper people rarely showed fear of anyone. A more plausible reason for the expurgation was to show contempt by ignoring him. In refusing to identify Hardin, the newspapers denied him publicity. The *Times* considered him unworthy of discussion.

Nevertheless, a *Times* reporter berated the city. "El Paso has lost her nerve, and she can't play tough anymore," the reporter snorted. "Two years ago no man on earth would have walked

Gem Saloon dice. (R. G. McCubbin Collection)

Interior of Gem Saloon. (R. G. McCubbin Collection)

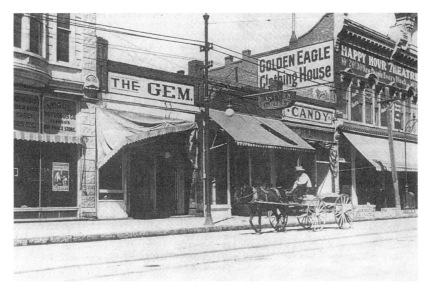

Gem Saloon exterior. During Hardin's time, a second floor existed. (Aultman Collection. El Paso Public Library)

into a house in this city and held up a game in that style and got out of the house alive. No sir. El Paso…is cornered, and I wouldn't be at all surprised to see the stranger hold up the entire police force. Why the other night he took charge of a jackpot in a social game of poker in the same manner, and there was not grit enough in the crowd to make a kick, and I guess if I had been there I would have broke the door down getting out."[11]

On May 4, John Wesley Hardin told the *El Paso Times* and *Herald* that his reason for taking the money was "to acquit myself manly and bravely." With regards to the Acme jackpot, he had confiscated the cash without threatening violence or drawing a gun. At the Gem, "I was grossly insulted by the dealer in a hurrah manner, hence I told him he could not win my money and hurrah me too. Hardin ordered Phil Baker "to deliver me the money, and you bet he did it."

His own ambition was to be a man, Hardin was quoted as saying, and I "wish to say right here once and for all that I admire pluck, push and virtue wherever found. Yet I contempt and despise a coward and assassin of character, whether he be a reporter, a journalist or a gambler. And while I came to El Paso to

16th of September Street in Juarez, Chihuahua, in 1896. Notice Nuestra Señora de Guadalupe Mission in background. (Frank Mangan Collection)

The Wigwam Saloon became the Wigwam Theater (shown here), and later the State Theater. Except for the facade, the building has changed little. U.S. Deputy Marshal George Scarborough shot Constable John Selman in this alley near Exit Door about a year after Hardin's murder. (Frank Mangan Collection)

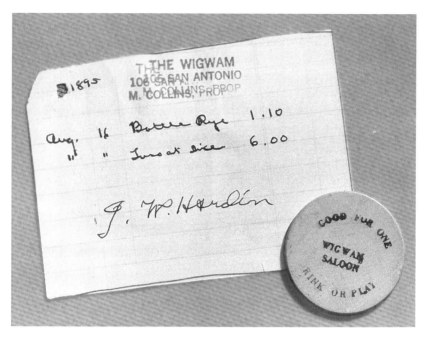

Wigwam Saloon chip, plus bar tab signed by John
Wesley Hardin. (R. G. McCubbin Collection)

prosecute Bud Frazer, and did it on as high a plane as possible,
I am here now to stay."

Hardin further announced that he had purchased a half interest in the Wigwam Saloon at 104 San Antonio street, half-way
between the Gem and the Acme. M. W. Collins, owner and manager, charged him $2,000, plus a 50 percent share "in an unfinished
book about the life of John Wesley Hardin." Hardin paid one thousand dollars down, and agreed to ante-up the other thousand
within five months, by September 30, 1895. The contract stipu-
lated that the book would be finished within one year. Until then,
the two men would equally manage the saloon, but would not
share profits and liabilities until Hardin paid the second thousand dollars. After Hardin squared the final installment, the firm's
name would change to "Hardin's Wigwam Saloon."[12]

To pay the $1,000, plus other expenses he had accrued, Hardin
borrowed $1,575 from Beulah, and gave her an undated note to
pay it back "within a reasonable time."[13] Meanwhile, those who

admired pluck and fair play were invited to a new management celebration in the Wigwam on May 4th.

That blowout was transferred to Washington Park for the benefit of Wigwam customers, both present and potential. Here Hardin demonstrated his riveting skill of shooting bullets through playing cards, blowing out the spades, diamonds, clubs and hearts. Some he signed and gave away; others he swapped for drinks, or used for chips when he ran short of cash.

DEPUTY SHERIFF WILL TEN EYCK arrested Hardin on May 6 for "unlawfully carrying a pistol" in the Gem Saloon, the .41 caliber Colt which the officer confiscated.[14] Hardin was now indicted on two separate county charges: one for carrying a gun, and one for gambling, both offenses being technically illegal in El Paso. On May 8, the state grand jury added a third indictment: "armed robbery" of the Gem Saloon. He posted bond for the latter, and filed for a continuance—which was granted—until October 1, 1895.

County Judge Frank E. Hunter held court on May 16 as John Wesley Hardin went to trial first on the charge of illegally carrying a firearm. Arguments started at three that afternoon. Witnesses testified that Hardin was carrying a gun because they had seen him use it while robbing the Gem crap game.

Phil Baker, the dealer, claimed Hardin had dropped a sheath (holster) while tugging the revolver from beneath his vest. Baker leaned down, picked it up and, with a grin, returned it.

An observer professed he happened to be present simply because Hardin was there. The bystander said he could not afford to play because he had been broke ever since Grover Cleveland became president of the United States.

Another witness testified that as Hardin went downstairs someone near the table made a disparaging remark about John's sportsmanship. Well, Hardin's sportsmanship might have been weak, but there was nothing wrong with his hearing. The attorney rushed back upstairs and challenged those who did not like his sportsmanship to get in line and show their manhood. "Since no one showed their manhood," the onlooker explained, "I guess we all liked his sportsmanship."[15]

Hardin responded that he needed the gun for self defense, that

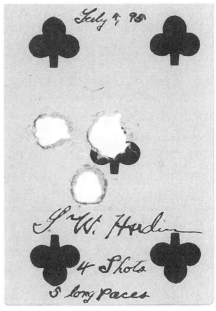

On July 4, 1895, in Washington Park, John Wesley Hardin drunkenly entertained the crowds. He placed playing cards on trees and against adobe walls, then paced off several steps, aimed and fired. All cards were then signed by Hardin. He also scribbled the distance from where he stood in relation to the target. Upper left, king of hearts, three bullet holes, "J.W. Hardin For: Mrs. H." Upper right, five of clubs, 3 or 4 bullet holes, "July 4, 95, J. W. Hardin, 4 Shots, 5 long paces." Left, ace of spades, four bullet holes, "Shot July 4, 1895, 5 Paces, John W. Hardin." (Michael Bernstein Collection)

carrying a six-shooter was justifiable. His life was in danger from the M'Rose faction. Jeff Milton even became a principal Hardin witness. While history has generally treated Milton and Hardin as wary enemies, the facts are that they shared a mutual respect. Milton voluntarily gave a written statement. Hardin's attorney, Jay Good, read it:

> My name is J. D. Milton and I live in El Paso, Texas. I know defendant John Wesley Hardin. I know that he was the attorney for Martin Morose and Mrs. Morose. I know that the friends of this man Morose...were antagonistic to him. One of them told me that they had John Wesley Hardin and another man afraid to cross the river [Rio Grande] and intimated that they would use violence toward him if they got a chance.
>
> Would also like to state that at two different times I went over the river with Mr. Hardin...and I told him (Hardin) to take his pistol with him, that we might need it. On two different times I told him to get his gun.
>
> Hardin came to me and asked me to protect him, and I told him that I would do so. I believe that John Wesley Hardin's life was in danger if he was found by these men without a gun.[16]

The prosecution countered that the "gang" across the river consisted of five men: M'Rose, Queen, Coffin, Fennessey and McKensey. M'Rose and Queen were in a Juarez, Chihuahua jail. Coffin would not enter El Paso because of cattle rustling warrants against him from New Mexico. When Fennessey and McKensey crossed the Rio Grande to El Paso from Juarez, Hardin asked Chief Milton to search them. Both men were unarmed. Furthermore, the prosecution argued, Hardin had never applied for a permit to carry a pistol.[17]

Both sides then made closing arguments. The jury thereupon took its time, but nevertheless found John Wesley Hardin guilty of unlawfully carrying a firearm. Judge Hunter assessed a fine of $25. The court refused to return the revolver, or two other six-shooters of Hardin's confiscated by Sheriff Frank Simmons.

As the trial ended, prosecutor D. Storms casually said to Hardin that he would have preferred to arraign him for gambling rather than carrying a pistol. Hardin responded, "Oh! Well, I would have pled guilty to that."[18]

Vic Queen (left) was murdered by unknown parties in Silver City, New Mexico. He is buried within a few feet of Catherine Antrim, mother of Billy the Kid. (Author's Collection) Jeff Milton (right) as a police chief in El Paso. (R. G. McCubbin Collection)

ALTHOUGH HARDIN HAD RETAINED his own attorney, Jay Good, the gunman did most of the legal work himself. In his own handwriting, he appealed the decision, citing ten errors of law. The last act of this drama occurred on July 1 when Hardin went to trial on the second charge: "betting at a table and game played with dice," a reference to the Gem Saloon affair. The authorities prosecuted Phil Baker at the same time for "exhibiting a gaming table and bank for the purpose of gaming on or about May 1, 1895." George Look and J. J. Taylor, co-owners of the saloon, made Baker's bond, although Baker was fined twenty-five dollars and went to jail for ten days. Hardin, who robbed the crap game, pleaded guilty to gambling, and paid a ten dollar fine.[19]

Adios, Martin

E L PASO IN 1895 WAS A WATERING HOLE for practically
every over-the-hill gunman left in the country. Hardin was
just one of several. Charles C. Perry, sheriff of Chaves County,
New Mexico, was two years younger than Hardin, but a prolific
drinker and gambler who saw himself as another shooter coming to the end of the trail…and no reputation to live on after him.

In May 1895, Perry invited his friend, the Eddy County, New
Mexico sheriff, Dee Harkey to visit El Paso with him. Along the
way he confided that, given the opportunity, he would kill John
Wesley Hardin.

At the Wigwam Saloon he encountered Hardin visiting with
George Gladden, who had served time with Hardin in the Travis
County jail. Gladden, a Mason County Feud survivor along with
John Ringo, had drifted around Texas from one killing to another
until winding up in El Paso.[1]

Perry reportedly challenged Hardin before turning his attention to Gladden. When Gladden showed he was unarmed, Perry
pulled two pistols and offered Gladden one. Gladden still refused,
so Perry laid both pistols on the bar, slapped Gladden and
demanded that he take one. Gladden thereupon retained John
Wesley Hardin to file assault charges against Perry. Constable

John Selman arrested Perry, and the court charged him with assault and battery, plus displaying a pistol. It assessed a fine of five dollars. Perry retreated back to Roswell in Chaves County.[2]

BY THIS TIME, HARDIN had come under immense personal pressure. He was an aging gunfighter too insecure to lay the gun aside. His skills, his nerve, his confidence, all had degenerated. He still had pluck, or liked to think he still had pluck, but now he confused pluck for rashness, and intoxication for courage. For the first time in his life, he probably wasn't sleeping well. Maybe the nights were haunting him. The days couldn't have been much better.

John Wesley Hardin might have bluffed the town by scooping up gambling pots at the Acme and Gem saloons, but serious enemies sensed his insecurities. They suspected the old dog had a frightening bark because he had lost so many teeth. Portions of the crowd who followed Hardin around were not there so much to see him kill, as to see him killed. They sensed the sweet, pungent odor of fresh blood and speculated that some of it might be Hardin's.

An alive and threatening Martin M'Rose and his loyal group of southeastern New Mexico thugs presented the greatest hazard to Hardin's longevity. Furthermore, an alive Martin M'Rose menaced Hardin's steadily deteriorating relationship with Beulah. She might even heed Martin's pleas and return.

M'Rose had written Beulah letters saying he wished to talk with her in El Paso since she had shown no inclination to backtrack to Juarez. He conferred with U.S. Deputy Marshal George Scarborough about slipping across the Rio Grande into Texas some night and talking with Beulah. M'Rose wanted the money his wife held, and he likely offered Scarborough a cut of the cash for arranging the meeting.

For a few days, Scarborough put M'Rose off, pleading that he had prior business in Sierra Blanca, Texas. On June 29th, the two met again in Juarez. This time M'Rose was hesitant, suspicious about crossing. George pretended indifference. Finally, M'Rose snapped, "By God, I believe I will go over to El Paso tonight." Scarborough agreed to meet him in the middle of the bridge before the sun went down and the electric light came on.

The old train trestle across the Rio Grande. Martin M'Rose and
George Scarborough crossed this trestle prior to the slaying of M'Rose
on the El Paso side. This trestle no longer exists.
(El Paso County Historical Society Collections)

El Paso Street in center of downtown during the 1880s.
(R. G. McCubbin Collection)

Scarborough returned quickly to El Paso and recruited U.S. Deputy Marshal Jeff Milton and Texas Ranger Frank McMahan. As darkness fell, the three lawmen hurried toward the river alongside the Santa Fe dump, an eyesore obscuring the north end of the Mexican Central Railroad bridge. Milton and McMahan took cover.

Deputy Marshal Scarborough claimed he met M'Rose two-thirds of the way across the trestle, the wanted man wearing a sombrero to make any observer suspect he was Mexican. Martin still had reservations about crossing, but after ten minutes of soothing talk by Scarborough, he sucked in his stomach and continued walking. They proceeded to the north end of the bridge into Texas where both jumped off and shuffled up the trail leading through the dump. Scarborough led the way.

Suddenly, Milton and McMahan shouted, "Hands up!" Scarborough jerked his own revolver and whirled. M'Rose leveled his weapon as the marshal shot four times. McMahan and Milton commenced firing. M'Rose fell, sprang up, was shot repeatedly, and toppled heavily on his back, still feebly trying to rise. As M'Rose groaned, "Boys, you've killed me," Scarborough put his foot on the rustler's chest and retorted, "Stop trying to get up, and we will quit shooting."

M'Rose died within minutes. Meanwhile, Dr. Alward White arrived, as did additional law officers. A superficial investigation occurred. The body went off to Powell's Funeral Home where an examination revealed seven or eight bullet wounds. According to the hand-written report of Dr. White, two bullets went directly through M'Rose's heart. Since the officers admitted M'Rose was still talking when flat on his back and a foot on his chest, the only explanation for the heart wounds is that someone shot him twice more while he was down and helpless, all in the name of making certain he was dead.

Sixteen hours later, undertaker Powell hired four men off the street to bury the body in Concordia Cemetery. The only two mourners were the bereaved widow, Helen Beulah M'Rose, and her (and Martin's) attorney, John Wesley Hardin. As John said, there are some people you just can't help.

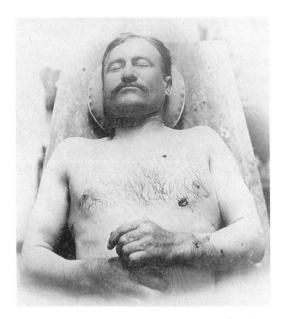

The body of Martin M'Rose reposing in death.
(R. G. McCubbin Collection)

THE KILLING OF M'ROSE did not receive good press in El Paso. Few residents sympathized with the outlaw, but death by a law officer pretending to be a friend, somehow rubbed citizens the wrong way. Eddy County, New Mexico did not know how to react either. Although the *Eddy Current* published an article implicating M'Rose in the murder of five men, the newspaper immediately turned around and renounced its own statement. It printed another assertion referring to Martin as a good-natured, well-meaning, mild-mannered cattle thief who never harmed anybody. "There was never a charge of murder or any other crime against M'Rose until he married a prostitute at the saloon town of Phenix last spring," the newspaper contended. "M'Rose was not a dangerous man and would not have made a very desperate resistance. Though the killing is much to be deplored, the step Martin took when he entered into a matrimonial contract was the prime cause of all his trouble."[3]

From across the Rio Grande in Juarez, Vic Queen angrily denounced Scarborough and Beulah M'Rose. He accused the marshal of "a systematic course of deception to inveigle Martin M'Rose into going across the river on the pretense of getting a division" of his wife's money.

Queen claimed to have encountered two Mexican smugglers returning from the Texas side of the border after observing the killing. According to them, the officers had fired for no reason, held their foot on M'Rose until he died, then found the dead man's pistol and laid it on the ground close to his hand. The smugglers, who were never identified, vanished into Mexico.[4]

The *El Paso Times*—following up on rumors already rampant around town—on June 30 hinted at a possible motive for the murder other than the New Mexico reward: "M'Rose had made several threats that he would kill John Wesley Hardin." That made it even easier to suspect, as author and historian Robert K. DeArment put it, "that Hardin, in the interest of self-preservation, must have somehow been involved in the elimination of M'Rose."[5]

And the question of Hardin's involvement was as natural as it was legitimate. First, consider the reward. Scarborough and Milton went to great lengths to explain in the newspapers that prior to luring M'Rose across the river, they had gotten the New Mexico reward figures on their man. They never publicly acknowledged if the reward was paid.

Second, John Wesley Hardin stood to gain the most from M'Rose's death. A dead M'Rose ended the threat to Hardin's life; it circumvented any possibility of Beulah going back to her husband; and it provided Hardin with a more open-ended access to Beulah's money. Using her bank account, he might even have financed Martin's trip to the graveyard.

Third, the M'Rose body contained a blood-soaked letter to Beulah with two bullet holes in it. The authorities read the message, and then passed it on to Beulah. The *Herald* quoted her as saying, "The letter I received after he was killed was a request for me to meet him in a certain place in El Paso, but I did not get it until after he was dead."[6]

So the letter said that M'Rose was coming to meet Beulah who of course did not know he was on his way because Martin hadn't told her. If that isn't strange enough, then consider why Martin M'Rose, a wanted outlaw with a price on his head, would trust any lawman to lead him to his wife. That makes no logic whatsoever, although it obviously happened.

And finally, Martin M'Rose would never have needed guidance from a lawman, or anyone else, to cross a simple railroad bridge into El Paso. El Paso and Juarez were tiny communities separated by a foot of water. People forded that stream all the time.

What probably happened is this. Although M'Rose hated his attorney, he also had to depend upon him. Using Beulah as bait, Hardin encouraged M'Rose to take the risk and cross the river in order to get his money. But M'Rose was frightened, distrustful. He needed guarantees. So what better security than a United States Deputy Marshal? Either Hardin or Beulah (or both) assured M'Rose that the fix was in, that with Marshal Scarborough leading the way, M'Rose's safety was assured.

John Wesley Hardin conferred with all lawmen involved, and together they reached an agreement. The pay could have been the New Mexico reward, a specific chunk of money from Beulah's purse, the cash in Martin's pockets, or all three. Martin M'Rose did not know it, but he was a dead man days before he ever got up enough nerve to cross the railroad bridge into El Paso.

As for the law officers, even the El Paso grand jury had trouble believing their story. All three were charged with murder, although it took two years to get them into court. When no one showed up to testify against then, the jury voted for acquittal.[7]

Vic Queen, suspecting he too might be marked for assassination, returned to Eddy from Mexico and offered to stand trial. In April 1896, a grand jury refused to indict him. Queen then announced his "bad-man" retirement, saying he was going into business and settling down.[8]

Autobiography
of a Sinner

ON THE DAY FOLLOWING M'ROSE'S DEATH, all seemed well with Hardin. A *Herald* reporter of July 2, 1895, quoted him as vowing to become a reformed man, to "quit drinking and gambling and to apply himself to the practice of law and to writing a history of his life."

Yet, just the opposite happened. The killing did nothing to ease Hardin's mind. It neither stopped his shakes, slowed his drinking, eased his turbulent relationship with Beulah, backed off his enemies or relaxed his troubled spirit. El Paso was the end of his line. He had no place else to go.

Annie Williams, his landlady, amply illustrated his reeling state of consciousness. "It is difficult to describe how Mr. Hardin's presence influenced me," she began:

> I did not hesitate to talk saucy to him when he got drunk and damaged my furniture, and yet I feared him. I would feel my very bones chill when he looked at me with his darting little serpentine eyes. He would bring his whiskey up here [to his room] by the gallon and I could hear him at all hours of the day and night stirring his toddy. But I never saw him staggering drunk. I could only tell he was drunk by his extreme politeness and the peculiar snake-like glitter of his eyes....
>
> He frequently talked to me about his book—the history of his life that he was writing. One day I walked in and asked: "What

are you doing now, telling how you killed a man or stole a horse?"
He replied that he was stealing a horse just then. He commenced
talking about his history, and said he had just one more man to
kill. He said that there was living near here a man who had assisted in lynching his brother in Comanche. [Hardin] intended to
go to that man's house, call him to the door and kill him and no
one would ever know who did it. He said that hereafter he intended to do his work on the sly, as other people did. He declared
that he had no confidence in human nature, that the human heart
was rotten and that everything living was deceitful. He made me
shudder when he said, "I would not trust my own mother but
would watch her just as I watch everyone else."

Hardin would walk the hall for hours at night with a pistol in
his hand. I think he was crazy with fear, for no matter who knocked
at his door he would spring behind a table where a pistol was
lying before he ever said, "Come in." He never allowed a living
soul to enter his room when he was sitting down.

Mr. Hardin was certainly a quick man with his guns. I have
seen him unload his guns, put them in his pocket, walk across the
room, then suddenly spring to one side, face around and, quick as
a flash, he would have a gun in each hand clicking so fast that the
clicks sounded like a rattle machine. He would place his guns inside his britches, in front with the muzzles out. Then he would
jerk them out by the muzzle and with a toss as quick as lighting
grasp them by the handle and have them clicking in unison. He
showed me how he once killed two men that way. They demanded
his guns and he extended them, one in each hand, he holding the
muzzle as if to surrender, and when the men reached for his guns,
he tossed the pistols over, catching the handles, and killed both
men while their hands were yet extended for the weapons. Oh, he
was a wonderful man. He practiced with guns daily, and I liked
to see him handle them when they were empty.[1]

Whether Hardin started writing his autobiography while in
prison, or just considered it, is uncertain. Another writer, had
already written an account about him, but with deplorable accuracy. In May of 1883, a "penny dreadful" hit the market entitled
The Bandits of the West: Their Lives, Crimes and Punishments. A sub-
title referred to *The Adventures of the Most Famous Road Agents,
Train Robbers, Highwaymen and Murderers of the Great West*. It de-
voted a paragraph to John Wesley Hardin:

John Wesley Hardin who infested Texas and the adjoining
states was one of the most desperate outlaws that ever lived. His
series of crimes would fill a large sized volume. He was born in

Emanuel "Mannie"
Clements, Jr.
He had plenty of enemies,
so it surprised no one
when he was shot dead
in 1909 on the Coney
Island Saloon floor.
(Author's Collection)

San Antonio, stood six feet in height and was a giant in strength. He made DeWitt County, Texas, his headquarters. He is credited with having killed twenty-one men. The officers of the law looked away when he passed. This was largely owing to the fact that two families, the Suttons and Taylors, carried on a terrible warfare, in which a large part of the population took part. But the law got Wesley Hardin into its clutches at last. Most of the Taylors and Suttons were killed. DeWitt county is now very orderly, as its chief terror is carrying a life sentence with little chance of ever escaping the clutches of justice again.[2]

The fallacies involved in this paragraph probably bothered Hardin not at all. The publicity, the acknowledgement that the world had noticed, is what mattered. He knew people recognized his name, and he knew the name made good newspaper and book copy. Hardin had consulted with various publishers while he was in prison, and then again when he was in Gonzales. Some biographers have taken this to mean that he was well along with the writing prior to El Paso, but not necessarily.

Hardin needed guidance for writing an autobiography. He needed answers to questions like, where to start? What order to follow? How much detail was necessary? Should he write in first or third person? Should he tell everything? How large a book would this be? Who would edit his spelling and grammar? What about sketches and maps?

Although Hardin might have written a few manuscript pages while in prison, considering the difficulties of acquiring paper, chances are the project never seriously got underway until he reached El Paso and met Beulah. The only known available photo shows her in a dress suit with bows, her light-brown hair piled neatly on her head. She looked every bit the secretary stereotype. While she was a lady addicted to thunder and lighting in terms of emotions and personal relations, she was also intelligent and articulate, a woman in possession of a moderate grasp of grammatical skills even though they were enclosed in a brothel body.

Beulah recognized that Hardin had a superb idea bound to go nowhere unless someone took charge. And she did. She brought to the manuscript a sense of organization and commitment.

The manuscript was probably written in longhand, and dictated by Hardin. Awkward constructions, bad spellings, unclear meanings and details left dangling or missing altogether were the result as much of unedited copy as inept writing.

During late June, Hardin sold his interest in the Wigwam Saloon, and announced again that he had quit drinking and gambling, and would hereafter commit himself to the practice of law and the completion of his life history.[3] That was Hardin's way of admitting that his existence was falling apart, that due to his drinking and gambling, he could neither handle money nor his business and personal affairs. In a tacit acknowledgement that he owed Beulah for her manuscript labors, he made her an associate in his forthcoming book:

> I, John W. Hardin, on this day [June 18, 1895], take Mrs. Beulah M'Rose as a full partner in my manuscript and all business matters. Also as a confidential correspondent clerk.[4]

But if Hardin was too intoxicated to work or concentrate on his own history, Beulah had her own instabilities. On August 1, with Hardin out of town, a drunken Beulah wandered down San Antonio Street after midnight and paused in front of Charlie's Restaurant. When police officer John Selman, Jr. happened by, she at first flirted and then threatened to shoot him. As Selman confiscated two .41 caliber Colt six-shooters from her parasol, she "rose up in her wrath and turned her vocal batteries loose on the officer's head...until the paint scaled off the neighboring woodwork."

Selman jailed her for carrying a gun. She bonded out, showed up sober in court, paid a fifty-dollar fine and said she was sorry. Later, Hardin drunkenly berated her for apologizing to the policeman. Landlady Annie Williams, who often had Hardin's ear, said he "hated young John Selman and Officer [Joe] Chaudoin," although he usually spoke well of Constable John Selman.[5]

As liquor continued to loosen the tongue and cloud the judgment of John Wesley Hardin, he visited Phenix in Eddy County, New Mexico. There in early August, while Beulah was being arrested in El Paso, he tried his Gem Saloon stunt. Hardin gathered up gambling currency from one of the tables and walked off. However, this time one of the players drew a gun and forced him to replace the money.[6]

Back in El Paso, a depressed Hardin implied to a *Times* reporter on August 5 that he would soon have something to say about the M'Rose killing. Hardin hinted darkly that he was not pleased with Deputy Marshal Scarborough. Such thoughts quickly reached Scarborough's ear, and Hardin apologized to the marshal for his thoughtless remarks.[7]

The Scarborough confrontation sent Hardin home in a foul mood to Beulah, and he found her just as intoxicated as he was. One word led to another, and their subsequent fighting carried over into the street. Beulah ran screaming downstairs into the *El Paso Tribune* offices. The editor dryly remarked that he was "an admirer of sensational drama in its proper place, but not caring to have his office transformed into a stage for blood curdling theatrics, he ordered Beulah to skip out into the alley." In the meantime, the landlady and lodgers in the Herndon House fled the building a couple of jumps ahead of a drunken, rampaging John Wesley Hardin.

Mrs. Williams, often a referee and counselor to Hardin and

Beulah, explained to the local newspapers what living in the same building with John Wesley Hardin was all about. The editors delighted in quoting Annie about scandalous events in the life of El Paso's most notorious attorney.

Annie revealed how Beulah carried a gun in the pocket of her dress, and while she wasn't as fast on the draw as John, she was quick. From downstairs, Annie heard the shouting, so she scurried to their room and entered just in time to see Beulah pointing her pocket six-shooter at Hardin. Hardin's pistol lay on a table across the room, but a cocked weapon in the trembling hands of a hysterical woman, and stuck in his face, caused Hardin to hesitate in reaching for it. As it was, Annie wrestled Beulah's revolver away, and screamed, "For God's sake, I don't want a killing in this house."

The two women scrambled out onto the back steps where Beulah said, "Mrs. Williams, I hate to do it in your house, but I must kill that man Hardin tonight or he will kill me." Beulah sobbed that "she would wait until he went to sleep and then put her pistol to his head and blow his brains out."

Mrs. M'Rose and Annie Williams then went back inside the furnished rooms where Beulah handed her landlady a letter, which Hardin snatched away. "Mrs. Williams, he forced me to write that letter saying I had committed suicide," Beulah wailed. "He wanted that letter found on me after he had killed me."

Annie Williams told the newspapers that "I was so completely put out that I told them to please get out of my house to kill each other."[8]

Nevertheless, Annie did not abandon Beulah. They both visited a justice of the peace where Beulah swore Hardin "had kept her on her knees [all afternoon] praying for her life." Officers Frank Carr, Joe Chaudoin and John Selman, Jr. arrested Hardin in the Acme Saloon. At the city jail he posted a peace bond of one hundred dollars. When D. Storms assessed five dollars in court costs, an example arose of Hardin's deteriorating financial condition.

Hardin asked Storms to remit the costs, and Storms refused, pointing out that he had remitted ten dollars in the Gem Saloon court case. However, Storms offered to remit half of the five dollar fine, if Hardin would pay the remaining $2.50 immediately.

Hardin could not. Instead, he requested time to come up with the five dollars. Storms granted it.[9]

In his inebriated condition, Hardin made drunken, imprudent statements for the second time about hiring officers to kill Martin M'Rose. On Saturday, August 10, Deputy U.S. Marshal George Scarborough grabbed Hardin by the ear, stood him on his toes, and marched him down to the *El Paso Times*. The newspaper printed Hardin's humiliating public apology:

> Yesterday morning John Wesley Hardin, accompanied by United States Marshal Scarborough, called at the Times office, where Mr. Hardin wrote the following card for publication:
> "To the public: I have been informed that on the night of the 6th while under the influence of liquor, I made a talk against George Scarborough, stating that I had hired Scarborough to kill M'Rose. I do not recollect making any such statement and if I did the statement was absolutely false and it was superinduced by drink and frenzy."
>
> John W. Hardin
>
> The above is published at the request of Mr. Scarborough for whom it was written.[10]

Within hours, Beulah and her son left on a Southern Pacific westbound train "to grow up with the country." However, she reached Deming, New Mexico, a hundred miles distant, and had a sense of impending tragedy. She wired Hardin, "I feel you are in trouble, and I'm coming back."[11]

She did return and he was in trouble. This time none of her magic helped. She left within a week, and they never saw each other again. Her leaving was one of the few stable decisions she ever made.

Four Sixes
to Beat

THE LAST DAYS OF JOHN WESLEY HARDIN can never be documented precisely, but sufficient evidence exists for an evaluation, and one of the best instruments for that is his Wigwam Saloon bar tab. Hardin drank in every saloon in town, and there were a couple of dozen in El Paso, at least, and plenty more in Juarez. Even taking into consideration that portions of his bar tab covered libations he bought for others, that factor is balanced by numerous people also buying him drinks.

Consider that a shot of whiskey cost between seven and fifteen cents, and a glass of beer about ten cents, maybe fifteen at the better class institutions. To consistently run up a bar bill of between one and three dollars a day, in just one saloon, indicates a hefty, two-fisted drinker.

On May 1, Hardin accumulated a Wigwam bar tab of three dollars. Considering that this figure amounted to at least thirty beers, or twenty shots of whiskey, or a combination of both, and more if he received a discount—which he probably did—that in itself represented an awesome amount of quaffing. Yet, late that night he was still tipping the glass and gambling for hours up the

Acme Saloon sign directed customers to the card room.
(R. G. McCubbin Collection)

Acme Saloon dice and bar chips. (R. G. McCubbin Collection)

John Wesley Hardin's long running Wigwam Saloon bar tab.
(R. G. McCubbin Collection)

street at the Gem Saloon where he ultimately removed ninety-five dollars from the dealer. On the following day, May 2, Hardin paid his bar bill in full at the Wigwam, a total of $13.30 for six days of libations.

On May 8, when the state grand jury indicted him for armed robbery of the Gem, Hardin took home a half-gallon of whiskey and a pint of rye. On July 3, before John Selman, Jr's. arrest of Beulah, Hardin bought "Johnny" (meaning police officer Selman), fifty cents worth of drinks. Hardin purchased a bottle of liquor

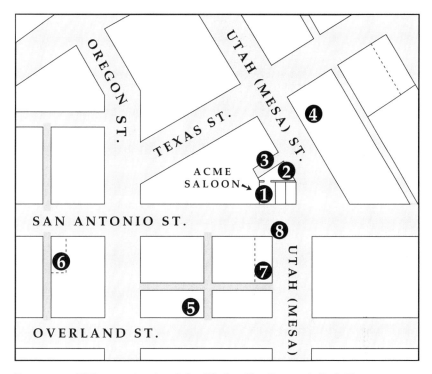

Downtown El Paso at the time John Wesley Hardin was killed. This map was made by pioneer El Pasoan Stanley Good who, as a small boy, sneaked into the Acme Saloon minutes after Constable Selman fired the fatal shots. Good numbered points on the sketch that were related to the killing. (1) The Acme Saloon (on San Antonio Street). (2) The Acme gambling room in back (facing Utah [Mesa] Street). (3) Short alley to gambling room from Utah [Mesa] Street. (4) Vacant lot which was later occupied by the Popular Dry Goods Company. (5) Herndon Lodging House, home of John Wesley Hardin and Beulah M'Rose. (6) Wigwam Saloon, one of Hardin's favorite gambling and drinking establishments. (7) Clifford Brothers grocery store. (8) Grocery boxes on sidewalk, young John Selman's intended firing position.

for eighty cents and gave it to Jeff Milton. The refreshment helped Milton get through the 4th of July celebrations.

The record shows Hardin drinking copious amounts at the Wigwam during the last week of his life. That was the period when Beulah left, and George Scarborough marched him down to the *Times* where John Hardin scratched out his chastened public apology.

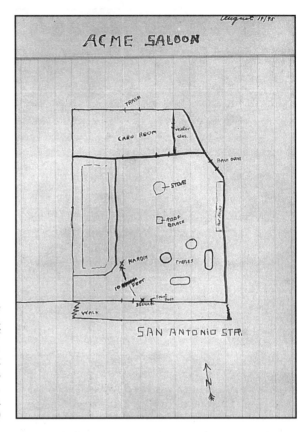

Map of the
Acme Saloon
on night of
Hardin slaying.
Sheriff Frank
B. Simmons
did the sketch.
(R. G. McCubbin
Collection)

As his final days became a blur, he lost seventy dollars at cards
in the Wigwam on August 18, and had run up a $3.15 bar bill by
the afternoon of the 19th. The balance due had reached $198.25—
the largest figure yet—and Hardin could not pay it. He had no
money, he had no income, and he had no clients.

Constable John Selman accosted Hardin in the street that afternoon, snorting that he understood Hardin had threatened John
Selman, Jr. Hardin allegedly called Young John a cowardly son-
of-a-bitch who had arrested his woman, Beulah. When Selman
defended his son and offered to shoot it out, Hardin claimed to
be unarmed. Hardin said, "I'll go get a gun and when I meet you,
I'll meet you smoking and make you shit like a wolf all around
the block."[1]

The two men separated, Selman going off to brood, Hardin likely stumbling into the Wigwam and tanking up.

At ten o'clock on the Monday night of August 19, 1895, Hardin swayed into the Acme Saloon and found it crowded. According to later testimony, Selman and an investor friend named E. L. Shackelford entered the saloon two or three times and even played a game or two of cards with Hardin. If so, they were checking positions and plotting strategy. For most of the evening, Selman sulked on a barrel near the Acme front door. At eleven o'clock, Shackelford came outside, nodded, turned around and walked back in. Right behind him, Selman put his hand on his gun and stepped through a door wide open due to the heat. He paced three or four steps quickly through the cigar smoke and haze as he focused on Hardin standing almost sideways against the bar and rolling dice down the polished counter. Hardin turned to grocer Henry S. Brown, and said, "Brown, you've got four sixes to beat."

At that instant, Constable John Selman started shooting. A .45 caliber bullet slammed Hardin in the head, and he crashed backwards onto the wooden floor. He never felt the two other slugs ripping into his body.

To a
Higher Court

THE ONLY FACT EVERYONE AGREES upon regarding the death of John Wesley Hardin, is that John Selman killed him. In spite of a dozen or more patrons drinking, talking and gambling, the why and how, and the circumstances of Hardin's murder are as murky and as controversial today as they were over a century ago.

One motive involves that curse so destructive to mankind: jealousy. Selman might have shot Hardin merely to keep himself center-stage among gunmen. The reason for Hardin's murder could have been as uncomplicated as that.

Selman claimed he fired the shots because he had been threatened and insulted, and because he wanted to keep Hardin from assaulting John Selman, Jr. Never mind that his story reeked with weaknesses, platitudes, and contradictions. The constable stuck by that account, and it is the version most accepted by historians. In a court of law, justice was often decided not on the basis of whether a threat was actually made, but whether a killer *perceived* a threat as being made.[1]

This perceived threat may have been a cover-up for the real motivation behind Hardin's death, a motive harking back to the M'Rose killing. El Paso residents widely speculated that there

In 1895, soon after Hardin's death, a national periodical ran this dramatic,
if entirely incorrect, engraving of Hardin's slaying. The caption read, "The
most noted of Texas man-killers slain at El Paso, Aug. 19, by Constable
John Selman—How the king of Southwestern man-killers has finally
fallen victim to violence." (R. G. McCubbin Collection)

was more behind the M'Rose killing than just three officers shooting one outlaw. They suspected Hardin had paid the policemen
for that night's work, a suspicion confirmed in some circles when
Hardin signed a newspaper statement apologizing for saying he
had hired Scarborough. He also said the same regarding Milton.[2]

The M'Rose conspiracy could be one of the reasons Beulah left.
She may have been stunned at Hardin's involvement, and left in
shame and horror; or she might have decided to vanish before he
implicated her too.

The story is that Hardin had not hired just Scarborough, Milton
and McMahan to murder M'Rose, but that he also had retained
Selman. In the darkness and confusion of that night along the
Rio Grande near the trestle, Selman might have slipped away
before other lawmen arrived. Perhaps he had not even reached
the bridge in time to participate.

IF ANYBODY KNEW EVERYONE in town, including John Wesley Hardin, as well as police officers and politicians, it had to be George Look. George Look arrived in El Paso during 1880, and stayed to invest in railroads and business enterprises. His fingers penetrated deep into politics, as well as into the liquor and gambling interests. He owned a half-portion in the Gem Saloon, El Paso's most prominent watering hole. He nurtured numerous secrets, and few affairs went on in El Paso that he did not know about or participate in. By the 1900s, he recognized that the gunfighter era had passed before his observant eyes. Look became an avid collector of gunfighter memorabilia, acquiring weapons, papers, and badges. In 1909 he wrote his memoirs, describing how John Selman had approached him in early August 1895, complaining that Hardin had "cut with Scarborough. But he has not cut with any of the rest of us. What do you say—shall I get the son-of-a-bitch."

Look acknowledged that the only alternatives were for Selman to let the matter rest, or kill Hardin. Old John chose the latter option, shooting Hardin dead in the Acme Saloon "because he [Hardin] would not give him (Selman) his cut of the M'Rose money."[3]

Therefore, the shooting evolved from either one, or a combination of possibilities: jealousy, the insulting threat, or the M'Rose money. They remain the murder theories with credibility. The absolute truth will never be known because Selman himself never understood the underlying emotions and insecurities that led him to perform the most noted killing in El Paso's history.

EVEN MORE CONTROVERSIAL is *how* Hardin died. John Selman said he walked into the saloon, looked Hardin in the eye and shot him there. When Hardin struck the floor, Selman shot him in the right chest near the nipple, and once in the right arm. Either another bullet, or a round already fired, nicked the little finger on the left hand. Three bullet holes formed a triangle in the wooden planks.[4]

Frank Patterson, the Acme bartender, testified that Hardin was standing at the bar with his back to the door. John Selman walked in, shouted something, and blasted away.

M. E. Ward, a railroad man, testified that he had heard John Selman

El Paso bicyclers. The two in front, mounted, are James Hibbert and
W. F. Paine. The three standing from left to right are S. H. Bailey,
Fred Feldman, and Henry Brown. Henry Brown was the grocer/dairyman
in the Acme Saloon to whom Hardin said, "Brown, you have four sixes
to beat." (Mr. & Mrs. Robert H. Brown Collection)

remark in the street that Hardin had threatened him. Ward said
Selman was waiting for Hardin to leave the Acme Saloon.

E. L. Shackelford, a broker and the man who signaled Selman
to enter the barroom, said Selman—under the influence of drink—
had been in and out of the saloon once or twice, and growled that
Hardin had threatened him. Shackelford admitted that he walked
inside the barroom first, and Selman followed him. "Then I heard
shots fired," Shackelford testified. "I can't say who fired those
shots as I did not see it. I did not turn around but left immediately.

El Paso police officer
John Selman, Jr.
(R. G. McCubbin Collection)

The room was full of powder smoke, and I couldn't have seen anything anyhow."

Grocer and dairyman Henry Brown testified that he had entered the saloon shortly before eleven, and Hardin offered to shake dice with him for twenty-five cents a throw. Hardin rolled his, turned and softly said, "Brown, you have four sixes to beat." The words were followed by an explosion, a flash, and Hardin crashed to the floor on Brown's left. Brown claimed Hardin's back was toward the direction the shot came from.

Shorty Anderson explained how he had gone into the Acme, had a drink of beer, watched the men rolling dice, and then seated himself in the back room. His chair put him in a position to observe the barroom. He saw Hardin suddenly "straighten up, turn and throw his hand upon his hip as he threw his coat back. Then I heard the pistol shot and he fell."

Constable John Selman
as he appeared on
the night he killed
John Wesley Hardin.
(R. G. McCubbin
Collection)

John Selman, Jr., gave a hearsay statement that his father and Hardin had exchanged words and that Hardin had threatened to kill the constable. When the gunfire subsided, young John rushed into the saloon, grabbed his father's arm and shouted, "Don't shoot him any more, he's dead." He took his father's gun.[5]

However, if what El Pasoan Stanley Good wrote was correct—and it has a ring of truth—John Selman, Jr., was an accessory to Hardin's murder.

Stanley Good grew up in El Paso and was just a young boy when the shooting occurred. Years later, he had a vivid recollection of the slaying that had stamped a strong imprint on his mind.

Good later claimed that on the evening Hardin died, Good and his childhood friends were playing in a vacant lot at the corner of

Utah (Mesa) and Texas streets. Since they were across from the alley entrance to the Acme, they hustled to investigate the shots. After crawling through a forest of legs, they saw a man sprawled on the floor, his face turned away from them. He had dark brown hair, and there was a hole in the back of his head with blood oozing out onto the floor.

When he became a teenager, Good learned that Young John had arranged with the clerk at Clifford Brothers Grocery on the corner directly across San Antonio Street from the Acme to leave shipping boxes on the sidewalk. They were stacked high enough to get a good view of the saloon interior. When the Selmans were ready, and the boxes were in place, Young John grabbed his Winchester and climbed up on top. Aiming through the window, alongside the front door, he planned to shoot Hardin from across the street if his father encountered difficulties. (See Appendix E)

Hardin entered the saloon at the San Antonio Street entrance and stepped up to the bar, moving down several feet before finding a vacant space. He called for the dice box, saying he wanted to play "Ship, Captain and Crew." After rolling three times, he passed the dice box to Henry Brown, saying, "Four sixes to beat."

Meanwhile, so many people were lined up along the bar, that Young John couldn't see Hardin. He never fired a shot.[6]

HARDIN'S BODY LAY ON THE FLOOR a couple of hours while the whole town passed by to gawk. The police retrieved two .41 caliber Colts from Hardin's body and took Constable John Selman away for questioning. The newspapers reported no sign of a mail shirt on Hardin, since rumor had it that he always wore one.

Starr Undertakers removed the body, and during an examination at the mortuary, they recorded numerous scars. Two side-by-side gunshot wounds were above the right hip bone. The left thigh midway between the knee and the groin had a gunshot wound, and a similar abrasion existed on the inside of the right thigh. A wound glistened on the back of the right elbow, and a large knife scar with several adjoining smaller scars appeared below the rib on the left side.[7]

MOST OF THE WITNESSES TESTIFIED that Selman shot Hardin in the back of the head. Justice Howe also took the testimony of

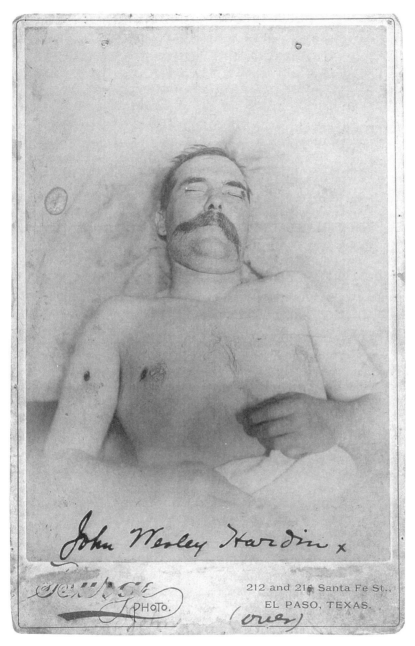

The late John Wesley Hardin. It cannot be seen in the photo, but one of Selman's bullets knocked off the tip of Hardin's left little finger. (R. G. McCubbin Collection)

doctors S. G. Sherard, W. N. Vilas and Alward White. They examined the gunshot wounds of John Wesley Hardin and swore that "It is our opinion that...the bullet entered at the base of the skull posteriorly and came out the upper corner of the left eye."[8]

Photographer J. C. Burge snapped Hardin's body from the waist up on the following day, and the picture sold briskly all over town. While his testimony was not sought by Justice Howe, the *El Paso Herald* published the "expert opinion" of Mr. Burge:

> Burge says that he has had thirty-five years experience on the border, and [has made] critical examinations of any number of gunshot wounds. He declares that Hardin was shot directly in the face, and not in the back of the head. He says that had the bullet entered the back of the head, it would have torn the eyeball and environment from its exit. The bullet hole in the left eye is so clean and well defined that Mr. Burge asserted at once that there was where the bullet entered.

Perhaps the most scientific account came from D. Storms, the county attorney who prosecuted John Selman for murder. On Tuesday, Aug. 20, 1895, in his own hand, he wrote:

> I learned of the shooting of Hardin and during the day I went to the undertaking rooms with Maurice McKelligon and Joe Woodson. I had Dr. Race's tape line, and Tom Powell [undertaker] and I took the following measurements on Hardin's body. Bullet hole in back of head was even in height with large cavity of right ear, and 3 and one-fourth inches from edge of rim of right ear. Bullet hole exited from left eye between eye brow and edge of eye, and at the extreme edge of eye lid, thus: [see sketch in doctor's report on page 275] Hardin apparently fell to the floor, flat on his back.
>
> I further found another bullet hole in Hardin's back just 9 in. from base of neck and about 1 and one-half in. from back bone on right side thus: [see sketch in doctor's report on page 275] It entered at right of right nipple where Powell reported Drs. said it went in. Another [bullet went] through right arm. Drs. said it went in back side. It went in back of arm ten in. from point of elbow, and exited on front side 8 and one-half inches from point of elbow.
>
> We three (Maurice, Joe and I) then went to Acme Saloon where Hardin was killed. I measured from edge of bar, where they said Hardin stood, to where bullet struck back of bar, and it was just 6 feet.... There were three holes in the floor and closest one was 37 in. from door....
>
> Since the doctors said the ball entered Hardin's head on the

Tuesday, Aug. 20, 1895.

I learned of the shooting of Hardin and during the day I went to the undertaking rooms with Maurice McKilligon and Joe Woodson and I had Dr. Race's tape line and Tom Powell and I took the following measurements on Hardins body. Bullet hole in back of head was even in height with large cavity of right ear and $3\frac{1}{4}$ in from edge of rim of right ear. Bullet hole in left eye between eye brow and edge of eye lid and at the extreme left of eye lid, thus: ⟨sketch⟩ Bullet hole just 9 in from base of neck and about $1\frac{1}{2}$ in from back bone on right side. thus: ⟨sketch back / arm⟩ and just at right of right nipple where Powell

District Attorney D. Storms, along with doctors and undertaker, wrote this report and took measurements of Hardin's body. Above, this portion of the hand-written account includes small sketches locating bullet holes. (D. Storms File, El Paso Public Library)

Death certificate of John Wesley Hardin. (Ron Futrell Collection)
Death certificates are in themselves impersonal, which if nothing else demonstrates the equality of the grave. John Wesley Hardin never saw, or even thought about, death certificates of the men he killed. And of course, he never paid any attention to his own, either.

back side, I was wondering how it could have struck so low after passing through his head. I got Dr. Sherard to go with me and re-examine the wound and he found that the ball struck the lower side of the arched cavity of bone above the eye and ruffled that bone for some little distance and deflected downward.

D. Storms then went before Justice of the Peace Walter Howe, and both men questioned Acme Saloon witnesses. C. B. Patterson excitedly walked in and said he was the defense attorney. He objected to the prosecution asking questions without his pres-ence. Howe then terminated the inquest, saying he had sufficient testimony to retain Selman until a hearing scheduled the next day at nine o'clock in the morning.

A deputy sheriff found Selman down at city hall swapping stories with policemen. The officers said they had Selman in custody.[9]

JUSTICE HOWE REACHED the conclusion that John Selman, "with malice aforethought, did shoot John Wesley Hardin with a revolver, the bullet taking effect three inches behind the right ear and leading to the death of said Hardin." Howe set bond at one thousand dollars.

The Recorder's Court then took charge, and "It was packed with interested listeners. The golden words of learned counsel were frequently punctuated by the cheerful spatter of tobacco juice on the bare floor in sublime disregard of the cuspidors con-veniently [placed] by the janitor for the reception of the nicotine cataracts."[10]

Prosecutor D. Storms wrote the following:

> Wednesday, Aug. 21.
> Murder of J. W. Hardin. W. D. Howe and I went to Recorder's Court at 2 p.m. Judge Davis and Kemp represented Selman. Rec. Patterson asked me if I had any testimony to introduce for the State. I was sitting outside the rail and I went up to his table and said that as he and Howe both claimed jurisdiction, I did not think I ought to be compelled to appear in both courts and asked to be excused from appearing here. Patterson excused me and then I asked to sit and listen as a citizen and he said certainly. I went outside the rail and sat down until ct. adjourned. No one was present to represent the State. They had quite a time and finally sent Howe after testimony he had taken in inquest case, and swore

him that it was the testimony taken. Then Howe read a part of all of it and McPherson testified for defendant. Ct. said he had read the newspapers and he thought def. justified. He would bind him over and fix his bond at $1,000 which was given.[11]

THE JOHN SELMAN MURDER TRIAL began in El Paso on April 29, 1896. The State subpoenaed twenty-nine witnesses, the defense thirty-two. Most of the witnesses testified as previously stated, bartender Frank Patterson expanding a little by saying the muzzle of Selman's gun was between one-and-one-half and two feet from Hardin's head. Hardin had his back to Selman and was leaning with both hands on the counter. Dr. Sherard testified that Hardin was shot in the back of the head, whereas J. A. Brock, a livestock merchant, testified that he had examined the wound, and in his judgment the ball had gone in the eye and exited the back of the head. Frank Carr, the night police captain, testified that he was the first to take hold of the dead man, "that Hardin's right hand was resting near the handle of his pistol, which had been drawn partly out, but was caught fast in the tight waistband of the dead man's trousers."[12]

The jury voted ten to two for acquittal, and a new trial was reset for the following year.

ON APRIL 1, 1896, YOUNG JOHN SELMAN took a fifteen-year-old girl—the daughter of a prominent Mexican family—to Juarez, allegedly to marry her. The mother and chief of Juarez police caught the two in a hotel. John Selman, Jr. went to the Juarez jail; the daughter went home with mother.

On the following day, Easter Sunday, Constable John Selman was obeying anything but the Lord's commandments when he became intoxicated in the Wigwam Saloon. At four in the morning, he wandered down the outside stairway into the alley where he encountered U.S. Deputy Marshal George Scarborough. The most prevalent account is that Selman wanted Scarborough's assistance in getting Young John out of the Juarez prison. There was an argument, followed by gunfire, with Selman absorbing four of Scarborough's bullets. He died that afternoon in Sisters Hospital on the operating table. The newspapers said the Selman murder trial for killing Hardin had been transferred to a higher court.[13]

The Immaculate Conception Church handled the last rites, plus the burial of John Selman in the Catholic section of Concordia Cemetery. Since Catholic record-keeping did not commence until 1912, all efforts to locate Selman's grave have failed.

John Selman, Jr., broke jail in Juarez and escaped back to El Paso, too late to be of any assistance to his father. He thereafter became something of a wanderer, dying of a heart attack at Belton, Texas, at the age of sixty-seven.

THE STATE INDICTED George Scarborough for murder, but acquitted him during an El Paso trial. He resigned his commission as a U.S. deputy marshal, and was working as a lawman in southern New Mexico, pursuing rustlers in April 1900. One of them shot him through the leg with a .30-40 rifle. He lay in the desert until a wagon reached him, at which time he was taken to Lordsburg and then transferred by train to Deming. He died on the operating table at Deming, New Mexico on April 5, one day short of four years after John Selman died on the operating table in El Paso. Scarborough was buried in Deming.[14]

JEFF MILTON JOINED THE IMMIGRATION service soon after leaving El Paso. By 1930 he had retired in Tombstone, Arizona. He died at the age of eighty-five in 1947, and his ashes were scattered in the desert.

EMANUEL "MANNIE" CLEMENTS, a son of Manning[15] who followed his cousin John Wesley Hardin to El Paso, continued to hang around town, working as a police officer, deputy sheriff and constable. After an unsuccessful attempt to kill Albert Bacon Fall, Clements was himself shot dead in the Coney Island Saloon on December 29, 1908, as he walked across the barroom floor. In a jammed room, no one saw a thing. Clements was buried in El Paso's Evergreen Cemetery, a couple of miles from Concordia and John Wesley Hardin.[16]

JEFFERSON DAVIS HARDIN, John's brother, owned livery stables, saloons, meat markets, farms, and whatever it took to make a living. On October 26, 1896, he married Creed Taylor's daughter, Mary. They had three sons. Jeff Hardin was shot and killed by John Snowden, a son-in-law of Jeff's cousin, at Clairemont, Kent County, Texas in November 1901. Jeff Hardin had recently slain a cattle thief, and he and Snowden had quarreled about it. Snowden claimed self-defense and never went to trial.

JAMES (BARNETT) GIPSON "GIP" HARDIN, the other surviving brother of Wes Hardin, taught school in Junction, Texas in 1897, and eloped in January 1898 with one of the local belles, Pearl Turner. Two months later on March 28, Gip shot and killed deputy sheriff John Turman, his best friend, as a result of an argument at a dinner table. A jury found Gip guilty of murder in the second degree, and the judge sentenced him to thirty-five years in the penitentiary. However, a new trial at Fredericksburg led to a lighter sentence, and Gip spent only a couple of years at Huntsville. After his release, he and his wife separated following the birth of two daughters, and Gip worked in the stockyards of Fort Worth. When World War I started, he took a job transporting horses to Europe for the United States government. Two box cars on board a ship shifted and crushed him to death somewhere off the Florida coast in 1918.

JOHN WESLEY HARDIN, JR., continued to live in Gonzales County, Texas, as a mail carrier and oil salesman. He married Lillie House on February 17, 1898. They had three children, the first named John Wesley Hardin, III, and called Wesley. John Wesley Hardin, Jr. died of a coronary at Nixon, Gonzales County, Texas on October 24, 1931.

MARY ELIZABETH "MOLLIE" HARDIN married Charles Billings. They had twelve children, none of whom were named John or Wesley. She died in 1938 in Nixon and is buried in the Billings Cemetery in Gonzales County.

THE YOUNGEST HARDIN CHILD, Jane "Jennie" Hardin, married John Ross Lyons. They had no children, and spent their lives managing ranching interests as well as a cafe in Kenedy, Texas. She died of a stroke on October 12, 1931, in the Kenedy Cafe in Karnes County, just twelve days before her brother, John Wesley Hardin, Jr.'s death.

Throughout their lives, the three Hardin children lived within thirty-five miles of each other.

UPON THE DEATH OF JOHN WESLEY HARDIN, Beulah returned to El Paso from Phoenix, Arizona, where she was visiting her parents. She paid $77.50 for the entire cost of Hardin's funeral.

Undertakers placed John Wesley Hardin in a coffin with AT REST engraved on the plate. The *Herald* wryly noted that this was probably Hardin's first rest since childhood. A "quiet, even peaceful, smile had spread over the somewhat disfigured features." The undertaking parlor filled with the curious, as "hundreds of people filed through in the afternoon to take a last look at the late noted character whose hand had been against every man and every man's hand was against him."

Reverend C. J. Oxley, of El Paso's Trinity Methodist Church, officiated both at the undertaker's and at graveside.[17] Two carriages and two buggies with friends followed the hearse to Concordia Cemetery where Hardin was laid to rest at four o'clock in the afternoon of August 21.

John Wesley Hardin died intestate at El Paso. In addition to the manuscript, Hardin's earthly possessions were:
- $94.85 in cash.
- Five books, three relating to the General Laws of Texas, one being a small dictionary, and the other *The Rise and Fall of the Confederacy.*
- Several photographs, mostly tintypes.
- One gold ring, ruby or garnet setting.
- Another gold ring with hands clasped.
- A pair of gold cuff links.
- A gold watch chain.
- An Elgin watch.
- A trunk and key.
- A leather valise.
- A pair of opera glasses.
- Assorted items of clothing.
- Two revolvers, a .41 and a .38 caliber. Two additional revolvers were still in possession of the authorities.
- 165-page autobiographical manuscript

The estimated value of the estate was set at one thousand dollars.

A court fight started between his children and Helen Beulah M'Rose, not over the odds and ends but for possession of what the newspapers and the official property inventory described as a 165 page autobiographical manuscript. The court papers referred to it as "196 pages of legal cap writing." The *Herald* noted that "the papers were under lock and key, and no one will be allowed access to them, as Austin publishers have practically completed arrangements to publish the book and pay the estate a handsome sum of money. One man is claiming that he can sell 50,000 copies. In view of this and the fact that publication beforehand in the newspapers would greatly injure the sale of the book, the estate under no condition will allow enterprising correspondents to glimpse the papers. But when the book is published, they can purchase copies and then sit up nights reading the same, if they so desire."[18]

Because Beulah M'Rose had taken charge of Hardin's body, and had paid his funeral expenses—for which no one objected and no one insisted upon reimbursing her—she requested that the court acknowledge her as the sole administrator of the Hardin estate. In particular, she claimed his autobiographical manuscript on the grounds of unpaid secretarial services. Her petition stated that the manuscript "was written by said Hardin and this applicant, at the dictation of said Hardin." Charles Patterson, her attorney, valued the manuscript at two thousand dollars. As she had loaned Hardin $1,575, and taken a note for half-interest in the book, she insisted upon reimbursement either at one-half the sales income, or with a flat $1,575. The court ruled against her.

Although the court gave no written reason for its verdict, justice did not prevail for Beulah M'Rose. She should have won because John Wesley Hardin, estranged from his family, intended for her to have his autobiography.

She had paid for a half-share, and she had a legitimate contract for her half of the autobiography. Beulah had written most of the manuscript. Had it not been for her, the manuscript likely would not have been as complete.

She lost the court battle because she was out-lawyered, and

because the grieving Hardin family received sympathy from the judge. She lost because she was a prostitute, because she had no standing or friends in the community, and because she was a woman. So far as is known, Beulah then disappeared forever from the streets of El Paso, vanishing into the mists of obscurity.[19]

THE HARDIN CHILDREN, through their attorney, P. S. Sowell, may have edited some of the manuscript before publishing it with Smith & Moore, out of Seguin, Texas. The paperback sold for fifty cents, but was of poor quality, the pages quickly turning yellow and brittle. The title read *The Life of John Wesley Hardin, from the Original Manuscript, as Written by Himself*. Following publication, the printers wadded up the manuscript and tossed it into a wastebasket.

The book sold fairly well but never made any of the money Hardin anticipated. The family, likely through embarrassment regarding their father's exploits, pulled it from circulation shortly after release. Over two thousand copies went into a San Antonio warehouse.

During the Callie period of Hardin's life, John visited Mason, Texas, to confer with the *Herald* newspaper editor regarding an "estimate on the cost of printing a small book, the story of his turbulent life." The *Herald* may or may not have expressed interest since the manuscript wasn't much more than just a concept in Hardin's head. Marvin Hunter, then a young boy, happened to be in the newspaper office at that time, and he later recalled Hardin as "a very mild-mannered gentleman, and not the desperado type whatever."[20]

As Hunter grew older, he became a publisher, plus a noted historian and author of the classic *Album of Gunfighters*. In 1925, Hunter reprinted the *Life* in a sixty page softcover along with comments regarding Hardin's death. The magazine *Frontier Times* followed with an "Introductory," and then serialized the book from September through December 1925. Today, Hunter's 1925 book is as rare as the original edition.

The University of Oklahoma Press has kept the book continuously in print since 1961. An outstanding introduction by Robert G. McCubbin explains the tortured trail of the original manuscript, and adds additional details regarding Hardin's death.

Given the contributions, skills and abilities of Beulah, Hardin wrote a good narrative. Readers might justifiably argue that it is self-serving, and so it is, but so are most autobiographies. Hardin left out numerous facts, details and events, perhaps intentionally. He loaded it with idle boasting, and he saturated the pages with maddening contradictions and inconsistencies. A portion of this is due to his and Beulah's lack of writing experience, and to the fact that since he never completed the manuscript, he also never edited it. Nevertheless, he told much that would not otherwise be known, and his first person account is an extraordinary contribution to Western history.

Hardin's prison years were an ideal stopping point, and he had almost written through them, reaching the year 1889 before Selman's bullet put a final period on the page. Given additional time (but with Hardin's drinking problem, and Beulah being gone, time may have been irrelevant), Hardin might have added additional prison experiences and details. He might also have discussed his pardon efforts, perhaps thrown in a couple of paragraphs about the Coleman-Jones race for sheriff of Gonzales County, mentioned El Paso, and concluded with plans for the future. In short, based on the length of material he had already written, Hardin was within ten to twenty manuscript pages of completion when he died.

An adequate editor would have retained Hardin's idle boasting and his prejudices. His points of view would have remained undisturbed. However, a skillful editor would have clarified his awkwardly constructed sentences; and would have insisted upon more particulars. For instance, Hardin wrote almost nothing about his wife, his mother and father, or his children. The characters he meets, and sometimes kills, the friends and relatives he associates with, are cardboard, incomplete figures. Hardin's autobiography is a masterpiece of facts and movements vs. discrepancies and evasions.

The true number of Hardin killings remains far from certain. A count by this author continued throughout this book, but that was dropped, and nothing more said, because an obvious conclusion is that the accuracy of any number is open to question.

The correct figures could have been as few as twenty dead men, or more than fifty. A primary question regarding his

John Wesley Hardin's grave in El Paso's Concordia Cemetery.
The grave is one of the city's premier tourist attractions where flowers,
both real and artificial, have often been left. Also found at the grave have
been decks of cards, toy six-shooters, dice, whiskey bottles (usually empty)
and notes. The grave has a reinforced, dirt-covered concrete apron
to discourage vandalism. The body of Martin M'Rose lies three
graves north of Hardin's. (Author's Collection)

autobiography is not "Did he kill all those people he claims he
did," but "How many other deaths did he neglect to mention?"

If Hardin was not so deeply entrenched as a Western figure,
a gunfighter with all of its accompanying mystery, legend and
myth, he would be identified as one of this country's leading
psychotic killers. What sets him apart from most others is that he

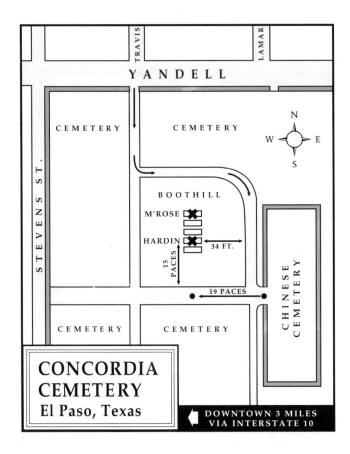

did not shoot women and children; and the men he killed were rarely the salt of the earth.

Another reason why Hardin never finished his autobiography is that as he progressed toward the end of his life, he understood less and less the age in which he lived. He understood himself least of all. In this respect, his own autobiography offered a lot of justification but scant personal insight.

The 1890s simply were not the 1860s and the 1870s. Hardin's youth had passed silently during the dark night of his prison years. At a little over forty-two years of age, John Wesley Hardin had outlived his era. He was an anachronism, a psychopathic gunman out of the past, a man more or less waiting to be buried.

John Selman not only killed John Wesley Hardin; more importantly, he did him a favor.

The Great Attempted Body Snatching Caper

AUGUST 19, 1995, MARKED the 100th anniversary of the death of John Wesley Hardin in El Paso. In early July, a small group of El Pasoans, including myself, Robert G. McCubbin, Bobby McNellis, Paul Northrop, and Herb Marsh met in the Hacienda Cafe. Mary Kime, owner of the Hacienda, joined us, as did Deen Underwood, a western writer and school teacher, and a local civic group of gun handlers known as the Paso del Norte Pistoleros.

We shared a common interest in John Wesley Hardin, El Paso's notorious resident of Concordia Cemetery.

Everyone agreed that this century-old killing should not pass unnoticed. Therefore, since the Hacienda had a bar similar to the Acme Saloon bar of 1895, we would reenact the shooting on August 19, 1995. McNellis agreed to handle publicity, and to stage bar scene shooting incidents utilizing the Pistoleros.

I would write a ten-page booklet entitled *Four Sixes to Beat*, and Bob McCubbin would handle the editing, designing and publishing of five hundred copies. They would sell on August 19 for five dollars each. The Concordia Cemetery Heritage Association, a non-profit El Paso organization seeking guardianship of the frontier cemetery, would be the recipient of all profits.[1]

The First Annual Reenactment of the Death of John Wesley Hardin (played by El Paso Police officer Bill Mansion), took place

High Noon at El Paso's Concordia Cemetery on Sunday, August 27, 1995. Five representatives from Nixon, Texas, attempt to disinter Hardin's body. Left to right are Randy and Donald Hoffman, Wendle Scott, Richard Faulkner and Donald Finch. (Jack Kurtz/El Paso Times)

at one o'clock on August 19. A second shooting, this one in slow motion, followed a few minutes later. From then on, the reenactment occurred every hour on the hour until seven o'clock. Observers paid two dollars admission. The fee also bought them a drink of their choice.

The final reenactment cost a little more, but the viewers received a meal, plus trolley transportation to the downtown area where I gave a ten o'clock walking tour of John Wesley Hardin's El Paso. From there the trolley moseyed to Concordia Cemetery where at one minute past eleven that night, the exact moment of Hardin's death, a few random but blank shots roared into the air, everyone had a drink on John Wesley Hardin, and the trolley returned to the Hacienda Cafe. Approximately one thousand people either watched the performances that day, or participated in the ceremonies that evening. One of these was Ernest Spellman, a great-grandson of Hardin, and a dentist in Beeville, Texas. His father, Elmer Spellman, had been largely responsible for marking Hardin's grave in 1965.[2]

In the meantime, vague rumors had been circulating that a group in Nixon, Texas (east of San Antonio in Gonzales County) planned to remove Hardin's body from Concordia Cemetery. It would be transported to Nixon and reburied. No one in El Paso gave credence to such a preposterous story.

Innocence changed at four-thirty on Friday afternoon, August 25, 1995, when I received word from an East Texas friend that several Nixon people, including an undertaker, would be in El Paso's Concordia Cemetery at seven o'clock Sunday morning, August 27. They planned to dig up Hardin, load him into a box, and take him east on I-10 before anyone in El Paso realized what had happened.

Although I suspected this story was a hoax, I nevertheless notified several El Paso history buffs. We all agreed to meet in Concordia Cemetery on Sunday morning at six o'clock.

Some of our group took the grave robbing possibility more seriously than I, however. Several showed up on Saturday, anticipating that the scavengers might arrive a day earlier. In their zeal, though, some of the good guys, meaning people on our side, fearful that a twenty-four hour vigil over the grave could not be maintained, decided to remove the tombstone. They theorized that the Nixon bunch would be unable to identify an unmarked grave.

The plot thickened, and other well-meaning people, coming along later in the day, noticed the absent stone and assumed the grave had already been breached. They filed a police report. Archaeologists determined that the grave was still occupied even though the marker was missing.

Other concerned citizens prevailed upon El Paso Judge Sam Paxson to write an injunction preventing Hardin's removal until the issue had been resolved in court. Because it was a weekend, and county offices were closed, Paxson hand-wrote the restraining order. Mayor Larry Francis ordered police to place an around-the-clock police guard on Hardin's grave.

On Sunday morning, August 27, approximately fifty people, a couple of police officers, and a swarm of media representatives were at Hardin's grave a little after six. At seven o'clock, two locally-retained grave diggers arrived, and were told there would be no work for them that day.

At 7:20, in a scene right out of High Noon, minus weapons, six men from Nixon, Texas, led by funeral director Don Finch, strode into the cemetery and up to Hardin's grave. Finch presented a legitimate, signed Texas Department of Health certificate giving his group permission to disinter Hardin's remains. A police officer handed Finch the Paxson injunction forbidding any removal until the controversy had been legally resolved.

The Nixon group consisted of Finch, Donald Hoffman (businessman and civic leader, plus chairman and organizer of the Rancho Nixon Historical Society), Randy Hoffman (Donald's son), Thomas Lindley (Nixon historian), Richard Faulkner (Nixon-Smiley school superintendent), and the Nixon editor of the *Cow County Courier*, Wendle Scott.

The resultant "testy" conversation swung back and forth, the Nixon people (truthfully) claiming they represented the Hardin descendants, although none were present. Their plan called for the removal of Hardin's remains to Nixon (where they said he grew up), and to bury him beside his first wife, Jane. The El Paso contingent refuted the argument, pointing out how Nixon did not even exist until 1906, that Hardin had not grown up in Gonzales County, and that the Hardin family had never, until now, shown any interest in placing Hardin next to Jane. She, incidentally, lies in the Bowen cemetery in Gonzales County but not in Nixon.

Each side accused the other of planning to use Hardin for publicity purposes. Interestingly, each group vigorously denied it, although Hardin, as a significant historical figure, justly deserves to be a cornerstone of any tourism program.

The Concordia Heritage Association retained El Paso attorney Chris Johnston to keep Hardin's remains intact and in El Paso. On the following day, Monday, Johnston took the case to El Paso's 205th District Court where Visiting Judge James Onion continued the temporary injunction. On August 31, Chris Johnston and the El Paso Concordia Heritage Association, in a long planned move now made more imperative, filed for legal guardianship of Concordia Cemetery in El Paso County Court-of-Law No. 5. The guardianship outlined an ambitious $1.4 million plan to restore and promote the cemetery. It would include the construction of a visitor's center, restoration of graves, protection of property, lighting, plus informational packets and trails to dozens of historically significant graves.

In the meantime, the Hardin gravestone turned up on the sidewalk alongside the El Paso Saddlery, owned by Bobby McNellis. The stone wasn't damaged, and was returned to Hardin's grave.[3]

On September 2, El Paso residents, led by Mission Trail Association's Sheldon Hall, poured a reinforced concrete apron on Hardin's grave. The object was not to frustrate the Nixon people, but to prevent local vandals from taking advantage of the publicity and digging up the old gunman as a prank.[4]

Nearly two weeks later, on Monday, September 11, El Paso 205th District Judge Kathleen Olivares set a trial date for January 29, 1996.

The nonjury trial started at one o'clock in the afternoon, and ended the following day (Tuesday, January 30), at noon or shortly thereafter. Attorneys Christopher R. Johnston and Victor F. Poulos defended the El Paso Concordia Heritage Association while attorneys Frank E. Billings, a great-great grandson of John Wesley Hardin and a name partner of Houston's Billings & Solomon, and Gene F. Stevens, himself a Hardin descendant, represented the Nixon, Texas contingent. During the eight to ten hour bitterly fought case, all four attorneys did a remarkably fine, professional job of defending their clients and attacking the opposition.

Nixon funeral director Don Finch testified that the Texas Department of Health had given him a valid permit to remove Hardin's body. However, that permit came under close scrutiny when it was revealed that a grave digger had signed off as cemetery caretaker. The actual ownership of the grave also came under question, the Hardin descendants insisting that they were the rightful owners. However, a hundred or more years before, Beulah M'Rose, Hardin's final lady love, had paid all funeral costs. No record exists that she signed any ownership papers over to the family.

John W. Billings, a Hardin great-grandson, testified that "all I had heard or read out of El Paso was that they [presumably the Concordia Heritage Association] portrayed him [Hardin] as a mad-dog killer, or a Texas gunslinger. There's no denying he killed a few people. In Gonzales County he's gonna be considered a family man who got caught in the aftermath of the Civil War."

Billings denied that financial considerations had anything to do with transferring the Hardin remains to Nixon. "The primary thought was to reunite Hardin and Jane," he stated.

When a Hardin great-granddaughter took the stand, she reiterated that the purpose of removing Hardin was to unite him and Jane. The family wanted Jane out of an abandoned cemetery in an overgrown, weed-covered pasture. She and her husband John should lie side by side.

When Attorney Vic Poulos questioned the witness, he asked that should the Nixon contingent lose its case, would she consent to moving Jane from Gonzales County to the Concordia Cemetery in El Paso? She stammered "No." So much for togetherness.

Not all descendants were in agreement on the need to move Hardin, however. Elmer C. Spellman and Audrey Spellman Corder, great-grandchildren of Hardin, traveled from Beeville, Texas, to testify in court for the Concordia Heritage Association. They pointed out that their parents had marked Hardin's grave during the 1960s, adding that they did not think Hardin should be relocated. Both Spellman descendants felt the same way. Finally, the question arose as to whether Hardin even occupied the grave with his stone on it. The Nixon faction gave an emphatic "Yes;" the El Paso group expressed numerous uncertainties. When El Pasoans insisted on DNA testing prior to any possible removal, the Nixon supporters countered that they could do any necessary analysis down in central Texas, the implication being that if they had the wrong body, they would simply bring it back to El Paso and exchange it for another.

Oddly, one other factor never arose in court obviously because neither side had ever researched the question. Yet, it might have had far reaching, decisive significance especially for the Concordia Heritage Association. That involved moving Jane out of the Bowen family cow pasture plot in Gonzales County. It might have strengthened the Nixon case if she had already been transferred to this pleasant hillside in the Nixon Cemetery. She wasn't, because the Bowen family might have protested that the cemetery where she lay was not abandoned. By some accounts, they would have fought vigorously to keep her from being transferred into Nixon.[5]

After final court arguments ended, Judge Olivares took the case under advisement, stating that she would re-read the testimony and check pertinent, applicable laws. Her decision would be handed down in a few weeks.

On Monday, February 19, 1996, she found in favor of the Concordia Heritage Association. Hardin would stay where he was. Judge Olivares cited nine points of law, one being that the Nixon faction had failed to comply with the Texas Health and Safety Code in getting the proper and necessary cemetery signatures and authorizations. Furthermore, the evidence persuaded her that "the location and identification of the remains of John Wesley Hardin cannot be precisely determined and the attempted removal of the body from Concordia Cemetery will cause irreparable harm to the graves and remains surrounding the alleged grave of John Wesley Hardin." She also noted that the trend of court decisions indicate that "the disinterment of dead bodies is discouraged. Removal is not permitted except under circumstances indicating a necessity or for compelling reasons."[6]

In mid-1996, the Nixon attorneys requested "findings of fact and conclusions of law" from Judge Olivares. In other words, they asked for additional information regarding her verdict. Attorneys study material such as this, evaluating what it contains and how it is worded. She responded, but when the lawyers solicited even more data, Judge Olivares replied that her decision needed no further clarification. The case is being appealed to the 8th Court of Appeals in El Paso where a panel of three appellate judges will determine if any critical errors of law were made during the trial, or in the decision. If such is determined, the appeals court can reverse the trial verdict and render a verdict themselves, or send it back to Judge Kathleen Olivares for retrial. Should the appeals court approve the trial verdict, the case automatically terminates in El Paso's favor unless the Nixon attorneys take their final legal step and appeal to the Texas Supreme Court for a "writ of error."

But whatever happens, wherever the bones of Hardin eventually reside, the Great Attempted Body Snatching Caper will be just the latest incredible chapter in John Wesley Hardin's extraordinary career.

Acknowledgments

Appendixes

Notes

Bibliography

Index

Acknowledgments

SO MANY PEOPLE HAVE HELPED. So much is owed. Chuck Parsons sent enormous amounts of material, did research, read manuscript, and guided me along dirt roads and through cemeteries.

Margaret Waring simply "made" the Comanche portion of the manuscript. She knows history, she knows courthouses. As the Comanche librarian she understands the strengths and weaknesses of obscure records. She could be firm and tough, but still gentle, in expressing a point of view.

Eddie Day Truitt was invaluable in terms of the Feud. She read manuscript, she led me through old graveyards and county seats that no longer exist. She opened the door to the Taylor Party.

Marjorie Lee Burnett read manuscript, found a photo, and pointed out graves and buildings I would never have located otherwise.

Dale Walker gave me the benefit of hours of his time. He even walked me through certain portions of the manuscript, describing strengths and weaknesses.

Robert G. "Bob" McCubbin, of course, is a long-time treasured friend. He read manuscript, gave of his wise counsel, and supplied many of the photos for this book.

Bobby McNellis and his brother John assisted with their vast knowledge of John Wesley Hardin and the El Paso Southwest.

James Day, like the old friend he has always been, came through every time I needed him.

Randy Lee Eickhoff and Myrna Zanetell edited and suggested revisions for various portions of the manuscript.

The especially creative Vicki Trego Hill did such a splendid job of computer graphics.

Fain McDaniel taught me how to find graves, opened up the marvelous Comanche museum for my inspection, and sent numerous photos.

Bob Barron, a long-time friend, translated hand-written letters and documents into typed English that I could read.

Ralph Hamilton is not only a friend, but a computer genius. Time after time during the course of this manuscript, he dug me out of computer glitches that I constantly managed to toss myself into.

Nancy Hamilton, Ralph's wife, did the excellent job of indexing.

Joyce Hardin Cavett, Jo Foster, and Oran Hardin were genealogists on call. They read manuscript and provided the vital ancestral keys to the roots of John Wesley Hardin.

Donaly Brice, Supervisor for Reference Services at the Texas State Archives in Austin, was always cooperative, always patient. Donaly is one of the state's great archival assets.

Rick Miller and Doug Ellison sent material on Hardin and Bill Longley. A. J. Wright sent me Florida/Alabama information relating to the capture of John Wesley Hardin.

Walter Dixson helped me through many obscure Hardin trails, and never failed to assist when needed.

Patrick King considered writing his own biography of Hardin. He would have done it well, but he graciously shared his research with me.

Gary Fitterer, in the process of his own research, sent me numerous newspaper clippings relating to Hardin. Gary's letters were always filled with good will and good advice.

Bill Reynolds is a top gun at finding information on anyone who was anybody in the Southwest. Bill kindly shared whatever he found. Bill died before this book was finished.

Robin Gilliam, Curator of History at the Silver City, New Mexico museum, evaluated clothing worn by John Wesley Hardin.

Sam Tumlinson, a direct descendant of the "Fighting

Tumlinsons," was always kind and helpful in helping me unravel the Tumlinson story.

Deen Underwood read manuscript, did various pieces of Hardin research, and turned up several unknown items such as the interesting comparison of Hardin with the Cisco Kid.

Mary Betke, in a meeting by chance, researched a couple of thorny Hardin questions I would never have resolved without her.

José Andow made many photo copies for this book. Terry Hammond, an El Paso attorney friend, offered legal advice with respect to Hardin. Bill James offered insight regarding Jim Miller. Karen Mac Smith told me about Albuquerque, Texas. T. Lindsey Baker offered assistance regarding Martin and Beulah M'Rose, Frances Hartmann provided information on the Duderstadts. Drew Gomber, Judge Herb Marsh, George Atwood, Wayne Daniel, Arturo J. Ortiz, Sr., Bus Riley, Anita Miller, Sheldon Hall, Paul Northrop, Barry Worrell, Michael Bernstein and wife Carol, Phillip Steele, Ed Thormaehlen, Hollis E. Dowlearn, Jr., Herman Weisner, Rosa Sharp, Thomas B. Moore, Paul Hoylen, Jr., Virginia Short, Robert B. Wales, Bill Wood, Wiloise Blyth, Darrell Jepson, Loretta Kelldorf, Mike Cox, Bena Taylor Kirkscey, Jack and Ernestine Austin, Clinton Hartmann and Alan Richmond, gave of their time and hearts in answering my endless inquiries.

I thank my publishers, Frank and Judy Mangan of Mangan Books, who as usual did it all; and my wife, Cheryl, who never complained when I started every conversation with comments about John Wesley Hardin.

And finally, my thanks always goes out to librarians, the priceless ingredients for any research. What would writers do without them?

Appendixes

APPENDIX A

BENJAMIN HARDIN II was born between 1705 and 1710,[1] whereas his son Joseph was born near Richmond, Virginia on April 18, 1734. Because father and son believed the Church of England was persecuting them (the Hardins were strict Presbyterians and religious dissenters), the family moved to the west side of the Catawba River, which separated North and South Carolina, and took up residence forty miles southwest of Salisbury, North Carolina. Joseph cleared a farm and built a family fort for defense against Indians.

When a revolutionary movement arose, Governor Tryon—a staunch British loyalist and professional soldier known as "The Great Wolf of North Carolina"—ruthlessly hanged his enemies. When he required male inhabitants to take an oath of allegiance to the Crown, he forced individuals like the Hardins into the wilderness backwoods where they migrated back and forth from North Carolina into the territories of Tennessee and Kentucky.

After participating in the 1760 Cherokee Indian wars, Joseph and his relatives, along with fifty neighbors, on August 14, 1775, wrote the "Mecklenburg Declaration of Independence," better known as the "Tryon Declaration" (named for Tryon County).[2] The opening statement denounced the "unprecedented, barbarous and bloody actions committed by British troops on our American brethren near Boston." It insisted that "the hostile operations and traitorous designs now carrying on by tools of ministerial vengeance and despotism…suggest to us the painful necessity of having recourse to arms…."[3]

Joseph Hardin was a Light Horse commander during the

Cherokee Indian Wars, as well as a minuteman captain in the Salisbury District during 1775. He engaged the British (actually a fight between Tories and Whigs) in the Battle of Ramsour's Mill on the south fork of the Catawba River in North Carolina. Following that came the Battle of King's Mountain in 1780 when rebels slaughtered part of the Lord Charles Cornwallis forces. Somewhere along these battlefield roads, Joseph became a major in the armed forces of North Carolina. There is no evidence of additional promotions, but by the time of his death in Tennessee, folks called him Colonel Hardin. Colonel Joseph Hardin is the way history remembers him.

Back in 1763, Joseph married Jane Gibson, and they raised fourteen children. Of these, Amos and Robert became Baptist and Presbyterian ministers. Two others were slain by Indians while small boys, and a son named John was killed by Indians at Lookout Mountain.

Before the Revolutionary War ended, Colonel Hardin moved his family to the northwest sector of North Carolina where he represented Greene County as a commissioner. When North Carolina failed to dispatch assistance against Indians in 1784, three northern counties separated from North Carolina and formed the independent state of Franklin, a rugged region named for Benjamin Franklin in the hope of getting his support. The area has often been referred to as the "Lost State of Franklin." The aspiring state wrote a constitution and elected its own governor. When North Carolina regained control of the errant Franklin in 1788, it pardoned Hardin and his cohorts, although Hardin was one of the last to take the oath of allegiance. Since Tennessee was now insisting upon statehood, North Carolina, tired of quarreling with its belligerent northwestern territory, ceded Franklin in 1790 to the United States. Washington allocated the land to Tennessee, and granted Tennessee statehood on June 1, 1796. The Hardin clan, plus the Lost State of Franklin, officially passed into Tennessee. Joseph Hardin chaired the "Government Formation Committee."

Because of his Revolutionary War and Indian fighting activities, the federal government awarded Colonel Joseph Hardin 3,000 acres in Tennessee. That area is now Hardin County, and borders on Mississippi. Joseph never lived on this grant, however, preferring to reside on 2,000-acres he purchased and called Hardin Valley,[4] fourteen miles from the then state capital, Knoxville. Hardin became an influential member of the legislature, as well as a trustee of Greeneville College. He died in Hardin Valley, Tennessee, in 1801. Although a staunch Presbyterian to the end, Colonel Joseph Hardin was buried in the Hickory Creek Baptist Cemetery, now known as the Mt. Pleasant Baptist Church Cemetery near Concord and Lenoir City, south of Knoxville[5]

Benjamin Hardin, the oldest son of Joseph, was born February 28, 1782 in what was North Carolina, but in 1796 became Tennessee. In 1801 (or 1802) the twenty-year-old Benjamin married the eighteen-year-old Martha Ann "Patsy" Barnett. Benjamin and Patsy would have four daughters and seven sons, one of whom became the father of John Wesley Hardin.

Since the War of 1812 stirred hopes of liberty among the Creek Indians, they overran Fort Mimms in Alabama. As panic spread across the southern frontier, Andrew Jackson organized a group of Tennessee militia. Ben Hardin served until December 1814 as a teamster. On March 27, 1814, Jackson's forces destroyed Creek power and ambitions at the Battle of Horseshoe Bend on Alabama's Tallapoosa River. Nearly eight hundred Indians died. The Creeks sued for peace. [6]

In the spring of 1816, additional Hardin relatives formed a colonizing expedition of twenty-six people. They divided into two parties, one by land and the other by flatboat on the Tennessee River. Ben took possession of a 1,000-acre grant in Wayne County where the Natchez Trace crossed Factor's Fork on Shoal Creek.

Commissioners forming Wayne County met at his house in 1817. Ben served as the first sheriff, and entered the Tennessee legislature with James K. Polk. Benjamin's principal income stemmed from the buying and selling of real estate, and he even sold land to the future United States President, James K. Polk. Although Benjamin was not primarily a slave dealer, sometimes he transacted slaves individually as with a sixteen-year-old black girl named Louise whom he sold for $500. He guaranteed her to be "sound and healthy in body and mind."[7] Otherwise, when slaves came with the property, Benjamin auctioned them after providing the legal twenty days notice in a Nashville or Columbia newspaper.

APPENDIX B

THE TENNESSEE-BORN WILLIAM BARNETT HARDIN was seventeen-years-older than his brother James. Barnett married Ann Holshousen in 1829, left Tennessee in 1831, and paused long enough to father a child in Arkansas before arriving in Polk County, Texas, in 1833. In November 1835, Barnett Hardin enlisted as a sergeant in a company commanded by Captain M. B. Lewis who recruited his men primarily from Jasper, Tyler and Polk counties. On November 16, the unit consolidated with the Republic of Texas army laying siege to San Antonio de Bexar. This force, led by colonist and military man Ben Milam, opened the battle on December 5, 1835 and defeated Mexican General Martín Perfecto de Cós. Hardin participated in bitter house-to-house fighting and took a bullet in the leg. He limped for the remainder of his life, but left the Texas army in September 1836 as a first lieutenant.

Barnett would have been a likely Hardin to sign the Texas Declaration of Independence from Mexico in 1836, and some descendants credit him with doing so. A Hardin did sign, but he was not Barnett or even of John Wesley Hardin's line.[1]

Barnett acquired his first-class headright at Moscow, Texas, and because of wounds received in the Republic of Texas army, he received two additional land grants near the Polk County seat of Livingston. In 1855, Barnett moved to his Livingston plantation on Long Tom Creek, four miles northwest of town.

Barnett never outgrew the poverty of his early life. Even when he became relatively affluent, he fretted. His letters contained a litany of complaints regarding his economic and medical woes. His relatives chuckled. Although he outlived practically everyone, "he was always about to starve, [or] some member of his family was always on the brink of death, [or] he expected death to overtake him momentarily."[2]

Still, Barnett donated land and helped organize the Methodist Church at Livingston. He befriended the Alabama Indians, a tribe forced out of its homeland in the Alabama/Mississippi region and compelled to settle near the Trinity River in East Texas about 1807. After the Texas War for Independence, the Alabamans returned from Louisiana to learn that white men had confiscated their Texas land. But they always found a friend and employer in Barnett Hardin. He served as an advisor (by other accounts an Indian agent appointed by Sam Houston) to chiefs Long King, Colita, Antone, Tempe, Long Tom and Bill Blout. On October 29, 1853, Barnett circulated a petition, calling for Texas to grant a reservation to the Alabama Indian tribe. A year later the state purchased and donated to the Indians a tract of 1,280 acres. It formed the initial unit of the present Alabama-Coushatta Indian Reservation.[3]

Although Polk County was Big Thicket country, Barnett Hardin likely made his living with cotton. He had sufficient land to consider himself a planter, and his home a modest plantation. He owned perhaps a half-dozen slaves, small by regional standards.

APPENDIX C

JOHN HUGH "IRISH JACK" DIXON MOVED from Indiana to Illinois to Missouri, and in 1858 migrated to Fannin County, Texas. Dixon farmed a grant of land in his wife's name at Pilot Grove in Grayson County.

Grayson, Fannin, Hunt and Collin counties intersected at a point called Four Corners where thickets lured renegades, desperados, Union sympathizers and Confederate deserters. This section had voted against secession in 1861. During Reconstruction, Jack entered the freight-hauling business with his sons Billy, Simpson (Simp), Bob and Charlie, plus Dick Johnson, a half-brother. Their wagons journeyed as far as Jefferson near the Louisiana border.

Bob Lee, one of Dixon's cousins, who was handsome, tall and muscular, had joined the South and fought alongside the brilliant cavalry commander General Nathan Bedford Forrest in the Tennessee and Louisiana campaigns. When he returned, Lee proved a difficult man to reconstruct. He clashed verbally and physically with Lewis Peacock, a former Missouri wagon-maker who lived near Pilot Grove in Grayson County. As the feud heated up, someone shot Lee in the back of the head, but he survived. Assassins killed the doctor who treated him. As killings mounted, the Fifth Military District out of Austin put a $1000 reward on Lee's head. With the Army woefully shorthanded, it depended upon civilians to maintain order. Lewis Peacock, a rising power in regional Republican circles, organized a Union League comprised of rowdies who hid in the thickets. Peacock recruited Henry Boren, a Unionist neighbor and a cousin of Bob Lee.

Peacock's Union League caught up with Lee in early June 1869, as Lee left his ranch house. Henry Boren fired the fatal shot, and sponsored a dance that night at his house.[1]

Bill Boren, Henry's nephew (and a Hardin cousin), who had served with Bob Lee in the Confederate cavalry, raced furiously to Henry's ranch after learning of the assassination. He found Enoch chopping wood. "Enoch," Bill screamed, "is your father home?" At that instant, Henry appeared at the door and ordered Bill off his property. Bill fired the first shot, and Henry died. Bill Boren went into hiding and did not return to Fannin County until the mid-to-late 1870s. Boren thereupon wrote Henry's brother, Dick, explaining that he hoped bygones could be bygones. Bill pointed out that he had done his best to understand Henry, saying:

> I know you are aware that my feelings were against the Union as was most of my countrymen, and Henry was with us at the first just as you were. I felt no anxiousness when Henry joined the Unionist cause as we had never seen eye to eye on matters anyway, and I thought this was just another [dispute], but his friendliness with the Peacock faction against cousin Bob Lee was a thorn in all our sides. Still I felt no anxiousness. Then Henry stained the proud Texas name of Boren with the blood of cousin Bob Lee.

Bill Boren also mentioned costs paid by most families. "Haven't we all lost a brother in this cause," he asked? "I know you will recall that my brother Isham died at the hands of the same Unionists and warmongers that Henry saw fit to join up with. He might as well have pulled the trigger and shot the ball that killed brother Isham."

Bill did not apologize for killing Henry, but he hoped Dick would understand and forgive him. Apparently Dick did.

After killing Henry, Bill Boren fled south and lived with Wes Hardin. Both became cowboys. Without being specific, Boren disapproved of the "ways" of Wes Hardin, but gave Hardin credit for being "a good friend [who] stood by me through it all."[2]

Meanwhile, the Dixons fared just as harshly as the Borens. They too had supported the Bob Lee faction.

Peacock partisans and Union soldiers surprised sixteen-year-old Billy and Charlie while the Dixons were hauling cotton to Jefferson. They captured both brothers at Hog-Eye, lashed them to a wagon wheel and whipped them. Billy died, and the slayers looted his body, stealing even the spurs.

The Peacock gang next ambushed Jack Dixon and his sons Bob, Charlie and stepson Dick Johnson while the Dixons were cutting timber at Black Jack Grove, now called Cumby. Bob died first, then Charlie. Jack and Dick suffered wounds, although both crawled into the brush and recovered. After the attackers rode away, Jack loaded his two dead boys into an ox cart and took them home for burial. Dick Johnson fled to West Texas.[3]

With his brothers dead, except for half-brother Dick Johnson, Simp Dixon scampered south to Navarro County and teamed up with cousin John Wesley Hardin.

As an afterword, Dick Johnson, the last male in the Dixon family, returned to Pilot Grove. His sisters and mother accused the Union League of threatening to burn them out. Johnson and two friends resolved his family's anxiety by waylaying Peacock with a shotgun. *Flake's Bulletin* of Galveston reported that

> "we are creditably informed that the famous Lewis Peacock, formerly chief-in-command of the Peacock Party, was shot to atoms this morning in his yard. You have heard of the foul murder of Billy Dixon at Hog-Eye three years ago, and also of the brutal murder of Elijah Clark. These are the cardinal points that prompted the destruction of Lewis Peacock. May God grant this sinful world, peace."

Johnson escaped to Missouri where he lived out his life free from arrest.[4]

APPENDIX D

ROBERT ECHISON HARDIN, John Wesley Hardin's uncle, born and raised in Tennessee, married Nancy Brinson Dixon. Uncle Bob arrived in Texas at Polk County in 1844-45, lived a brief time in Limestone County, and spent the majority of his life, and died, around Brenham in Washington County. Graham Lodge No. 20 in Brenham recorded that he served as a Masonic Senior Steward in 1855, rose to Tiler in 1856, and became a Junior Warden in 1859. According to the 1870 census, Robert Hardin had a real estate and personal property value of $8,000. He listed his occupation as farmer. His three boys (William, Aaron and Joseph) lived with him and also worked as farmers. Upon his death on February 6, 1881, the *Daily Banner* in Brenham referred to Uncle Bob as "a plain and unassuming farmer, a good neighbor universally honored and respected by the entire community." The Baptist Church held the services and parishioners buried him in the nearby Prairie Lee Cemetery.

The 1870 census also listed an eighteen-year-old "John Hardin," and this was John Wesley Hardin although he was only seventeen. While Robert had a son named John Dixon Hardin, in 1870 he lived in a separate household.

APPENDIX E

(The following letter, in possession of the author, was a handwritten copy. Excepts of site locations have been taken from the letter for description of the map on page 263, chapter 27).

To – Jake E. Manigold, (El Paso Probation Officer)
From – Stanley Good
        920 – 10th Street
        Alamo, New Mexico   15 August 1959

Dear J.E.

My wife told me that you had expressed a keen interest in early El Paso history and that you wanted to know where John Wesley Hardin was killed.

I have made a rough sketch of the area and have numbered these points that were related to the killing.

1. The Acme Saloon (on San Antonio.)

2. The gambling room in back.

3. Short alley to gambling room from Mesa.

4. Popular Dry Goods at Texas and Mesa was a vacant lot at that time.

5. Lodging House.

6. The Wigwam Saloon.

7. Clifford Brothers grocery store.

8. Corner of San Antonio and Utah Sts., now San Antonio and So. Mesa.—It was across the street and in line with the front doors of the Acme Saloon.

Now that we have identified the area, we will go into the story as I saw it.

Perry Greer, Jr. was a little boy about my age. He lived at the corner of Mesa and Texas in a red brick house. His father was a bar tender at the Acme Saloon. I don't know how old Mr. Greer was at that time, but his hair was almost white. He looked too old to have such a little boy as Perry, but he was Perry's father.

All the houses on the north side of Texas St. Where Perry lived had very small yards. The Good's had a very large yard with trees, a big lawn and wooden swing that held four children.

The children of the neighborhood spent a lot of their time in my yard in the day time, but after supper their folks tried to keep them at home, or at least in front of their homes. So they would play on the vacant lot across the street where their folks could keep an eye on them. Sometimes my mother would let me go down to the vacant lot too.

The evening Hardin was killed I was with the other children on the vacant lot. (Mesa and Texas) Parents had been calling their children to come home as it was reaching their bed time. Finally only Perry and I were left. We were digging in the sand among the roots of a big mesquite clump located close to Mesa Ave. Just across the street from the alley (3) entrance to the Acme gambling room. Our folks hadn't called us home yet.

Our attention was first drawn in that direction when Al Wood, the Negro porter at the Acme Saloon, came out of the alley like a bear might have been chasing him. He was almost to the middle of the street when we called to him and asked what he was running for. Al was scared and breathing hard. He barely checked his speed to say, "just killed a man in there," and kept going to the north on Mesa Ave.

Perry said, "I wonder if it was my Dad?" I said, "Let's go see." We ran across and went in the alley (3) to the back door of the gambling room (2). Everyone in the room was gathered at the half doors that led into the saloon (1) from the gambling room, so we went in. We couldn't see from the back of the group of men crowding the door way, so we started in between legs. I was ahead. The men were holding the half doors open so they could see.

I got to where I could see the man on the floor. He head was turned the other way. I couldn't tell who it was, but he had dark brown hair. There was a hole in the back of his head with blood oozing out of the hole.

I called back to Perry, "It's not your Dad?" Some man said, "What are you kids doing in here? Get out." We left as soon as we could wiggle back through the forest of legs. Perry went home in a run, and I did the same so that I could tell my Mother that I had seen the dead man.

When my Father got home, he had all the news. It is a matter of common knowledge that there had been trouble between Selman and Hardin for some time. Hardin played cards and did most of his drinking at the Acme Saloon. The day of the killing Selman's son, known as young John, arranged with a clerk at Clifford Brothers Grocery to leave some shipping boxes out on the sidewalk at (7) on the corner. He stacked the cases up high enough to see over the paint marks on the door and windows at the Acme saloon opposite.

When the Selmans got word that Hardin had gone into the Acme Saloon, young John got his Winchester and went to his stack of boxes. He was supposed to shoot Hardin from across the street through the windows if his Dad got caught trying to shoot Hardin in the back.

As it happened, there were so many people lined up at the bar that he couldn't see Hardin, so he never fired a shot.

Hardin entered the saloon at the San Antonio St. entrance. He had to walk to the far end of the bar before he found a vacant place. This was right next to the swing half doors into the gambling room. A bartender, (not Mr. Greer) went to wait on Hardin. Hardin called for the dice box to play "Ship, Captain and Crew" for his drink, or pay double. He rolled his three times and passed the dice box to the bartender saying, "Four Sixes to Beat."

Selman had word of Hardin's position. [Here, Good's observation of the slaying varies slightly from others.] He slipped to the swinging doors from the gambling room, stuck his arm through with his pistol cocked. The muzzle of the pistol was about two feet from the back of Hardin's head. Just as Hardin handed the dice back to the bartender Selman pulled the trigger. Hardin fell backwards and collapsed across the door to the gambling room.

Selman was charged with murder and made bond. Before he was tried, he was killed in the alley at (6) the Wigwam Saloon by George Scarborough. I believe that was less than three months later.

After I was older, I talked with two men on different occasions who had been in the Acme Saloon the night Hardin was killed. They both told substantially the events of that night, what I have related to you. My Father was a deputy sheriff under Frank Simmons at that time. He told me that the foregoing story was generally considered the truth of the killing.

I don't know what you have read about Selman and Hardin, but I doubt if anyone has ever written it in a book, because the Selman tribe today would probably try to sue some one for libel. I have talked to several of them and they feel that John Selman was a hero and did a noble deed.

Yours,
Stanley

Notes

Foreword

1. Joseph Gallegly, *From Alamo Plaza to Jack Harris's Saloon: O. Henry and the Southwest He Knew*. Paris, France: Mouton, 1970, 154-164; Keith Wheeler, *The Chroniclers*. New York: Time-Life ("The Old West" series), 1976, 180.

1. A Boy Named John

1. Walter Clay Dixson, *Richland Crossing: A Portrait of Texas Pioneers*. Everman, Texas: Peppermill Publishing Co., 1994, 25.
2. Ibid., 43.
3. Ibid; the *Hardin Newsletter*, April 1986, 74.
4. Jo Foster to LCM, June 29, 1994.
5. James Gibson Hardin family genealogy, by Joyce Hardin Cavett.
6. Adolphus Werry, *History of the First Methodist Church, Dallas, Texas, 1846-1946*, 9, 16-17. A few James Hardin descendants believe his name is carved in the cornerstone of the First Methodist Church of Dallas, now the First United Methodist Church of Dallas. During Hardin's time, the church was a log cabin. However, there is a plaque, erected in 1927, in the church foyer, which lists Hardin's name as the fifth minister.
7. Louise B. Robertson, "Church History of Reverend James Gibson Hardin," *Harden/Hardin/Harding Family Association*, Aug. 24, 1968.
8. Mrs. Martha Ann "Mattie" Smith, interview with C. L. Sonnichsen, Fort Worth, Texas, June 17, 1944.
9. Ibid.

10. John Wesley Hardin, *The Life of John Wesley Hardin as written by himself*. Norman: University of Oklahoma Press, 1961, 8-10. Hereafter, Hardin, *Life*.
11. H. D. Hamilton "Memoirs," published in the *Trinity County News*, Nov. 10, 1927; Flora G. Bowles, *The History of Trinity County, Texas*, Graduate Thesis, Master of Arts, The University of Texas, Aug. 1928, 30.
12. Bowles, *History of Trinity County, Texas*, 33.
13. William B. Teagarden, attorney-at-law, to Mrs. Charles Billings (Mollie), Nov. 2, 1931, C. L. Sonnichsen files.
14. Hardin, *Life*, 7.

2. The Hour of the Gun

1. Elizabeth Silverthorne, *Plantation Life in Texas*. College Station: Texas A&M Press, 1986, 157.
2. Hardin, *Life*, 10.
3. Ibid., 5-6.
4. Ibid., 5; H. D. Hamilton, *History of Company M: First Texas Volunteer Infantry*. Waco: W. M. Morrison, 1962, p. 9.
5. Hardin, *Life*, 5; Bowles, *The History of Trinity County, Texas*, 47-49.
6. Hardin, *Life*, 10-11.
7. John Lachuk, "John Wesley Hardin," *Guns of the Gunfighters*. Petersen Publishing Co.: Los Angeles, 1975, 79-84.
8. Hardin, *Life*, 11-12.
9. Ibid., 11-14.
10. William B. Teagarden to Mrs. Charles (Mollie Hardin) Billings, Nov. 2, 1931, C. L. Sonnichsen Papers.
11. Register of Letters Sent, Item 3774,

Record Group 105, Records of the Field Offices of the Bureau of Refugees, Freedmen and Abandoned Lands, National Archives, 112.

12. Return of Crimes Committed, Trinity County, 1870, 2, Texas State Archives.

13..Sheriff G. W. Barfield to James Davidson, Chief of Texas State Police, July 16, 1870, Texas State Archives, 4.

3. A Reputation Builds

1. Hardin, *Life*, 13-14, 28.
2. Ed Bartholomew, *Kill or Be Killed*. Houston: Frontier Press of Texas, 1953, 47.
3. Hardin, *Life*, 14.
4. Ibid.
5. Walter Clay Dixson, "The Barekman-Anderson Prelude to Comanche." *Quarterly for the National Association for Outlaw and Lawman History, Inc.*, Vol. XVII, #2 (April-June, 1994), 7.
6. In his autobiography, Hardin mistakenly referred to the building as the Old Word Schoolhouse. The Old Word was six miles distant across Pin Oak Creek. Eddie Day Truitt to LCM, Sept. 11, 1994. Also see the *Dallas News*, July 2, 1961 and the *Dallas Times*, Aug. 15, 1962.
7. James Gibson Hardin to "My Dear and most noble Sister [in law]," March 20, 1869, quoted from Dixson, *Richland Crossing*, 207-208.
8. Hardin, *Life*, 15.
9. Hardin, *Life*, 16-17; *National Police Gazette*, Oct. 5, 1878.
10. Hardin, *Life*, 17.
11. Ibid.
12. *Flake's Daily Bulletin*, reprinted in the *Waco Register*, Feb. 6, 1870; *Dallas Herald*, Feb. 19, 1870; Hardin, *Life*, 16-17. Cotton Gin is today in western Freestone County although very near the Limestone County line. The town itself no longer exists. Some authorities suspect Dixon might have been slain near Springfield since the Fort Parker Cemetery is only three miles distant. Cotton Gin was twenty to twenty-five miles from the graveyard, a long way to tote a body just to bury him catty-cornered and markerless.
13. A fifty-year-old James W. Page shows up in the 1870 Hill County census. He and his wife Martha had five children. The "Reports of Crimes Committed," File 864-35, Adjutant General's Records, Austin, reports that a James W. Page of Navarro County murdered an E. W. Abby in 1861. There is no known family relationship between the Pages and the Hardins. The name Towash comes from a Hainai Indian chief of the 1850s. The town vanished under the Whitney Reservoir in 1951.

14. Hardin's version of this account differs from that of researcher Chuck Parsons, "Tell Wes to be a good man: Examining an Early Hardin Killing," *National Outlaw/Lawman Association Quarterly (NOLA)*, Vol. VI, No. 3 (April, 1981), 3-8. Among other things, Parsons discovered that Hardin's Jim Bradly was actually Benjamin B. Bradley, and the shooting events occurred not on Christmas Day 1869 but likely on January 4, 1870. Parsons believes that Bradley was not a desperado, but an individual not much different from other Towash gamblers and rowdies. As for James Collins, Hardin referred to him as John Collins.

15. *El Paso Daily-Herald*, Sept. 4, 1895.
16. Hardin, *Life*, 19-22; *El Paso Daily-Herald*, Sept. 4, 1895; Parsons, "Tell Wes to be a good man," 5, 8.
17. Hardin, *Life*, 22-23.
18. Ibid., 23-24.
19. Ibid., 24.
20. Hardin, *Life*, 25; Jo Foster to LCM, June 29, 1994.
21. Hardin, *Life*, 25.
22. Chuck Parsons, *Phil Coe: Texas Gambler*. Wolfe City: Henington Publishing Co., 1984.
23. Parsons, *Phil Coe: Texas Gambler*, 11. Hardin, *Life*, 25; Bartholomew, *Kill or Be Killed*, 50. Bartholomew says Hardin was nicknamed "Little" Seven-up, a story not likely since Hardin was of average height and definitely not little.
24. Hardin, *Life*, 26.
25. Ibid., 25-28. Historians are divided over whether Hardin's autobiographical account of the Longley meeting is true. Hardin's statement is the only support for their encounter, but it seems innocuous enough, one hardly worth going to the trouble of lying

about. For an opposing view, see *Bloody Bill Longley*, by Rick Miller. Henington Publishing Co. Wolfe City, TX: 1996, 26-27.

26. Ibid., 27-28.

4. Death Ride

1. Elizabeth Hardin to Alec Joseph Dixon, Aug. 27, 1870, courtesy Joyce Hardin Cavett.
2. Lists of Arrests by State Police, 1871, pages 128-129, Texas State Archives, Austin. Hardin is listed as John R. Hardin.
3. An L. J. Hoffman of Waco served in the Union Army and returned to Texas as a man of property with opinions favoring the North. He joined the State Police in July 1870, but was dismissed in September when he was appointed a United States Deputy Marshal. No official record exists of his death. Captain of State Police to Col. James Davidson, Chief of Police, July 11, 1870, State Police letter files, Texas State Archives, Austin; Donaly E. Brice (Research Specialist, Texas State Archives) to LCM, Dec. 22, 1993; *Flakes Daily Bulletin*, Feb. 4, 1871, quoting from *Fairfield Ledger* of Jan. 28.
4. Hardin referred to Lt. Stakes as "Stokes," and to Private Smalley as "Smolly." Hardin, *Life*, 29-31.
5. Ibid.
6. Ibid., 30-32.
7. Hardin, *Life*, 32-33; *Denison Daily Herald*, Aug. 26, 1877.
8. Hardin, *Life*, 33. This remains one of the more startling and puzzling statements in Hardin's autobiography. Since Hardin did not explain his father's outburst, or amplify its meaning, it is possible that Hardin did not fully understand what he had written.

5. A Dead Man Every Mile

1. Martha Balch Hardin was born in Tennessee in 1817, Clements in Kentucky on May 10, 1813. They died in Freestone County, he in July 1864 and she in March 1867. Clements family genealogy sheets furnished by Joyce

Hardin Cavett; Jo Foster to LCM, June 29, 1994.
2. Historians and genealogists alike have gotten confused regarding the Clements clan. Emanual I (born in 1813, died in 1864), married Martha Balch Hardin. He used two "a's" in his first name. Emanuel II with one "a," (born 1845 and died in 1887), married Mary Ann Robinson. Emanuel was a first cousin to John Wesley Hardin, as well as one of his closest associates. He is referred to in Hardin's autobiography as "Manning," whereas others usually called him Mannen. Emanuel III (born in 1868 and died in 1908) married Sally Clements, and was usually called "Mannie." Mannie did not enter Hardin's life until a few months before John's death.
3. Jimmy M. Skaggs, *The Cattle-Trailing Industry: Between Supply and Demand, 1866-1890*. Lawrence: The University Press of Kansas, 1973.
4. Hardin, *Life*, 34.
5. Ibid.
6. Ibid., 35-36.
7. Ibid., 36.
8. Ibid., 35-37.
9. Ibid., 37-38.
10. See Hardin, *Life*, 38; Waldo E. Koop, "Enter John Wesley Hardin: The Dim Trail to Abilene," *The Prairie Scout*, Vol. II, The Kansas Corral of the Westerners, 5-6; "Touring Kansas and Colorado in 1871: The Journal of George C. Anderson," *The Kansas Historical Quarterly* (Autumn, 1956), 222; *Wichita Tribune*, June 1, 1871.

6. The Killing Trail

1. This entire description of the fight with the Mexicans came from the autobiography of John Wesley Hardin, 39-42.
2. *Wichita Tribune*, June 1, 1871.
3. Waldo E. Koop, "Enter John Wesley Hardin," 8-9.
4. *Kerrville Mountain Sun*, Feb. 24, 1938. Fred Duderstadt interview by K. S. White.
5. *Topeka Commonwealth*, May 11, 1871.
6. Hardin, *Life*, 43.
7. *Union* (Junction City, Kansas), Oct. 29, 1871.

7. Abilene, Kansas

1. Two credible books on the subject of Abilene are Robert R. Dykstra, *The Cattle Towns*. New York: Knopf, 1968; and *The Chisholm Trail*, by Wayne Guard. Norman: University of Oklahoma Press, 1954.

2. *The Union*, Aug. 10, 1871.

3. *Abilene Chronicle*, June 22, 1871.

4. Joseph G. Rosa, *They Called Him Wild Bill: The Life and Adventures of James Butler Hickok*. Norman: University of Oklahoma Press, 1974, 1-20; Also see Joe Rosa's, *The West of Wild Bill Hickok*. Norman: University of Oklahoma Press, 1982.

5. *The Union* (Junction City, Kansas), Aug. 19, 1871.

6. Hardin, *Life*, 43.

7. Ibid., 43. Historical authorities have dismissed this confrontation with Carson since Hardin implies it took place on June 1. Tom Carson did not become a policeman until June 14. However, since Hardin described the event from a recollection of over twenty years, the mistake of a couple weeks should not necessarily be deemed critical. Besides, Carson is supposed to have worked in this "notorious resort" as a special policeman. See Koop, "Enter John Wesley Hardin," 10; Nyle H. Miller and Joseph W. Snell, *Great Gunfighters of the Kansas Cowtowns, 1867-1886*. Lincoln: University of Nebraska Press, 1963, 64.

8. Hardin, *Life*, 44. Hardin's account of the Bull's Head painting incident is the first. Other writers have expanded upon it without citing sources. Kansas newspapers and city council minutes made no mention of the episode.

9. The feud between Hickok and Texas gambler Coe concluded in October, months after Hardin had left Abilene. Coe and fifty Texas cowboys drunkenly wandered from saloon to saloon, forcing hapless customers to either buy drinks or risk being thrown over the bar. After pausing in front of the Alamo Saloon, Coe fired at a stray dog. Hickok shouldered his way through the crowd to remind Coe of the city ordinances against firearms. At eight feet apart, both men started shooting, and what happened next did not say much for the accuracy of either. Coe fired four times and missed the marshal. Hickok rapidly fired both revolvers through clouds of gunsmoke, the fusillade accidently killing Mike Williams, a friend of Hickok's and a special deputy hired by the Novelty Theater to protect the dancing girls. Another slug churned through the stomach of Phil Coe. He died in agony three days later. Coe returned in a casket to Brenham, Texas. Hickok said he was sorry about the whole affair, and paid for the Williams funeral. *Abilene Chronicle*, Oct. 12, 1871; *Wyandotte Gazette* (Kansas), Oct. 12, 1871; *Kansas City Tribune*, Oct. 7, 1871; *Brenham Banner*, Oct. 19, 1871; Rosa, *They Called Him Wild Bill*, 196-200; and Chuck Parsons, *Phil Coe: Texas Gambler*, 16-33.

10. Hardin, *Life*, 44.

11. Ibid.

12. *Kerrville Mountain Sun*, Feb. 24, 1938, R. S. White interviews Fred Duderstadt.

13. *Abilene Chronicle*, June 29, 1871, in reference to a series of miscellaneous Abilene ordinances passed June 24, 1871.

14. Hardin, *Life*, 45-46.

15. Chuck Parsons, "Who Was the Fastest Gunman, James B. 'Wild Bill' Hickok, or Wesley 'Little Arkansas' Hardin?." *Newsletter of the National Association and Center for Outlaw and Lawman History*, Vol. 1, No. 3 (Autumn, 1975), 8-9.

16. Joe and Helen Clements, interview with C. L. Sonnichsen and Robert N. Mullin, Paso del Norte Hotel, El Paso, Texas, April 26, 1963, Sonnichsen Papers.

17. For versions arguing against the Border Roll (Road Agent Spin) ever happening, see Koop, "Enter John Wesley Hardin," 11-13; Rosa, *They Called Him Wild Bill*, 188-189.

8. Prairie Justice

1. Hardin, *Life*, 46; *Abilene Chronicle*, July 13, 1871. Incidentally, Hardin wrote Billy's last name as Coran. The *Abilene Chronicle* spelled it Chorn. However, the tombstone used Cohron, and that spelling will be followed here.
2. Hardin incorrectly referred to the stream as Bluff Creek, and to the town as Bluff City, which he called Bluff. Bluff City did not exist in 1871.
3. Hardin, *Life*, 49-50.
4. *Oxford Times* (Kansas), July 13, 1871.
5. Ibid., 50; *Kansas Daily Commonwealth*, July 11, 1871; *Kansas State Record*, July 12, 1871; Koop, "Enter John Wesley Hardin," 17-18.
6. Hardin, *Life*, 51.
7. Ibid., 50; *Kansas Daily Commonwealth*, July 11, 1871; *Kansas State Record*, July 12, 1871; Koop, "Enter John Wesley Hardin," 17-18.
8. Hardin, *Life*, 50-51.
9. *Kansas City Commonwealth*, July 11, 25, 1871, Aug. 22, 1871.
10. Colin W. Rickards, "Vengeance: Kansas 1870s Style," *The English Westerners' Brand Book*, Vol. 4, No. 1 (Oct. 1961), 2-9.
11. *Topeka State Record*, July 28, 1871; *Topeka Daily Commonwealth*, July 20, 1871; Koop, "Enter John Wesley Hardin," 19.
12. Hardin, *Life*, 53.
13. Ibid., 53-56.
14. Ibid., 58.

9. Death by Snoring

1. Hardin, *Life*, 58-59.
2. Ibid., 58.
3. *Abilene Chronicle* and *Sabine County Weekly Journal*, Aug. 10, 1871. The *Journal* referred to this slaying as Hardin's "sixth murder."
4. Ibid., Aug. 17, 1871.
5. *Topeka Daily Commonwealth*, Aug. 9, 1871; *Sabine County Weekly Journal*, Aug. 10, 1871.
6. Robert B. Dykstra, "Exit John Wesley Hardin," *Los Angeles Corral Brand Book 6*, Los Angeles, CA., 1956, 123-129; Koop, "Enter John Wesley Hardin," 26-29.
7. *Life and Adventures of Sam Bass*. Dallas: Dallas Commercial Steam Print, 1878, 69. This reference mentions an Austin newspaper interview which quotes Hardin as saying, "They tell lots of lies about me. They say I killed six or seven men for snoring, but it isn't true. I killed only one man for snoring." This interview has never been located, and is probably bogus.
8. *West Texas Free Press*, Sept. 8, 1877.
9. *Denison Daily Herald*, Sept. 21, 1877.

10. A Three-Gun Man

1. Chuck Parsons, "A Texas Gunfighter," *Real West* (July, 1980), 32-34; Joe and Helen Clements, interview with C. L. Sonnichsen and R. N. Mullin, Paso del Norte Hotel, El Paso, Texas, April 26, 1963, Sonnichsen Papers.
2. Marjorie Hyatt, *Fuel for A Feud*. Smiley, TX., 1990, 39, quoting from the *Galveston Daily News*, March 8, 1876.
3. Hardin, *Life*, 62-63; Gonzales County Indictment #1005, Oct. 24, 1871, Wesley C. Hardin for Murder, Texas State Archives, Austin; Gonzales County Census, 1870. Green Paramore (Hardin spelled the name Paramoor), was twenty-eight years old and born in Georgia.
4. Gonzales County census, 1870. Lackey was married to an Indian woman, and owned $600 worth of personal property.
5. Hardin's Gonzales County indictment of Oct. 24, 1871 (#1005) is in the Texas State Archives. It refers to him as Wesley C. Hardin, and dates the slaying as Oct. 19, which is incorrect. Also see Gonzales County, List of Special Police, 1871, p. 122, and the Texas Adjutant General's Report, 1872, p. 12, both in the Texas State Archives; *The Daily Journal* (Austin), April 11, 1873.
6. Hardin, *Life*, 63.
7. *San Antonio Daily Herald*, Oct. 31, 1871. As an aside, James T. Matthieu, the 50-year-old sheriff from Gonzales, was born in the West Indies. (Census, Gonzales County, 1870.) The Reconstruction government placed him in office, but he was removed on Nov. 10, 1871 when Reconstruction ended. Also see, Hardin, *Life*, 62; *Daily State Journal*

(Austin), quoting from an undated article in the *Gonzales Index; San Antonio Daily Herald*, Nov. 9, 1871.

8. Governor's Proclamations, Nov. 5, 1871, Texas State Archives, Austin; *San Antonio Daily Herald*, Nov. 9, 1871.

9. *San Antonio Daily Express*, Jan. 4, 1892.

10. Hardin, *Life*, 63.

11. Chuck Parsons, "Forgotten Feudist," *Frontier Times*, Vol 50, #1 (Dec.-Jan., 1976), 28-29, 44-45. Ann and Jim altogether had eleven children, eight of them girls.

12. J. W. Hardin to Mrs. Jane Hardin, Jan. 9, 1879. Hardin Collection.

13. The Gonzales County Historical Commission, *The History of Gonzales County, Texas*. Dallas: Curtis Media Corporation, 1986, 333; Memoirs of Jo Foster, 1986.

14. Hardin, *Life*, 64-65.

15. Hardin, *Life*, 66-67; *Austin Daily Democratic Statesman*, Aug. 30, 1877; Adjutant General's Report, 1872, 12. Sonny Speights lived to marry and father eight children. He died on Sept. 4, 1900. The Adjutant General's report states that the wounding of Speights occurred in Milam, Texas, roughly ten miles north of Hemphill. However, since there was no reason for Hardin to lie, he should certainly remember who he shot and where he shot him. That same Adjutant General's report shows a William M. Speights, a sergeant in the State Police and believed to be the father of John Henry Hopkins Speights, as dying at Milam, Texas, on May 17, 1872. Since the name of the elder Speights is not on the State Police killed or wounded list, his death is surmised to have stemmed from natural causes.

16. Hardin, *Life*, 67.

17. Ibid., 70.

18. Ibid., 69-71.

19. Trinity County Indictment of Aug. 29, 1874. Copy in Texas State Archives, Austin.

20. Ellen Reagan to Chuck Parsons, April 30, 1959. Ellen Reagan was Sheriff Richard Reagan's granddaughter.

21. Hardin, *Life*, 73-74.

22. The sheriff's son was William B. Reagan, a nineteen-year-old farmer according to the July 18, 1870 census of Cherokee County. When he was small, everyone called him Dood. Ten years later on Oct. 27, 1881, a Belton, Texas newspaper, reported that city marshal Marlow arrested Will Reagan for drunkenness and abusive language. On the way to jail, Reagan drew a Smith & Wesson revolver and fired at the marshal, the ball barely missing his head. Marlow and Deputy Allen, plus bystanders, overpowered Will Reagan and locked him up. The outcome is unknown. Chuck Parsons to LCM, Feb. 22, 1994.

23. Hardin, *Life*, 74.

24. *Austin Daily Democratic Statesman*, July 10, 1874.

25. Hardin, *Life*, 75.

26. Ibid., 76.

27. Hardin, *Life*, 75-77; *Austin Daily Democratic Statesman*, Aug. 30, 1877,

28. John Wesley Hardin to *The Drag Net*, Gonzales, Texas, Nov. 2, 1894.

29. *San Antonio Daily Herald*, March 25, 1873. On Aug. 10, 1877, the *Austin Daily Democratic Statesman* reported the figure as only $100, and said the sheriff offered that.

11. A Bullet for Tom Haldeman

1. Nordyke, Lewis, *John Wesley Hardin, Texas Gunman*. New York: William Morrow & Co., 1957, 142-143.

2. Chuck and Marjorie Parsons, *Bowen and Hardin*. College Station, Texas: Creative Publishing, 1991, 18-30.

3. Texas Court of Criminal Appeals, "Bowen v. The State," 1878, 627-628; Parsons, *Bowen and Hardin*, 35-36.

4. *Report of the Adjutant General of the State of Texas for the Year 1873*. Austin, Texas, 1874, 122.

5. *Gonzales Inquirer*, April 13, 1878, as reprinted in Parsons, *Bowen and Hardin*, 45-46.

12. The Sutton-Taylor Feud

1. The two best books regarding Texas troubles are C. L. Sonnichsen's, *Ten Texas Feuds*, Albuquerque: University of New Mexico Press, 1957; and *I'll Die Before I'll Run: The Story of the Great*

Feuds of Texas. New York: Devin-Adair, 1982.
2. The most documented account of this war is found in *Fuel For A Feud*, by Marjorie Hyatt. Smiley, TX: Privately printed, 1990. This work is an extension of an earlier book by Marjorie Hyatt, *The Taylors, the Tumlinsons and the Feud*. Smiley, TX: Privately printed, 1988.
3. Austin *Daily Democratic Statesman*, Sept. 18, 1874, "Letter From Pidge." Reprinted in *Pidge: A Texas Ranger From Virginia*, by Chuck Parsons. Privately Printed: 1985, 42.
4. Interview with Taylor descendants at the Taylor Reunion, Cuero, Texas, Sept. 23-24, 1994.
5. D. E. Kilgore, *A Ranger Legacy: 150 Years of Service to Texas.* Austin: Madrona Press, 1973, 33-72.
6. Ibid., 49. There are stories afloat in the Taylor family, with no evidence cited, that Joe Tumlinson murdered his first wife, Johanna. According to these rumors, her death is what started the Sutton-Taylor Feud.
7. Richter, *The Army in Texas During Reconstruction*, 124.
8. Ibid., 174-180.
9. *Taylor Family News*, Vol. 3, #2 (March 1992), p. 7 and Vol. 4, No. 1 (Jan., 1993), p. 7; *Victoria Advocate*, Sept. 23, 1869; Hyatt, *Fuel For A Feud*, 57.
10. Ibid., Sept. 23, 1868, Aug. 19, 1869.
11. *San Antonio Daily Herald*, Aug. 31, 1869.
12. Tise, Sammy. *Texas County Sheriffs.* Albuquerque: Oakwood Printing, 1989, 167.
13. Sworn statement of Amanda J. Kelly to Justice of the Peace O. K. Tuton, Oct. 15, 1870, reprinted in Truitt, *The Taylor Party*, 212-213.
14. Truitt, *The Taylor Party*, 93-94.
15. Parsons, *DeWitt County History*, 35-37.

13. Exit Jim Cox and Jack Helm

1. *San Antonio Daily Herald*, March 14, 1873.
2. This entire conversation comes from Hardin, *Life*, 77-79.
3. Ibid., 64-65.
4. Ibid., 79.
5. Ibid., 81.

6. Hardin, *Life*, 79-80; Austin *Daily Democratic Statesman*, Dec. 5, 1874, reprinted from *Pidge*, by Chuck Parsons, 53.
7. Hardin, *Life*, 79-80; *The Standard* (Clarksville, Texas), April 26, 1873; Dixson, *Richland Crossing*, 247. Dixson claims Morgan was a chief deputy for Jack Helm, and had been ordered by Helm to arrest Hardin; Rose, *The Texas Vendetta; or, the Sutton-Taylor Feud* (quoting an undated item from the *Victoria Advocate*, a newspaper whose issues for this period have been lost), 30.
8. Hyatt, *Fuel for A Feud*, 35-37.
9. Alfred Creed Day, alias Creed Day and/or Jessie Mayfield, was called Alf by his friends. He turned 18 in 1873, and in addition to the usual misdemeanors such as playing cards and carrying a pistol, he was wanted for robbery with intent to kill in Gonzales County, willful murder in Karnes County, assault with intent to murder in DeWitt County, and bank robbery in Goliad County. These were just the known charges. Alf served time in the Huntsville Prison in 1880 for second-degree murder in Guadalupe County, and dropped from sight at Rusk, Texas in 1883. Alf Day and Jim Taylor became as close to John Wesley Hardin as the Clements had been. Truitt, *The Taylor Family*, 29, 66.
10. Hardin, *Life*, 82
11. Hardin spelled the name Albukirk, and identified it as in Wilson County, understandable since a corrected survey did not place it in Gonzales County until 1914. A forgotten veteran of the Civil War's New Mexico Campaign named it Albuquerque. The village existed from 1870 to 1883, when business activities shifted two miles south to Union Valley. Sylvan Dunn, "Life and Times in Albuquerque, Texas," *Southwestern Historical Quarterly*, Vol. LV, #1 (July, 1951), 62-76.
12. According to Chuck Parsons, Helm applied for his patent on Nov. 16, 1872, and the government granted him Patent #13902 on May 20, 1873. Parsons, *DeWitt County History*, 37.
13. Hardin, *Life*, 83-85. Thus far, this account of the Helm killing has been taken entirely from the Hardin autobi-

ography. Hardin always referred to Helm as "Helms."

14. *Fayette County New Era*, Aug. 8, 1873.
15. *San Antonio Daily Express*, July 31, 1873.
16. Austin *Daily Democratic Statesman*, Nov. 8, 1874, "Letter from Pidge," reproduced in *Pidge*, by Chuck Parsons, 49.
17. Hardin, *Life*, 84.

14. Too Mean to Arrest

1. *Galveston Tri-Weekly News*, May 26, 1873; *The Standard* (Clarksville, TX.), June 7, 1873; Dixson, *Richland Crossing*, 120-125, 249-250; Dixson, "The Barekman –Anderson Prelude to Comanche," 11-13.
2. Sam Tumlinson to LCM, Nov. 5, 1991; Sam Tumlinson, "Joe Tumlinson: Was He All Bad," *Taylor Family News*, Vol. 2, #1, 6-7.
3. Hardin, *Life*, 84-85.
4. The *Houston Telegraph* of Aug. 20, 1873, reprinted the article from the *Gonzales Inquirer*. Also see *Cuero Star*, Aug. 12, plus the *San Antonio Express* and the *San Antonio Herald*, Aug. 20, 1873
5. The treaty is reproduced in full in Hyatt's, *Fuel for a Feud*, 14-15.
6. L. B. Wright to Governor E. J. Davis, Aug. 16, 1873, Texas State Archives, Austin.
7. Austin *Daily Democratic Statesman*, Nov. 12, 1874, "Letter from Pidge." Reprinted in *Pidge*, by Parsons, 47-48.
8. *Austin Weekly State Gazette*, Oct. 11, 1873.
9. *Cuero Star*, Dec. 31, 1873.
10. Parsons, *DeWitt County History*, 38.
11. Parsons, *DeWitt County History*, 38; *Cuero Weekly Star*, Jan. 9, 1874.

15. Joe Hardin and the Good Earth

1. Minutes of Comanche County Commissioners Court, Vol. 1.
2. Record of Appointment of Postmasters, 1832—Sept. 30, 1971, Castro through Ellis Counties, Texas, National Archives Microfilm Publication M841.
3. Elizabeth and the twenty-three-year-old Cobb had ten children. Lizzie died in 1930. Comanche County Marriage

Records Vol. 1856-1872, 112; Vol. A., 58; T. R. Havins and James M. Day, *Twenty-Five Years on the Outside Row: Autobiography of Rev. Peter Gravis*. Brownwood, Texas: Cross Timbers Press, 1966, ix; Dixson, *Richland Crossing*, 244-245; Family records, Joyce Hardin Cavett.
4. Commissioners Court Minutes, Feb. 1874 term, Vol. 1, p. 228; Lockwood, Frances B., *Comanche County Courthouses*. Comanche, Texas: Comanche Public Library, 1969.
5. Records of the District Court, Comanche, Texas.
6. Deed Records, Comanche Co., Vol. C, 270-272.
7. Ibid., 270.
8. Ibid. Page 277 contains much of the Hazle Dell information, but the material sources are scattered all through the volumes. Hardin did not file the plat until March 28, 1874. The Hazle Dell spelling is as the post office spelled it.
9. Conversation with Margaret T. Waring, and the examination of documents in Comanche, Texas, Oct. 9-11, 1994.
10. Mollie Moore Godbold, "Comanche and the Hardin Gang," *Southwestern Historical Quarterly*, LXVII, #2 (Oct., 1963), 247.

16. Goodby Bill Sutton

1. #310, Criminal Docket, Dist. Court, Comanche County, Feb. 10, 1874.
2. *Cuero Weekly Star*, Feb. 17, 1874.
3. Austin *Daily Democratic Statesman*, Aug. 30, 1877.
4. Hardin, *Life*, 86.
5. *The Sutton-Taylor Feud*, by Robert C. Sutton, Jr. Quanah, TX.: Nortex Press, 1974, 52.
6. *Victoria Advocate*, May 21, 1874.
7. *Cuero Weekly Star*, Jan. 23, 1874.

17. Charlie Webb Goes Down

1. Cox, *The Cattle Industry of Texas*, 67; *Austin Daily Democratic Statesman*, Aug. 30, 1877.
2. Chuck Parsons, "Doc Bockius Survived Civil War, Texas Feud,"

Newsletter of the National Association and Center for the Study of Outlaw and Lawman History, Vol. II, No. 4 (Spring, 1977), 9-10; *San Antonio Daily Express*, June 19, 1874.

3. J. D. Bonner recollections, *Comanche Chief*, May 20, 1932.

4. Bill of Sale, Book E, 61-62, Office of the District Clerk, Comanche County, Comanche, Texas.

5. David and John Carnes vs. J. B. Waldrip, Civil Case #193, Nov. 1, 1873, Suit pending in District Court of Comanche Co., Nov. term, Dist. Clerk's office, Comanche Courthouse.

6. Ibid., 89.

7. Ibid., 91.

8. Ibid., April 25, 1874, 93-94.

9. Civil Case #193, Nov. 1, 1873 & May 11, 1874, District Clerk's office, Comanche.

10. Bill of Sale, Book E, May 19, 1874, 121.

11. Donovan Duncan Tidwell, *Freemasonry in Brownwood*. Fort Worth, Texas: Department of Printing, Masonic Home and School, 1966, 67.

12. T. R. Havins, *Something About Brown [County]*. Brownwood, TX: Banner Printing, 1958, 28.

13. *Daily Houston Telegraph*, June 5, 1874. Three years later in May 1877, a posse led by Constable W. T. Still from Kaufman, Texas, shot and killed a "William" Beard. This almost certainly had to be James Beard since he had claimed to be one of John Wesley Hardin's "right bowers," meaning a right-hand man or sidekick. No reason for the shootout was given. See *San Antonio Daily Express*, May 27, 1877.

14. Hardin, *Life*, 90.

15. Hardin claimed the saloon was on the northwest corner of the square with the door facing south. However, Comanche citizens later identified it as on the northeast corner. *Comanche Chief*, Golden Anniversary Edition, June 6, 1924.

16. Mollie Moore Godbold, "Comanche and the Hardin Gang," 71-73.

17. This incident and the conversation comes from Hardin, *Life*, 92-93. This is the only time in the autobiography where someone refers to Hardin as "Jack," although the reference was likely quite common.

18. Parsons, *DeWitt County History*, 39-40.

19. Mollie Moore Godbold, "Comanche and the Hardin Gang," 71-73.

20. Except for the newspaper account, Hardin's drinking and gambling, the slaying of deputy sheriff Charles Webb, and the escape from Comanche are all described in Hardin's, *Life*, 90-95; The *Houston Daily Telegraph* of June 3, 1874 published a long article, and is the source for the Ware shots that missed.

18. A Whale Among Little Fishes

1. Petition from the citizens of Comanche to Governor Richard Coke, May 28, 1874, Texas State Archives, Austin. The date of Webb's death has generally been considered as the 26th, rather than the 25th, as in the supplication.

2. Capt. John R. Waller to Major John B. Jones, May 30, 1874, Texas State Archives, Austin.

3. Monthly Report of Capt. John R. Waller, Co. A, Frontier Battalion, June 1874, Texas State Archives, Austin; Hardin, *Life*, 95.

4. Hardin, *Life*, 95-96; Report of Co. A., Capt Waller Comd, June 27, 1874, Texas State Archives, Austin.

5. Hardin, *Life*, 96, 98; "Report of Co. A Capt. Waller Comd for the Month of May [1874]," May 28.

6. Hardin, *Life*, 99-100.

7. Dixson, "The Barekman-Anderson Prelude to Comanche," 14-16; Godbold, "Comanche and the Hardin Gang," 251-253.

8. J. R. Waller, Monthly Return for June entitled, "Record of Scouts," June 30, 1874; Report of Co. A Capt. Waller Comd For the Month of May [1874], Tx. State Archives, Austin.

9. Chuck Parsons, "Destroying the Hardin Gang," *Quarterly of the National Association and Center for Outlaw and Lawman History*, Vol. 4, #4 (July, 1980), 4-5.

10. Havins, *Something About Brown*, 29-30.

11. *Comanche Chief*, Aug. 11, 1933.

12. Ibid., May 20, 1932.

13. Commissioners Court minutes, Sept. 28, 1874, 252; Donovan Duncan Tidwell, *Freemasonry in Brownwood*. 67-70.

14. Commissioners Court minutes, Sept. 28, 1874, 252; Tidwell, *Freemasonry in Brownwood.* 67-70.

15. Lightfoot, *The History of Comanche County, Texas, to 1920*, 132-133.

16. Godbold, "Comanche and the Hardin Gang," 257-259.

17. Hardin, *Life*, 103-104.

18. Ibid., 104.

19. Ibid.

20. Commissioners Court paid $21 for sixty-three meals to the seven prisoners. Commissioners Court Minutes, June 20, 1874, 239; J. D. Stephens, Attorney at Law at Comanche, to Governor Richard Coke, June 10, 1874; Waller to J. D. Stephens, June 10, 1874, Texas State Archives, Austin; *San Antonio Daily Express*, June 19, 1874.

21. Hardin, *Life*, 107. Hardin claimed the rangers turned Taylor, Tuggle and White over to the Tumlinson crowd, knowing that the Tumlinson mob would kill them.

22. Parsons, *DeWitt County History*, 40; *San Antonio Herald*, July 1, 1874; *Cuero Weekly Star*, June 27, 1874.

23. Truitt, *The Taylor Party*, 232. The account comes from an unidentified newspaper clipping to the Citizens of Gonzales County, and labeled "Sheriff's Card."

24. *Daily Democratic Statesman*, July 14, 1874.

25. Parsons, *DeWitt County History*, 41-43.

26. L. H. McNelly to Gen'l Wm. Steele, Aug. 31, 1874, Texas State Archives, Austin.

27. Chuck Parsons, *Pidge*, 40.

28. Austin *Daily Democratic Statesman*, Nov. 8, 1874, "Letter from Pidge," Reprinted in *Pidge*, by Chuck Parsons, 48.

29. Austin *Daily Democratic Statesman*, Dec. 5, 1874; *Pidge*, by Chuck Parsons, 52-53.

30. Austin *Daily Democratic Statesman*, Sept. 24, 1874; *Pidge*, by Parsons, 42.

31. Parsons, *Pidge*, 43.

32. Walter Prescott Webb, *The Texas Rangers: A Century of Frontier Defense*. New York: Houghton Mifflin, 1935, 233-238.

33. Parsons, *DeWitt County History*, 43-44.

34. Chuck Parsons to Taylor Family, Cuero, Texas, Sept. 24, 1994.

35. Chuck Parsons, "Bill Sutton Avenged: The Death of Jim Taylor," *Quarterly of the National Association and Center for Outlaw and Lawman History*, Vol. IV, #3 (March, 1979), 3-5; and Parsons, *DeWitt County History*, 44-45. The only remaining feud killing of significance occurred on Sept. 19, 1876 when Sutton partisans unexplainably killed Dr. Philip Brassell and his son James W. Some of those arrested were Dave Augustine, Jim Hester, William W. Cox (son of James Cox), William Meador and Jake Ryan. The legal battles lasted for years with only Augustine being convicted. W. W. Cox fled to near Las Cruces, New Mexico, where he became a prominent rancher, bank president and civic leader who nevertheless was involved in the mysterious death of former Lincoln County, New Mexico, Sheriff Pat Garrett on Feb. 29, 1908.

19. Capturing the Grand Mogul

1. W. J. Maltby to Maj. John B. Jones, June 17, 1874, Adjutant General's Papers, Archives, Texas State Library.

2. Hardin, *Life*, 109-110; *Victoria Advocate*, Sept. 8, 1877; Parsons, Chuck, *The Capture of John Wesley Hardin*. College Station, Creative Publishing, 1978, 34.

3. Ibid., 110-111; A. J. Wright, "John Wesley Hardin's Missing Years," *Old West* (Fall, 1981), 6-7.

4. *Victoria Advocate*, Sept. 8, 1877.

5. General Correspondence, Adjutant General's Office, Texas State Archives, Austin.

6. Legislative Proceedings, Jan. 14-15, 1875, printed in the *Daily Democratic Statesman*, Jan. 15, 1875; also see *General Laws of the State of Texas*, Session of the 14th Legislature, Joint Resolution 1, Houston: A. C. Gray, 1875. During a personal interview with John Wesley Hardin, the *Victoria Advocate* of Sept. 8, 1877, printed Hardin's denial that he had threatened Senator Stephens, or any legislative member. The newspaper closed with a comment that the Austin jail held some seventy dangerous prisoners, many as anxious to escape as Hardin. "It is not altogether improbable," the *Advocate* said, "that Mr. Hardin will yet have a chance to get at the Senator from Comanche.

7. Hardin, *Life*, 112; *Victoria Advocate*, Sept. 8, 1877; Jack DeMattos, "Gun-

fighters of the Real West: John Wesley Hardin," *Real West* (April, 1984), 48.
8. Hardin, *Life*, 112; Parsons, *Capture of*, 39.
9. Hardin, *Life*, 112-113; A. J. Wright, "A Gunfighter's Southern Vacation," *Quarterly of the National Outlaw and Lawman History Association*, Vol. VII, #3 (Autumn, 1982), 12-18.
10. *Mobile Register*, Nov. 12, 1876.
11. J. H. H. Swain to Mrs. Swain, June 6, 1877, Hardin Collection, San Marcos State University, San Marcos, TX.
12. Chuck and Marjorie Parsons, *Bowen and Hardin*. College Station: Creative Publishing Co., 1991, 72.
13. Ibid., 60.
14. Michael Whittington, "Six Telegrams That Tell A Story: The Arrest of John Wesley Hardin," *Quarterly for the National Association and Center for Outlaw and Lawman History*, Vol. XI, No. 2 (Fall 1986), 9.
15. Rick Miller, *Bounty Hunter*. College Station, Texas: The Early West, 1988; *Galveston News*, Aug. 23, 1895.
16. Chipley wrote Governor Hubbard on Aug. 28, 1877, and confirmed that Brown Bowen had indeed assaulted him, and had been almost beat to death in the process by his own weapon. The letter is on file with the governor's papers in the Texas State Archives, Austin; Also see Chuck and Marjorie Parsons, *Bowen and Harden*, 74-76; Miller, *Bounty Hunter*, 84-86; *Pensacola Gazette* (reprinted from *The Advertiser and Mail*, Aug. 26, 1877; *Atlanta Daily Constitution*, Sept. 1, 1877; Hardin, *Life*, 115-116.
17. State of Florida vs. Martin Sullivan, Escambia County, Circuit Court, Criminal Records, Oct. 4, 1877. A Florida grand jury indicted Sullivan for the killing, but nothing came of the trial. Other versions of the conflict have Mann reaching the depot passenger platform before deputies shot him dead.
18. Hardin to Jane Bowen Hardin, Aug. 25, 1877, Hardin Collection.
19. Hardin, *Life*, 120.
20. Telegram to Adj. General Steele, Aug. 23, 1877, Adj. General's Records, Texas State Archives. A total of six telegrams are on file in the Archives.; *Dallas*

Morning News, Aug. 22, 1895; *Galveston News*, Aug. 29, 1877; Whittington, "Six Telegrams, 9-11.
21. *Galveston News*, Aug. 23, 1895.
22. Hardin, *Life*, 121; Parsons, *Capture of*, 137.
23. *Atlanta Daily Constitution*, Sept. 1, 1877.
24. Ibid.
25. The telegrams from Armstrong to Duncan are in the Attorney General's file in the Texas State Archives; also see Parsons, *The Capture*, 59-60, and Miller, *Bounty Hunter*, 92-94.

20. I Am A Human Being

1. *Montgomery Advertiser*, Aug. 28, 1877.
2. *Galveston News*, Aug. 23, 1895.
3. Hardin, *Life*, 122.
4. *Galveston News*, Aug. 23, 1895.
5. Ibid., Aug. 28, 1877.
6. *Dallas News*, Sept. 6, 1895, as reprinted in *El Paso Daily Times*, Sept. 8, 1895.
7. Dian Malouf, *Cattle Kings of Texas*. Hillsboro, Oregon: Beyond Worlds Publishing, 1991, 108.
8. Wright, *Quarterly*, 13-18; *Montgomery Advertiser*, Oct. 12, 1877.
9. Austin *Daily Democratic Statesman*, Sept. 19, 1887, quoting from the *Fort Worth Democrat*.
10. James G. Gillett, *Six Years With the Texas Rangers*. New Haven and London: Yale University Press, 1963, 86.
11. *Daily Democratic Statesman*, Sept. 19, 1877; *Lampasas Dispatch*, Sept. 27, 1877.
12. T. U. Taylor, Dean of Engineering, U. of Texas, "New Light on John Wesley Hardin," *Frontier Times*, Vol. 2, No. 11 (Aug. 1925), 16; *Victoria Advocate*, Sept. 22, 1877.
13. Letter from Mervyn, *Galveston News*, Oct. 8, 1877; Chuck Parsons, "John Wesley Hardin and the Texas Rangers," *Newsletter of the National Association and Center for Outlaw and Lawman History*, Vol. II, #2 (Spring, 1976), 9-11.
14. *Dallas Weekly Herald*, Sept. 26, 1877.
15. Hardin mentions only the first three men as his attorneys, and it seems unlikely that the other two played much of a part in the trial. Hardin, *Life*, 124. Renick specialized in land titles and land litigation. Nugent was a former

Methodist minister and populist lawyer who served on the Constitutional
Convention of 1875, and in 1879 as a
judge for the 29th Judicial District. He
unsuccessfully ran twice for governor
of Texas (1892 & 1894) as a candidate
of the People's (Populist) Party. One
wonders if he got Hardin's vote.

16. Fleming was born in Kentucky, joined
the Confederate Army, and later became a Texas newspaper publisher,
lawyer, banker and businessman prior
to serving on the Constitutional Convention in 1875. He was elected judge
at Comanche in 1875 but resigned in
1880; *Galveston Weekly News*, Oct. 15,
1877.

17. *Galveston Weekly News*, Oct. 2, 15, 1878;
Book C., District Court Minutes,
Comanche County, 324, 326, 327, 445-
446.

18. The appeals court transcript uses
"Henry" Carnes instead of David.
Since there was no "Henry," it is as-
sumed that the clerk meant David.

19. *Cases Argued and Adjudged in the Court
of Appeals of the State of Texas During the
Austin Term, 1878, and the Early Part
of the Tyler Term, 1878*. Reported by
Jackson & Jackson. Vol. IV. St Louis:
The Gilbert Book Co., 1879, 355-372.

20. Hardin, *Life*, 93-94; Fain McDaniel to
LCM, March 27, 1995. The Hardin let-
ter was written on April 8 and
published in the *Austin Gazette*. The
Dallas Daily Herald reprinted it on
Saturday, April 13, 1878.

21. *Cases Argued*, 367.

22. Hardin, *Life*, 124-125.

23. Richard Marohn, *The Last Gunfighter*:
John Wesley Hardin. College Station,
TX.: Creative Publishing, 1995, 170.

21. State Prison

1. Elizabeth Hardin to My Own Precious
Son, Oct. 16, 1877, Feb. 15, & Feb. 20,
1878, Hardin Collection.

2. "Total Wreck" apparently was one of
Lee Hall's rangers. *Galveston Daily
News*, Dec. 26, 1877.

3. *Gonzales Inquirer*, April 13, 1878.

4. "Brown Bowen v. The State," Third
Texas Court of Appeals Reports, 1878,
627-628.

5. Quoted in Parsons, *Bowen and Hardin*,
88-91.

6. *Galveston News*, May 17, 1878.

7. John Wesley Hardin to "My Dear and
Loving Wife," May 18, 1878, Hardin
Collection.

8. *Daily Democratic Statesman*, May 11,
1878.

9. *Gonzales Inquirer*, May 11, 18, 1878;
Sweet, Alex E. and Knox, J. Armory, *On
A Mexican Mustang, Through Texas,
From the Gulf to the Rio Grande*. Chicago:
Rand McNally & Co., 1891, 423-425.
Sweet and Knox witnessed the Bowen
hanging as invited guests but wrote a
slightly different version than what has
been given in this text.

10. Douglas G. Ellison, "Rivals in Texas:
Hardin and Longley," *Quarterly of the
National Association and Center for Out-
law and Lawman History*, Vol. XII, #4
(Spring, 1988), 10.

11. *Galveston News*, Aug. 31, 1877.

12. Portions of this correspondence furnished by Douglas Ellison.

13. John W. Hardin to "My Dear and Loving Wife," June 11, 1878, Hardin
Collection.

14. *San Antonio Daily Express*, Sept. 12, 20,
1878.

15. *Austin Weekly State Gazette*, Oct. 12,
1878.

16. *Victoria Advocate*, Oct. 19, 1878.

17. *Fort Worth Democrat*, Oct. 2, 1878.

18. *Houston Item*, Oct. 18, 1878.

19. John Wesley Hardin, "Certificate of
Prison Conduct," Texas State Peniten-
tiaries, March 15, 1894; second file
provided through the courtesy of Texas
Senator Peggy Rosson, March 27, 1995.

20. Hardin, *Life*, 127-128; John Hardin to
Jane, Dec. 28, 1878, Hardin Collection.

21. Hardin, *Life*, 129-130.

22. John W. Hardin to "My Dear and Loving Wife," Jan. 26, 1879, Hardin
Collection.

23. *Austin Statesman*, Jan. 11, 1880.

24. John Wesley Hardin, "Certificate of
Prison Conduct," Texas State Peniten-
tiaries, March 15, 1894.

25. Hardin, *Life*, 132-133.

26. *San Antonio Daily Express*, May 25,
1879.

27. *Gonzales Inquirer*, July 20, 1879.

28. Hardin, *Life*, 130.

29. John Wesley Hardin to Mrs. Jane

Hardin, Dec. 5, 1877, Hardin Collection.
30. Hardin, *Life*, 133.
31. Hardin to McCulloch, Aug. 26, 1885, Hardin Collection.
32. *Burnet Bulletin*, Oct. 25, 1881; the *Longview Democrat*, Dec. 2, 1881.
33. Hardin, *Life*, 135.
34. Ibid., 133-134; Prison petition written and signed by John Wesley Hardin and convicts, Southwest Texas State University Library, Hardin Collection.
35. J. W. Hardin to Jane Hardin, June 24, 1888, Hardin Collection.
36. Ibid., Feb. 9, 1879.
37. Ibid., Aug. 14, 1881.
38. Ibid.
39. Ibid., Nov. 2, 1890.
40. Neither of these notes are dated, but they are attached to one of Hardin's letters to Jane, Jan. 22, 1888, Hardin Collection.
41. The DeWitt County courthouse presently has no files or indictments relating to John Wesley Hardin. However, handwritten copies of Hardin's indictment are available through private sources, and this author has one.
42. *San Antonio Daily Express*, Jan. 2, 1892, quoting from the *Cuero Star*.
43. Ibid., Jan. 3; Henry R. Small, Bureau of Records and Identification, Huntsville, to Kenneth Major, Record Clerk, Oklahoma Penitentiary, McAlester, OK., Aug. 18, 1870.
44. W. S. Fly to John W. Hardin, Jan. 8, 1892, Hardin Collection.
45. *El Paso Daily Herald*, Aug. 30, 1895, quoting a dispatch from Corpus Christi.
46. John Wesley Hardin to J. B. Cobb, Nov. 6, 1892, & J. B. Cobb to Gov. Hogg, April 13, 1893, Hardin Collection.
47. Ibid., June 24, 1888.
48. No. 3029, Dept. of State, Reasons for Executive Clemency for John Wesley Hardin, Murderer, filed March 16, 1894, Texas State Archives; Petition to Hon. James S. Hogg, Gov. of the State of Texas, Jan. 1, 1894, Hardin Collection.
49. J. B. Cobb to Gov. Hogg, April 13, 1893, Hardin Collection.
50. *Gonzales Inquirer*, Feb. 11, 1892.
51. The *San Antonio Daily Express*, Jan. 30, 1892, quoting from the *Cuero Star*.
52. *San Antonio Daily Express*, Feb. 18, 1894.

22. Tell Wes to be A Good Man

1. *San Antonio Daily Express*, Feb. 21, 1894.
2. This series of letters are all found in the Hardin Collection, this one specifically being "Bell to Glover," April 14, 1894; also see Parsons, "Tell Wes to be a good Man," 6-8.
3. Chuck and Marjorie Parsons, *Bowen and Hardin*, 137-150.
4. Fly to Hogg, March 10, 1894; Restoration of Citizenship, #15075, March 16, 1894, Governor Hogg Papers, Texas State Archives, Austin.
5. Hardin papers, The Hardin Collection; *San Antonio Daily Express*, Feb. 18, 1894.
6. *La Opinion del Pueblo* (Gonzales, Texas), Oct. 13, 1894; James L. Sievers, *Selected Correspondence of John Wesley Hardin: From Capture to Parole*. Thesis for Master of Arts, Southwest Texas State University, San Marcos, TX., Nov. 15, 1972, 26.
7. Scattered letters in Hardin Collection.
8. *Gonzales Inquirer*, March 8, 15, 1894.
9. Ibid., Oct. 8, 1894.
10. *The Drag Net*, Oct. 12, 1894.
11. *Gonzales Inquirer*, Nov. 1, 1894.
12. After the death of James Gipson Hardin, most of the family started calling Barnett after his father, James.
13. *Recorded Landmarks of Kimble County*, by the Kimble County Historical Survey Committee. Junction: Privately printed, 1971, 205; O. C. Fisher, *It Occurred in Kimble County*. Houston: Anson Jones Press, 1937, 236.
14. John Wesley Hardin to Callie Lewis, Jan. 1, 1895, Hardin Collection.
15. Callie Lewis to Mr. Hardin, Jan. 2, 1895, Hardin Collection.
16. Bettie Lewis to "Dear Friend and Son-in-Law," March 23, 1895, Hardin Collection.
17. Author's interview with Coke Stevenson, former governor of Texas, Junction, Texas, April 12, 1972. Mr. Stevenson said that as a small boy, he observed the marriage of John Wesley Hardin and Callie Lewis. During the ceremony, Callie stood with tears running down her cheeks, while Hardin was dead drunk. Stevenson said Hardin had won Callie during a card game with the father.
18. Hardin Collection.

19. Jim Miller apparently thought of M. Q. Hardin as a cousin of his as well as John Wesley Hardin, and said so in a letter. M. Q. Hardin also wrote John Wesley Hardin a letter which he opened with "Cousin John," and closed with "Your cousin, Mart Hardin." Nevertheless, genealogists have never yet established M. Q. Hardin in any particular line. See Hardin Collection.

20. University of Oklahoma Press, 1970, 28-30. John Denson was the son of Mary Jane Clements, a sister of Manning Clements.

21. Sallie Clements Miller to Mr. J. W. Hardin, Jan. 26, 1895, Hardin Collection; *El Paso Herald*, April 10-11, 1895; Case 1789, 34th Dist Court, El Paso, TX.

23. El Paso

1. Leon Claire Metz, *John Selman: Texas Gunfighter*. New York: Hastings House, 1966; Robert K. DeArment, *George Scarborough: The Life and Death of A Lawman on the Closing Frontier*. Norman: U. of Oklahoma Press, 1992.

2. *El Paso Times* and *El Paso Herald*, April 6, 1894; Metz, *Selman*, 148-150; DeArment, *George Scarborough*, 69-75.

3. Case No. 1753, 34th district Court, El Paso.

4. DeArment, *George Scarborough*, 79-81; J. Evetts Haley, *Jeff Milton: Good Man With A Gun*. Norman: University of Oklahoma Press, 1953, 211-214.

5. DeArment, *George Scarborough*, 48.

24. Just Return What I Lost

1. *El Paso Times*, April 2, 1895.

2. Ibid., April 7, 1895.

3. DeArment, *George Scarborough*, 96-97; Dee Harkey, *Mean As Hell*. Albuquerque: University of New Mexico Press, 1942, 88-90.

4. *El Paso Times*, April 21, 23, 25, May 1, 1895, *El Paso Herald*, May 30, 1895.

5. *El Paso Evening Tribune*, June 13, 1895.

6. *Eddy Current*, June 13, 1895.

7. *Eddy Argus*, July 7, 1893, Aug. 17, 1894.

8. *El Paso Times*, April 24, 1895.

9. Ibid.

10. Ibid., May 2, 4, 1895.

11. Ibid., May 2, 1895.

12. Bill of Sale between M. W. Collins and J. W. Hardin, May 1, 1895. Original in possession of Robert G. McCubbin, El Paso.

13. Document copy in author's possession.

14. Case No. 1814, 34th Dist. Court, El Paso; *El Paso Times*, May 10, 16, 17, 1895.

15. *El Paso Times and Herald*, May 4, 16, 17, 1895.

16. Sworn statement of J. D. Milton to D. Storms, May 10, 1895; D. Storms File, #510, Southwest Room, El Paso Public Library, May 9, 1895.

17. D. Storms File, #510, May 15, 16, 1895.

18. Ibid., May 11, 1896.

19. El Paso County Court of Law, July 1, 1895.; Richard C. Marohn, "El Paso Has Lost Her Nerve," *Arms Contents Gazette*, Vol. 5, No. 10 (July 1978), 26-30; *El Paso Times*, June 2, 29, 30, July 3, 1895.

25. Adios, Martin

1. Dave Johnson, "G. W. Gladden—Hard Luck Warrior," *National Association and Center for Outlaw and Lawman History*, Vol. XV, No. 3 (July-Sept., 1991), 1-6.

2. Ibid.; Memoranda of Court Cases, D. Storms, County Attorney, El Paso County, Vol. 2, p. 17-18, El Paso Public Library, El Paso, Texas; Harkey, *Mean As Hell*, 94-95.

3. *Eddy Current*, July 5, 1895.

4. *El Paso Times*, July 2, 1895.

5. DeArment, *George Scarborough*, 110; *El Paso Times*, June 30, 1995.

6. *El Paso Herald*, July 1, 1895.

7. Ibid., April 27, 28, 1897.

8. *Eddy Current*, Jan. 30, April 16, 1896.

26. Autobiography of A Sinner

1. *El Paso Times*, Aug. 23, 1995.

2. No author cited, *The Bandits of the West: Their Lives and Punishments*. New York: Richard K. Fox, Publisher, Vol. 1, No. 9 (May 1, 1883), 45.

3. *El Paso Times*, June 30; *El Paso Herald*, July 2, 1895.

4. El Paso County Leases Deed Book, # 41, 40.
5. *El Paso Times*, Aug. 23, 1895.
6. *Eddy Current*, Aug. 15, 1895.
7. Ibid., Aug. 7, 1895.
8. Ibid., Aug. 7, 23, 1895.
9. D. Storms File, #510, Aug. 7, 1895, El Paso Public Library.
10. Ibid., Aug. 11, 1895.
11. George Look Manuscript, copy in possession of author.

27. Four Sixes to Beat

1. *El Paso Herald*, Aug. 20, 1895.

28. To A Higher Court

1. Testimony of John Selman before Justice of the Peace Walter Howe, Aug. 19, 20, 21, 1895.
2. Haley, *Jeff Milton*, 245.
3. George Look Manuscript, copy in possession of author.
4. *El Paso Times*, Aug. 20, 1895; testimony of John Selman before Judge Howe.
5. Judge Howe took the testimony of these individuals. All of their statements appeared in the *El Paso Times* and *Herald*.
6. Stanley Good manuscript.
7. *El Paso Times*, Aug. 20, 1995.
8. Sworn testimony of doctors S. G. Sherard, W. N. Vilas and Alward White before Justice Walter Howe.
9. D. Storms File, #510, El Paso Public Library, Southwest Section.
10. Ibid.
11. D. Storms File, #510, El Paso Public Library, Southwest Section.
12. Case No. 1874, 34th Dist. Court, El Paso; also note local newspapers of day and time.
13. DeArment, *George Scarborough*, 142-156; Metz, *John Selman*, 197-203.
14. DeArment, *George Scarborough*, 210-229.
15. Emanuel "Mannie" has historically been mistaken for his father, Emanuel "Manning" Clements.
16. Patrick King, "Manen Clements: Last of the Breed," *True West*, Feb., 1995, 44-49.
17. *El Paso Herald*, Aug. 21, 1895

18. Ibid.
19. 34th Dist. Court, Sept. Term, 1895, Judge Frank Hunter, presiding.
20. J. Marvin Hunter and Noah H. Rose, *The Album of Gunfighters*. San Antonio: Rose & Hunter, 1951, 123-25; Chuck Parsons to LCM, March 13, 1995.

The Great Attempted Body Snatching Caper

1. Metz, Leon C. *Four Sixes to Beat: The Death of John Wesley Hardin*. El Paso: Published by Robert McCubbin, Aug. 19, 1995, softcover, limited to 500 copies.
2. *El Paso Times* & *El Paso Herald-Post*, Aug. 20, 21, 1995; *Cow Country Courier* (Nixon), Aug. 24, 31, 1995.
3. *El Paso Times* & *El Paso Herald-Post*, Aug. 27-31, 1995; El Paso County Court-at-Law No. 5, In Re: Concordia Cemetery, No. 95-11014.
4. Ibid., Sept. 3-5, 1995.
5. This author is in possession of various letters indicating that the Bowen family would never have released Jane from the family cemetery without a substantial court fight. Therefore, the Nixon contingent argued only for Hardin. They probably would have taken Jane later if possible, but if her removal was contested or difficult to achieve, the main thrust of their mission (in grabbing Hardin) would still have been accomplished.
6. Concordia Heritage Assn. Inc. et al. v. Finch, et al., No. 95-10636, 205 District Court, El Paso. Also see *Texas Lawyer*, Feb. 26, 1996 (a publication of American Lawyer Media), plus *El Paso Times* and *El Paso Herald-Post*, Jan. 28-Feb. 20, 1996. Media television, plus newspapers and radio, both national and international, ran stories regarding the trial.

Appendix A

1. There is puzzlement about the birthplace of Benjamin Hardin II, most authorities listing Virginia but others believing England. Joyce Cavett to LCM, Dec. 29, 1992.

2. Tryon County was named for Governor William Tryon, a despot who supported the British so intensely that after the colonies gained independence from England, the citizens of North Carolina obliterated Tryon County from the map.
3. Joyce Cavett to LCM, Dec. 29, 1992.
4. Hardin Valley begins at Ball Camp Pike and runs along Conner Creek which empties into the Clinch River. Hardin Valley Road was formerly Buttermilk Road. The western boundary was the Knox County Line. Hardin built himself a two story log cabin which burned in 1930. Unidentified Tennessee newspaper clipping, August 25, 1982.
5. Ibid; Adam Kuykendall, "Colonel Joseph Hardin," *The Hardin Newsletter*, Vol. 4, 1987, 64-69.
6. Pension application of Martha Hardin for the service of Benj. Hardin during the War of 1812. The application date is 1855. A scattering of military records indicate that a Benjamin Hardin was paid $3.40 a day for operating a five-horse team while transporting provisions for the Army. The records do not say if the pension was granted. Joyce Cavett Papers.
7. The Deed Records in Wayne County, Tennessee, are filled with Benjamin Hardin land transactions. For those described here, see Old Book A, p. 35-36, and Old Book C, 148.

Appendix B

1. Swan and Jerusha Blackburn Hardin shifted their family out of Franklin County, Georgia to Maury County, Tennessee, in 1807. In 1825, they moved to Texas and settled along the Trinity River. Benjamin Hardin, the eldest son of Swan, was a member of the 9th Congress of the Republic of Texas in 1844. Augustine Blackburn Hardin, the second son, was a representative from Liberty County to the Convention of 1833, the Consultation of 1835, and the Convention of 1836. Augustine Blackburn Hardin signed the Texas Declaration of Independence, and soon thereafter retired to Liberty County

where he died in 1871. Hardin County, Texas, is named for this branch of the Hardin family. So far as is known, John Wesley Hardin never met any of the Hardin County Hardins. Mary Lou Proctor, *A History of Hardin County*. Master of Arts Thesis, University of Texas, Aug. 1950, 18-21; Camilla Davis Trammell, *Seven Pines: Its Occupants and Their Letters*. Austin: Whitehead & Whitehead, 1986, 20, 29.
2. Louise Robertson to Mrs. Gus Warner, Dec. 3, 1973, *Harden/Hardin/Harding Association* newsletter.
3. Information on William Barnett Hardin derives mostly from the research and assistance of Joyce Hardin Cavett. Included in the Official Record of William Barnett Hardin's service in the War for Texas Independence, Public Debt Paper, Texas State Library, Archives Division, Austin; Patent B 556 for 640 acres of land, General Land Office, Austin; Petition for a reservation for the Alabama Indian Tribe, Memorials and Petitions to the Texas Legislature, Texas State Library, Austin, Texas; Texas Historical Marker, Holshousen Cemetery, Moscow, Texas, 1967.

Appendix C

1. T. U. Taylor, "The Lee-Peacock Feud," *Frontier Times*, Vol. 3, No. 8 (May 1926), 19-28; Nick Jones, "The Lee-Peacock Feud," *Real West* (Jan., 1979), 12-14, 52-54.
2. Bill Boren to Dick Boren, addressed to "My Dear Relative." Undated, but probably written in 1874 or '75. Courtesy Mrs. Virginia Short.
3. Sonnichsen, *I'll Die Before I'll Run*, 22, 32; Joyce Cavett notes to LCM, undated; T. U. Taylor, "The Lee-Peacock Feud," 25; Dixon Genealogy Sheet furnished by Walter Dixson.
4. Nick Jones, "The Lee-Peacock Feud," 52-53; *Flake's Bulletin*, June 28, 1871.

Bibliography

PRIMARY SOURCES

Hardin, John Wesley. *The Life of John Wesley Hardin as written by himself*. Norman: University of Oklahoma Press, 1961.

Hyatt, Marjorie. *The Taylors, the Tumlinsons and the Feud*. Smiley, TX., Privately printed, 1988.

——. *Fuel For A Feud*. Smiley, TX: Privately printed, 1990.

Jackson & Jackson. *Cases Argued and Adjudged in the Court of Appeals of the State of Texas During the Austin Term, 1878, and the Early Part of the Tyler Term, 1878*. Vol. IV. St Louis: The Gilbert Book Co., 1879.

Kimble County Historical Survey Committee. *Recorded Landmarks of Kimble County*. Junction: Privately Printed, 1971.

Third Texas Court of Appeals Reports, "Brown Bowen vs the State," 1878.

Truitt, Eddie Day. *The Taylor Party*. Wortham, TX: Privately printed, 1992.

THESES & DISSERTATIONS

Bowles, Flora G. "The History of Trinity County, Texas" (Master's thesis, The University of Texas, 1928).

Lightfoot, Billy B. "The History of Comanche County Texas Until 1920" (Master's thesis, University of Texas at Austin, Aug. 1949.)

Proctor, Mary Lou. "A History of Hardin County." (Master's thesis, The University of Texas, 1950.)

Sievers, James L. "Selected Correspondence of John Wesley Hardin: From Capture to Parole." (Master's thesis, Southwest Texas State University, San Marcos, TX., 1972.)

TEXAS ARCHIVES, AUSTIN

Public Debt Papers; General Land Office; Memorials and Petitions to the Texas Legislature; Reconstruction Records; Return of Crimes Committed (Trinity County), 1870; Sheriff G. W. Barfield to James Davidson, Chief of Texas State Police, July 16, 1870; Adjutant General's Records; Lists of Arrest by State Police, 1871; State Police Letter Files; Gonzales murder indictments; Governors Proclamations; Trinity County indictments; Texas Extradition Papers; Texas Courts of Criminal Appeals, Brown Bowen vs the State; Comanche County Petition 166, July 2, 1882; Monthly Report of Capt. John R. Waller; Petition From the Citizens of Comanche to Governor Richard Coke, May 28, 1874; *1878 List of Texas Fugitives From Justice*.

NATIONAL ARCHIVES, WASH.

Register of Letters sent, Item 3774, RG 105, Records of the Field Officers of the Bureau of Refugees, Freedmen and Abandoned Lands; "Report of Persons Evading Arrest in the County of DeWitt for the Month ending on the 30th Day of April, 1869," RG 393, Part 1, Entry 4853; "Record of Felonies Committed in Texas, 1866-1867," RG 393, Part I, Entry 4853; Record of Appointment of Postmasters, 1832-1971, Castro through Ellis Counties, Texas, Microfilm Publication, M841;

SECONDARY SOURCES

Adolphus, Werry. *History of the First Methodist Church, Dallas, Texas, 1846-1946*. Privately printed, date and place unknown, but probably 1946 or '47 in Dallas.

Bartholomew, Ed. *Kill or Be Killed*. Houston: Frontier Press, 1953.

Bennett, Joseph E. *Sixguns and Masons*. Highland Springs: Va., Anchor Publications, 1991.

Cox, James. *Historical and Biographical Record of the Cattle Industry, and the Cattlemen of Texas, and Adjacent Territories*. New York: Antiquarian Press, 1959.

Day, Jack Hays. *The Sutton Taylor Feud*. San Antonio: Sid Murray and Son, Printers, 1937.

DeArment, Robert K. *George Scarborough: The Life and Death of A Lawman on the Closing Frontier*. Norman: University of Oklahoma Press, 1992.

Dixson, Walter Clay. *Richland Crossing: A Portrait of Texas Pioneers*. Everman, Texas: Peppermill Publishing Company, 1994.

Dykstra, Robert R. *The Cattle Towns*. New York: Knopf, 1968.

Fisher, O. C. *It Occurred in Kimble, and How*. Houston: Anson Jones Press, 1937.

Gallegly, Joseph. *From Alamo Plaza to Jack Harris's Saloon*. Paris, France: Mouton, 1970.

Gard, Wayne. *The Chisholm Trail*. Norman: University of Oklahoma Press, 1954.

Gillett, James G. *Six Years With the Texas Rangers*. New Haven and London: Yale University Press, 1963.

Gonzales County Historical Commission. *The History of Gonzales County, Texas*. Dallas: Curtis Media Corp., 1986.

Haley, J. Evetts. *Jeff Milton: Good Man With A Gun*. Norman: University of Oklahoma Press, 1953.

Hamilton, H. D. *History of Company M: First Texas Volunteer Infantry*. Waco: W. M. Morrison, 1962.

Harkey, Dee. *Mean As Hell*. Albuquerque: University of New Mexico Press, 1942.

Havins, T. R. *Something About Brown*. Brownwood, TX: Banner Printing, 1958.

———. and James M. Day. *Twenty-five Years on the Outside Row: Autobiography of Rev. Peter Gravis*. Brownwood: Cross Timbers Press, 1966.

Hunter, J. Marvin and Noah H. Rose. *The Album of Gunfighters*. San Antonio: Hunter and Rose, 1951.

Kilgore, D. E. *A Ranger Legacy: 150 Years of Service to Texas*. Austin: Madrona Press, 1973.

Lockwood, Frances B. *Comanche County Courthouses*. Comanche, TX: Comanche Public Library, 1969.

Malouf, Dian. *Cattle Kings of Texas*. Hillsboro, Oregon: Beyond Words Publishing Co., 1991.

Marohn, Richard C. *The Last Gunfighter: John Wesley Hardin*. College Station, TX.: Creative Publishing Co., 1995.

Metz, Leon Claire. *John Selman: Gunfighter*. Norman: University of Oklahoma Press, 1980.

Miller, Nyle H. and Joseph W. Snell. *Great Gunfighters of the Kansas Cowtowns, 1867-1886*. Lincoln: University of Nebraska Press, 1963.

Miller, Rick. *Bounty Hunter*. College Station: Early West, 1988.

———. *Bloody Bill Longley*. Wolfe City, TX: Henington Publishing Co., 1996.

Myers, Lee C. *The Pearl of the Pecos*. Carlsbad, NM: Lee Myers, 1974.

Nordyke, Lewis. *John Wesley Hardin: Texas Gunman*. New York: William Morrow & Co., 1957.

Parsons, Chuck. *The Capture of John Wesley Hardin*. College Station: Creative Publishing, 1978.

———. *Phil Coe: Texas Gambler*. Wolfe City, TX: Henington Publishing Co., 1984.

———. *Pidge: A Texas Ranger From Virginia*. Wolfe City, TX: Henington Publishing, 1985.

———. "The DeWitt County Feud." *DeWitt County History*. Dallas: Curtis Media Corp., 1991.

———. Chuck and Marjorie, *Bowen and Hardin*. College Station, TX: Creative Publishing, 1991.

Richter, William L. *The Army in Texas During Reconstruction, 1865-1870*. College Station: Texas A&M University Press, 1987.

Rosa, Joseph G. *They Called Him Wild Bill: The Life and Adventures of James Butler Hickok*. Norman: University of Oklahoma Press, 1974.

———. *The West of Wild Bill Hickok*. Norman: University of Oklahoma Press, 1982.

Rose, Victor. *The Texas Vendetta; or, the Sutton-Taylor Feud*. New York: J. J. Little & Co., 1880.

Skaggs, Jimmy M. *The Cattle-Trailing Industry: Between Supply and Demand, 1866-1890*. Lawrence: The University Press of Kansas, 1973.

Shirley, Glenn. *Shotgun for Hire: The Story*

of Deacon Jim Miller: Killer of Pat Garrett. Norman: University of New Mexico Press, 1970.

Silverthorne, Elizabeth. *Plantation Life in Texas.* College Station: Texas A&M University Press, 1986.

Sonnichsen, C. L. *Ten Texas Feuds.* Albuquerque: University of New Mexico Press, 1957.

——. *I'll Die Before I'll Run: The Story of the Great Feuds of Texas.* New York: Devin-Adair, 1962.

——. *The Grave of John Wesley Hardin: Three Essays on Grassroots History.* College Station: Texas A&M University Press, 1979.

Steen, George N. "When A Man's Word Was As Good as A Gilt-Edged Note," *The Trail Drivers of Texas,* compiled and edited by J. Marvin Hunter. Austin: University of Texas Press, 1985, p. 140.

Sutton, Robert C., Jr. *The Sutton-Taylor Feud.* Quanah, TX: Nortex Press, 1974.

Tidwell, Donovan Duncan. *Freemasonry in Brownwood.* Fort Worth: Dept. of Printing, Masonic Home and School, 1966.

Tise, Sammy. *Texas County Sheriffs.* Albuquerque: Oakwood Printing, 1989.

Trammell, Camilla Davis. *Seven Pines: Its Occupants and Their Letters.* Austin: Whitehead & Whitehead, 1986.

Webb, Walter Prescott. *The Texas Rangers: A Century of Frontier Defense.* New York: Houghton Mifflin, 1935.

Wheeler, Keith. *The Chroniclers.* New York: Time-Life Books ("The Old West"), 1976.

PRIVATE COLLECTIONS

Sonnichsen (Papers) Collection, UT El Paso Archives

Hardin Collection of Letters, University Library, University of Southwest Texas at San Marcos.

Minutes of Comanche County Commissioners Court.

Records of the District Court, Comanche.

Robert G. McCubbin Collection, El Paso, Texas

State of Florida vs Martin Sullivan, Escambia County, Circuit Court, Criminal Records, Oct. 4, 1877.

George Look Manuscript, copy in possession of author.

Tumlinson Collection, by Sam Tumlinson. Copy in possession of author.

JOURNALS, QUARTERLIES AND MAGAZINES

The Harden/Hardin/Harding Association. Crewe, Va.

DeArment, R. K. "Gunman Ambushes Sheriff, is Acquitted," *Tombstone Epitaph,* Vol. XVIII, #2 (Feb. 1991).

Dixson, Walter Clay. "The Barekman-Anderson Prelude to Comanche." *Quarterly for the National Association for Outlaw and Lawman History.* Vol. XVII, #2 (April-June, 1994).

Dunn, Sylvan. "Life and Times in Albuquerque, Texas," *Southwestern Historical Quarterly,* Vol. LV #1 (July, 1951).

Dykstra, Robert B. "Exit John Wesley Hardin," *Los Angeles Corral Brand Book 6,* Los Angeles, CA., 1956.

Ellison, Douglas G. "Rivals in Texas: Hardin and Longley," *Quarterly of the National Association and Center for Outlaw and Lawman History,* Vol. XII, #4 (Spring 1988).

Godbold, Mollie Moore. "Comanche and the Hardin Gang," *Southwestern Historical Quarterly,* Vol. LXVII, #2 (Oct., 1963).

Johnson, Dave. "G. W. Gladden—Hard Luck Warrior," *National Association and Center for Outlaw and Lawman History,* Vol. XV, #3 (July-Sept., 1991).

Jones, Nick. "The Lee-Peacock Feud," *Real West* (Jan. 1979).

Koop, Waldo E. "Enter John Wesley Hardin: The Dim Trail to Abilene." *The Prairie Scout,* Vol. II, Kansas Corral of the Westerners.

Lachuk, John. "John Wesley Hardin," *Guns of the Gunfighters.* Los Angeles: Peterson Publishing Co., 1975.

Marohn, Richard C. "El Paso Has Lost Her Nerve," *Arms Contents Gazette,* Vol. 5, #10 (July 1978).

Parsons, Chuck. "Who Was the Fastest Gunman, James B. 'Wild Bill' Hickok, or Wesley 'Little Arkansas' Hardin?" *Newsletter of the National Association and Center for Outlaw and Lawman History,* Vol. 1, #3 (Autumn, 1975).

——."Forgotten Feudist," *Frontier Times,* Vol. 50, #1 (Dec.-Jan, 1976).

——. "John Wesley Hardin and the Texas Rangers," *Newsletter of the National Association and Center for Outlaw and Lawman History,* Vol. II, #2 (Spring, 1976).

——."Doc Bockius Survived Civil War Texas Feud," *Newsletter of the National Association and Center for Outlaw and Lawman History*, Vol. 2, #4 (Spring, 1977).

——."Bill Sutton Avenged: The Death of Jim Taylor," *Quarterly of the National Association and Center for Outlaw and Lawman History*, Vol. IV, #3 (March, 1979).

——. "A Texas Gunfighter," *Real West* (July 1980).

——. "Tell Wes to be A Good Man: Examining An Early Hardin Killing," *National Outlaw/Lawman Association Quarterly*, Vol. 1, #3 (April, 1981).

Rickards, Colin W. "Vengeance: Kansas 1870s Style," *The English Westerners Brand Book*, Vol. 4, #1 (Oct. 1961).

Taylor, T. U. "New Light on John Wesley Hardin," *Frontier Times*, Vol. 2, #11 (Aug. 1925).

——."The Lee-Peacock Feud," *Frontier Times* Vol. 3, #8 (May, 1926).

Whittington, Michael, "Six Telegrams That Tell A Story: The Arrest of John Wesley Hardin," *Quarterly for the National Association and Center for Outlaw and Lawman History*, Vol. XI, #2 (Fall, 1986).

Wright, A. J. "John Wesley Hardin's Missing Years," *Old West* (Fall, 1981).

——. "A Gunfighter's Southern Vacation," *Quarterly of the National Outlaw and Lawman History Association* Vol. VII, #3 (Autumn 1982).

NEWSPAPERS

Abilene Chronicle
Atlanta Daily Constitution
Austin Daily Democratic Statesman
Austin Weekly State Gazette
Brenham Banner
Burnet Bulletin
Daily Houston Telegraph
Comanche Chief
Cuero Star
Daily Democratic Statesman
The Daily Journal (Austin)
Daily Austin Republican
Daily State Journal (Austin)
Dallas Herald
Dallas News
Dallas Times
Denison Daily Herald

Drag Net (Gonzales, TX)
Eddy Argus (New Mexico)
Eddy Current
El Paso Evening Tribune
El Paso Herald
El Paso Times
Fayette County New Era
Fairfield Ledger
Flakes Daily Bulletin
Galveston Daily News
Galveston Weekly News
Gonzales Inquirer
Houston Daily Telegraph
Houston Item
Kansas City Commonwealth
Kansas Daily Tribune Times
Kansas State Record
Kerrville Mountain Sun
Lampasas Dispatch
Longview Democrat
Mobile Register
National Police Gazette
New York Times
Oxford Times (Kansas)
Sabine County Weekly Journal
San Antonio Daily Express
San Antonio Daily Herald
The Texas Lawyer
Topeka Daily Commonwealth
Topeka State Record
Topeka Commonwealth
Trinity County News
The Union
Victoria Advocate
Waco Register
Weatherford Exponent
Weekly State Gazette
West Texas Free Press
Wichita Tribune
Wyandotte Gazette

Index